Learning
to Labor in
New Times

D0165560

The *Critical Social Thought* Series
edited by Michael W. Apple, University of Wisconsin—Madison

Contradictions of Control: School Structure and School Knowledge
Linda M. McNeil

Working Class without Work: High School Students in a De-industrializing Society
Lois Weis

Social Analysis of Education: After the New Sociology
Philip Wexler

Capitalist Schools: Explanation and Ethics in Radical Studies of Schooling
Daniel P. Liston

Getting Smart: Feminist Research and Pedagogy with/in the Postmodern
Patti Lather

Teacher Education and the Social Conditions of Schooling
Daniel P. Liston and Kenneth M. Zeichner

Race, Identity, and Representation in Education
Warren Crichlow and Cameron McCarthy, editors

Public Schools that Work: Creating Community
Gregory A. Smith, editor

Power and Method: Political Activism and Educational Research
Andrew Gitlin, editor

Critical Ethnography in Educational Research: A Theoretical and Practical Guide
Phil Francis Carspecken

The Uses of Culture: Education and the Limits of Ethnic Affiliation
Cameron McCarthy

Education, Power, and Personal Biography: Dialogues with Critical Educators
Carlos Alberto Torres, editor

Contradictions of School Reform: Educational Costs of Standardized Testing
Linda M. McNeil

Act Your Age! A Cultural Construction of Adolescence
Nancy Lesko

Tough Fronts: The Impact of Street Culture on Schooling
L. Janelle Dance

Political Spectacle and the Fate of American Schools
Mary Lee Smith with Walter Heinecke, Linda Miller-Kahn, and Patricia F. Jarvis

High Stakes Education: Inequality, Globalization, and Urban School Reform
Pauline Lipman

Rethinking Scientific Literacy
Wolff-Michael Roth and Angela Calabrese Barton

Learning to Labor in New Times
Nadine Dolby and Greg Dimitriadis, editors

Learning to Labor in New Times

Edited by

Nadine Dolby and Greg Dimitriadis
with Paul Willis

RoutledgeFalmer

NEW YORK AND LONDON

Published in 2004 by
RoutledgeFalmer
29 West 35th Street
New York, NY 10001
www.routledge-ny.com

Published in Great Britain by
RoutledgeFalmer
11 New Fetter Lane
London EC4P 4EE
www.routledgefalmer.com

Printed in the United States of America on acid-free paper.
Typesetting: BookType

10 9 8 7 6 5 4 3 2 1

Library of Congress Cataloging-in-Publication Data

Learning to labor in new times / edited by Nadine Dolby and Greg Dimitriadis.
    p.   cm. — (Critical social thought)
   Includes index.
   ISBN 0-415-94854-1 (alk. paper) — ISBN 0-415-94855-X (pbk. : alk. paper)
   1. Willis, Paul E. Learning to labour. 2. Youth—Employment. 3. Working class—
Education. I. Dolby, Nadine, 1964– II. Dimitriadis, Greg, 1969– III. Willis, Paul E.
Learning to labour. IV. Series.
   HD276.G7W5435 2004
   306.3'6'0835—dc22

                                                          2004041867

Contents

Acknowledgments   vii

Foreword   ix
  STANLEY ARONOWITZ

1   Learning to Labor in New Times: An Introduction   1
  NADINE DOLBY AND GREG DIMITRIADIS

Section I: Reflecting on *Learning to Labor*

2   Male Working-Class Identities and Social Justice: 17
  A Reconsideration of Paul Willis's *Learning to Labor*
  in Light of Contemporary Research
  MADELEINE ARNOT

3   Paul Willis, Class Consciousness, and Critical Pedagogy: 41
  Toward a Socialist Future
  PETER McLAREN AND VALERIE SCATAMBURLO-D'ANNIBALE

4   Between Good Sense and Bad Sense: Race, Class,   61
  and Learning from *Learning to Labor*
  MICHAEL W. APPLE

5   The "Lads" and the Cultural Topography of Race   83
  FAZAL RIZVI

v

Section II: Learning to Labor in New Times

6   Reordering Work and Destabilizing Masculinity   95
JANE KENWAY AND ANNA KRAACK

7   Revisiting a 1980s "Moment of Critique":   111
Class, Gender and the New Economy
LOIS WEIS

8   Learning to Do Time: Willis's Model of Cultural   133
Reproduction in an Era of Postindustrialism,
Globalization, and Mass Incarceration
KATHLEEN NOLAN AND JEAN ANYON

9   Thinking About the Cultural Studies of Education   151
in a Time of Recession: *Learning to Labor* and the Work
of Aesthetics in Modern Life
CAMERON McCARTHY

Section III: Critical Ethnography, Culture and Schooling: Paul Willis Reflects on *Learning to Labor*

10   Twenty-Five Years On: Old Books, New Times   167
PAUL WILLIS

Appendix
"Centre" and Periphery—   197
An Interview with Paul Willis
DAVID MILLS AND ROBERT GIBB

Notes on Contributors   227

Index   233

Acknowledgments

This book began as two panels at the 2002 meeting of the American Educational Research Association. We would like to thank Barry Fraser, then chair of the International Relations Committee, for his enthusiastic support. The panel participants—and the audiences—generated an enormous amount of energy and excitement about the work, and were the inspiration for developing a more sustained examination of the impact of Paul Willis's research and scholarly work on educational research over the last quarter century. We thank everyone who participated and the authors whose essays appear in this collection.

We thank the Office of the Vice-President for Research at Northern Illinois University for publication assistance. Joe Miranda and Catherine Bernard at RoutledgeFalmer were dedicated and wholly supportive—we are grateful for their commitment to this project. Samar Haddad provided outstanding support in the production process. Nadine would like to thank Stephen for his understanding during a hectic period of our lives, and for supporting her and this work. Greg would like to thank all his colleagues and students in the Graduate School of Education and the Department of Educational Leadership and Policy at the University at Buffalo.

Foreword

STANLEY ARONOWITZ

When I first read Paul Willis's *Learning to Labor* my first response was: Finally, someone has addressed schooling outcomes for working-class kids not as an instance of failure or victimhood. Instead Willis shows that working-class kids more or less consciously reject the cultural and political implications of buying into the curriculum and accepting school authority. In standard sociological terms, far from being labeled as "losers," the lads are exercising "agency" by choosing to "fail." I wrote the preface to the American edition of the book in these terms. My preface was, to say the least, incomplete. As several articles in this collection demonstrate *Learning to Labor* is suggestive in several additional dimensions. Because industrial labor has traditionally been associated with "manly" endeavor and intellectual labor has a distinctly feminine connotation, the "lads'" rebellion against school authority, in the first place against the classroom teacher, is an assertion of masculinity. As Willis himself points out, this gendered gesture mediates the lads' rebellion because it helps reproduce male superiority within gender relations as well as reproducing class relations.

Subsequently others, including myself, have situated Willis's superb ethnography in its historicity. Their entrance into the factory to which the lads gleefully escape after leaving school reproduces the class structure, but also reproduces the oppositional working-class culture inherited from their families, neighborhoods, and peers. Although in a wider context forms of working-class association are considered "sub" cultures, this does not proceed from a presupposition of inferiority to the dominant middle-class aspirations of social climbing and consumerism. In fact, the bonds of (male) class solidarity are forged on the shop floor as well as at the sites of working-class public spheres: the pub, the union hall, and noninstitutional sites such as the street corner. But the factory jobs that were still available in the early 1970s, when Willis engaged the lads, are now gone not only from the Midlands and from Hammertown—the city that is the sight of his study—but from many major industrial cities in Britain, continental Western Europe, and the United States. As subsequent studies of working-class life in cities demonstrate (notably Jay McLeod's *Aint No Makin' It* and William Julius Wilson's *When Work Disappears*, both about Chicago, among many others including my own analysis, with William DiFazio, *The Jobless Future*), those who leave school without acquiring a credential are almost invariably consigned to low-paying service jobs or long-term, sometimes permanent unemployment. And in many cities of the United States where the working class is composed mainly of Blacks, Latinos, and Asians, despite shrinking job opportunities, the patterns Willis discerns generally hold. Contrary to some observers like Moynihan and Glazer, Wilson, and anthropologists such as Oscar Lewis, it is not the "culture of poverty" that leads to and derives from the formation of an "underclass" of permanently unemployed people; casual and contingent work is the product of a new labor-market regime of Global Capitalism.

The historicity of Willis's great ethnography consists in its location in time and space. Since the late 1970s the political economy of global capitalism has radically altered conditions of life. The decentralization of production to all corners of the planet's geography has led to the disappearance of good jobs in the metropoles of the United States and other industrially developed societies, not only in low- and intermediate-technology industries, but also in high-tech sectors. The tale of the losses in textiles, garments, steel, and other major production industries is by now a commonplace. But in the last few years the easy assumption that services on the one hand and computers on the other would do more than take up the slack has suffered crushing repudiation. In 2003 no significant economic sector has elided massive reorganizations and steep job losses, but high-tech is no exception. After an explosion of hard- and software computer and computer-mediated manufacturing from the 1960s to the 1990s and the concomitant dot.com, boom both of which created employment for low-, moderate-, and fairly high-paid work, the turn of the 21st century has witnessed a pronounced bust. Chip makers have laid off low-paid Latino women in Silicon Valley just as software firms have shed computer programmers and engineers in the Microsoft Seattle empire and Silicon Alley in Manhattan. Recession tells only part of the story. Some of the best jobs have migrated to India and China, where, owing to good technical and scientific universities, engineers and computer scientists and technicians have proven able to design world-class equipment and software and earn a tenth of the salaries of their United States counterparts.

But overriding these considerations, the new regimes of computer-mediated industrial and service production—and the inability of labor unions to protect wages and benefits—have accelerated productivity, which far exceeds the economic growth rate, revealing the purpose of technological change: to reduce labor costs. Even without recession and job migration over time, cybernetic technologies reduce factory and service jobs absolutely and reduce them relative to the expansion of the labor force, even in growth periods. In the years between 2000 and 2003, even as the labor force grew by 3 percent the United States lost almost 3 million jobs, mostly in manufacturing, but increasingly in the services, including retail and wholesale trades and especially in financial services.

Having said this, working-class kids still drop out of school at alarming rates, while many others grimly hang in because they are well aware that there is no alternative to obtaining a credential of some sort, even if the credential carries no specific occupational qualifications. On the other hand, American colleges, technical institutes, and universities have, perhaps unwittingly, contributed to depressed salaries for credentialed computer workers by overproducing them in relation to the sagging job market. The hype of the 1990s—that computers would lead to almost infinite job and income opportunities—brought hundreds of thousands of students into a field that produced tens of thousands of good jobs. Armed with their associate and bachelor's degrees, many qualified computer technicians and programmers were delivered to a job market that offered only a small number of real jobs, but much part-time, contingent, and temporary work that usually carried no health benefits. For young people the first years of the new century have been disasterous. Many ended up waiting tables, working as construction laborers at nonunion sites, vainly trying sales, or entering rapidly declining financial services sector as licensed brokers, but with few clients. And others simply withdrew from the labor force and took work in the underground or informal economy.

The new working-class jobs—coded as forms of "professional" labor—bring with them neither good wages and benefits, nor do they reproduce working-class culture. As the first generation to have earned a post-secondary credential, many working-class kids have been inducted into the value systems and expectations of the salaried middle class, but without acquiring the accoutrements. Class identities have become ambiguous. Even as they seek professional and technical jobs, many retain their ties with the neighborhood and with their families because they have learned that the academic promises for social mobility have proven to be ephemeral. Yet, with some exceptions, neither the family nor the neighborhood provides a secure anchor missing in their work situations. Economic dislocation has pulled many families apart as siblings, frustrated with the dearth of jobs in their hometowns, move away in search of a better future, leaving parents and grandparents behind. And in the major cities of New York, Boston, Chicago, Los Angeles, and San Francisco, gentrification has driven millions from their once scorned ghetto and slum communities that nevertheless provided a sense of place for the Black and Latino working poor and the unemployed. What from outside appeared as ravaged neighborhoods were—and remain for many of their inhabitants—a haven in the heartless world, impoverished conditions notwithstanding.

Contemporary youth are frequently caught between still potent, although disintegrating, social networks of their childhood and youth and the stark reality that there are no good working-class jobs. Even as the struggle over loyalties never abates while they remain skeptical about the chances for good jobs, let alone genuine social mobility, school is perceived by a significant fraction of them as a necessary option. Needless to say, many working-class kids, Black, Latino, and white drop out of college because elementary and high schools have not prepared them, in either literacy or numeracy terms, for technical and scientific occupations much less the liberal arts.

Students who drop out of high school and community and senior colleges do not disappear from the face of the earth. Some, especially women, find full-time subprofessional or administrative jobs in government or in the health and education sectors. They work in so-called "caring" occupations such as nonprofessional nursing, dietary departments of schools and hospitals, and in commercial and residential building maintenance. These are now the "good" working-class jobs because they are usually unionized, provide health benefits, and are relatively protected from layoffs.

But most of them constitute the working poor. Contrary to ordinary belief, most work full-time for wages that are below the bogus official poverty line. They are the customers of the thousands of food pantries and kitchens because their meager take-home pay needs to be reserved for rent, which has skyrocketed almost everywhere in the Northeast and on the West Coast as well as in some cities of the heartland. Typically they live at home with their parent(s), relatives, and siblings. If they are fortunate to live in public housing, living conditions, although crowded, are somewhat better than in the tenements that, as everyone knows, were built to be slums. Or four or five take an apartment in order to pay the rent. And of course a certain number of dropouts enter the informal economy. They work off the books for subminimum wages or engage in illegal trade, mostly of drugs, and a few do become petty thieves.

In every state the period of deindustrialization corresponds to the burgeoning prison systems, which today house more than 2 million residents, the highest number and percentage of the population of any industrial country. Most are incarcerated for victimless crimes such as drug use and drug dealing and, in many states, are obliged to serve prolonged mandatory sentences. Prison culture may be brutal but it is the culture of the oppressed. For young Black and Latino men, often the consequence of their antiauthoritarian revolt is to find themselves, sooner or later, in the so-called criminal "justice" system, either as inmates, parolees, or probationers. According to some students of the process, a third of all Black men between 16 and 25 years old can expect to be within the purview of the criminal justice system sometime in their adolescent or adult lives.

Prisons are awful places, but, like families, neighborhoods, and peer groups, they are, perhaps, more important educational sites than the schools. For what Paul Willis has taught us—and this may be the most important contribution of *Learning to Labor*—is that schools are in constant competition for the hearts and minds of youth with powerful, oppositional cultural sites that regard schooling from an adversarial perspective. That in the context of urbanism the current form of these cultures is often coded in racial rather than class terms does not erase the fact that for the overwhelming majority of Blacks, Latinos, and Asians, segregation and economic deprivation are both class and race issues. More to the point, the constellation of circumstances—jobs or the lack thereof, segregated neighborhoods, common cohabitation in prisons, social relationships that form communities of class/race solidarity—reproduces an oppositional, if not an explicitly working-class culture, the representations of which in the media, rap music, and other popular forms are as ubiquitous as they are misapprehended by the dominant social formations.

CHAPTER 1

Learning to Labor in New Times
An Introduction

NADINE DOLBY AND GREG DIMITRIADIS

This book grew out of two panels at the 2002 annual meeting of the American Educational Research Association that honored the 25th anniversary of the U.S. publication of *Learning to Labor,* and the indispensable contribution of Paul Willis to educational research worldwide. Willis's many contributions during his (still flourishing) career speak to the importance of everyday worlds and lives, and to his commitment to ensuring that youth's realities—of school, of work, of home, of community, and of media culture—are consistently at the forefront of our agendas for research, and for political change. From the seminal *Learning to Labor,* to his more recent work on a major policy document, *The Youth Review,* Willis repeatedly insists that what youth *do* is important: they function as political actors, and they are not simply dupes of a wholly reproductive class system.

Several words continually reappear in the copious amounts of literature devoted to the study and critique of Willis's work over the past quarter century: *class, education,* and *ethnography.* An exploration of these three connected aspects of his writing and research structures this volume's engagement with his work. Such an emphasis is particularly appropriate at this moment, as all three terms are undergoing profound, substantive changes that reconfigure the way that educational researchers will approach their work in this century. First, as we discuss throughout this introduction and the book, "class"—as an explanatory category and a site of identification—is reemerging as a key locus of academic inquiry.[1] Second, "education" as a public good is under threat globally, as corporate practices and privatization are increasingly accepted as the norm (Apple, 2001; Klein, 2000; Stromquist, 2003). Finally, "ethnography," as a practice is reshaping itself in light of decades of harsh critique, so that it can continue to be a significant force in academic practices that help us to understand, and transform, social and cultural worlds. In this introduction, we map theses three trajectories in Willis's work, and then introduce the essays in this volume. As is evident throughout this volume, Paul Willis's remarkable contributions to the rich literature on class, education, and ethnography are formative sparks that will undoubtedly mold how educational researchers make sense of, and attempt to influence, this new terrain.

Learning to Labor: Twenty-Five Years Later

Learning to Labor: How Working Class Kids Get Working Class Jobs is arguably one of the most significant educational research studies of the 20th century. The book was originally published in Britain in 1977 by Gower Press. Since that time, it has been reprinted nine times in Britain, published in a separate U.S. edition in 1981, and published in German, Swedish, Finnish, Japanese, Spanish, Portuguese, and Korean. Based on an ethnographic study of a group of working-class boys in a secondary school in an industrial area of England in the 1970s, Willis's analysis of the lads' role in the production and reproduction of their position in the working class stands as major contribution to multiple fields, including education, anthropology, sociology, cultural studies, and political science. Within education, Willis's work precipitated a major shift in the way that researchers have come to understand the school as a site of political, social, and cultural struggle, and the way that youth's identities are constituted within schools, ground largely in their own particular autonomy.

Through the 1970s, the dominant approach to class analysis in education had been structural (see Morrow & Torres, 1995). Bowles and Gintis's influential *Schooling in Capitalist America* (1976) was perhaps the most important text in this regard. For Bowles and Gintis, schools had a key functional role in the reproduction of capitalism, preparing young people to take their places in a differentiated class hierarchy. Schools operated on what they called a "correspondence principle," and were anything but a meritocracy. One's class position was determined by family income rather than one's achievement in school. Schools helped, more often than not, to create and justify the *illusion* of meritocracy, but not its reality. For Bowles and Gintis, the pedagogical experience was about learning to take one's place in the capitalist system.

Ultimately, or "in the final instance," capitalism was reproduced. There was little room for transformative action, for an understanding of human agency, or for the rearticulation of ones circumstances.

Willis's *Learning to Labor* came out of a very different kind of history and academic tradition. Although Bowles and Gintis were both economists, trained in statistical methods, Willis situated himself within the more interpretive, humanistic, and ethnographic tradition of the Birmingham School for Cultural Studies. Here, there was an effort to understand the cultural dimensions of everyday life, how people lived through the structural conditions they found themselves in. There was, of course, a stress on agency and creativity in this regard, and an effort to understand social structures from the ground up.

Learning to Labor is an ethnography of working-class youth in an industrial town Willis calls Hammertown, conducted between 1972 and 1975. Hammertown is, for Willis, an "archetypal industrial town." It had first been industrialized over 200 years before Willis began his work (p. 6). As Willis explains, the total labor force in this town was about 36,000, with an extremely high percentage—79%—involved in manufacturing. Half of these jobs were in metal and metal goods, wherease the other half included the production of bricks, pottery and glass, and food, beverages, and tobacco.

For this study, Willis followed a small group—about 12—of working-class youth throughout their school day. He attended classes and leisure activities and at points accompanied them onto the shop floor. He interviewed individual youth, recorded group discussions, and interviewed parents, senior masters at the school, the youth's teachers, and career officers. As the study was multisited, Willis also interviewed and spent time with a smaller cohort of other youth.

Willis's findings are, by now, well known. These working-class boys create a culture of resistance and opposition to authority. As Willis writes, "The opposition is expressed mainly as style. It is lived out in countless small ways which are special to the school institution, instantly recognized by the teachers, and an almost ritualistic part of the daily fabric of life for the kids" (p. 12). These boys spend their days "dosing, blagging, and wagging." Above all else, "having a laff" is key. "Opposition to the school is principally manifested in the struggle to win symbolic and physical space from the institution and its rules and to defeat its main perceived purpose: to make you 'work'" (p. 26). These boys enact everyday resistances to all symbols of school authority—teachers as well as conformist youth.

Willis powerfully documents the emergence of an aggressive, White working-class masculinity. The youth in his study violently mark out the boundaries of their lives: They are aggressively territorial about their neighborhood and are quick to fight. The lads are also sexist and racist. Young women must be sexually attractive, but "giving in" to sex devalues them immeasurably. Courtship is complicated business. "The referent is the home—dependability and domesticity—the opposite of the sexy bird on the scene. If the initial attraction is based on sex, the final settlement is based on a strange denial of sex" (p. 44). A kind of "domestic code" rules the day (Weis, 1990). In racial terms, the boys define themselves against Asians and West Indians, seeing both as "foreign," "smelly," and "dirty" yet still differentiated (and threatening) in sometimes divergent ways.

Willis displays the counters of an emergent White working-class masculinity. He focused on these young men's resistance to school authority and the way they were able to subvert dominant culture on a local level through devaluing school life. Crucially, it also means that they are invested in masculine kinds of labor activities, the kinds of work associated with manual labor and heavy industry. Perhaps Willis's most important insight is that these young men are complicit in their own class reproduction. The kinds of dispositions they generate in school prepare them for life on the shop floor. In addition to the immediate financial rewards, they are more likely to "have a laff" on the shop floor. The culture of resistance generated in school is entirely continuous with work culture. It is a cruel irony. In one of the book's more trenchant moments, Willis asserts:

> For no matter what the larger pattern of working class culture and cycle of its continuous regeneration, no matter what the severity of disillusionment amongst "the lads" as they get older, their passage is to all intents and purposes irreversible. When the cultural apprenticeship of the shopfloor is fully worked out, and its main real activity of arduous production for others in unpleasant surroundings is seen more clearly, there is a double kind of entrapment in what might be seen, as the school was seen before, as the prison of the workshop. Ironically, as the shopfloor becomes a prison, education is seen retrospectively, and hopelessly, as the only escape. (p. 107)

This is only one of the study's most enduring findings. Along with this class reproduction, however, is the notion that there are cracks in this edifice. Reproduction is never total. In what Willis refers to as moments of "partial penetration," the lads understand that they are positioned as abstract labor. These are key insights: insights about the nature of the lads' labor and their control over it. However, as noted, these penetrations are largely subverted by their own resistant practices.

Youth, Common Culture, and The Ethnographic Imagination

One of the most sustained legacies of *Learning to Labor* is its focus on youth's agency. Though the lads' resistance and "victory" was pyrrhic, Willis drew attention to the importance of scrutinizing youth's everyday lives and practices through ethnography. In Willis's later work (*Profane Culture* [1978], *Common Culture* [1990], and *The Ethnographic Imagination* [2001]) he specifically extends and examines the substantive and methodological implications of what he terms youth's everyday cultural lives. The "ethnographic imagination perspective" that Willis develops is one that acknowledges the "art" of everyday life, that understands people make sense out of their lives in creative ways and that there are moments of penetrating insight worth exploring and documenting (Willis, 2001, p. xx). Youth are a critical focus for understanding contemporary societal dynamics, for, as Willis notes, youth are at the forefront of confronting and negotiating the new modes of technological and human transformation at the core of modernization. He writes,

> Young people respond in disorganized and chaotic ways, but to the best of their abilities and with relevance to the actual possibilities of their lives as they see, live, and embody them. These responses are actually embedded in the flows of cultural modernization, but to adult eyes they may seem to be mysterious, troubling, and even shocking and anti-social. (Willis, 2003, p. 391)

Yet, as Willis reflects, it is not enough to simply document or record the minutiae of youth's everyday lives, as if it existed in some pretheoretical world. Instead, researchers must creatively bring this experiential material into "some relation to theory," thereby "maximizing the illumination both of wider change and of the ethnographic data" (2001, p. 114). Indeed, Willis implores us to avoid the twin dangers in contemporary social scientific work—the danger of presenting empirical material divorced from theoretical reflection, as well as the danger of theoretical reflection divorced from an engagement with the empirical.

For Willis, there is something irreducible about the human experience. Reflecting on *Learning to Labor*, he noted that he had "a 'common sense' view which knew that your identity was always *more* than class, gender, or ethnicity, involving a whole set of points about the way you lived, how you fitted in, who you knew, what the myriad of your personal and domestic relations were: these things were separate from the theories that I picked up specifying obvious binary divisions" (Mills & Gibb, Appendix, this volume). Ethnography is a way at getting at some of this cultural complexity, a way to reflect on experience in ways that go beyond easy categories and distinctions.

Ultimately, this kind of work points us to a broader project that looks to understand the ways people creatively deal with their realities, which is one of the enduring lessons of *Learning to Labor*. Willis's politics center on capturing this spark "of creativity or aspiration"—which is at the core of the lads paradoxical "moment of partial penetration"—and using it to propel us into the terrain of new possibilities. Here we find Willis's hope, as he reflects that this spark is "routinely lost, distorted or alienated or turned into reified forms" though "never quite lost" (Mills & Gibb, Appendix, this volume).

Willis has spent much of the past few years extending these concerns, studying young people's cultural lives. In particular, his influential *Common Culture* documented the multiple uses to which a group of young people put popular culture, or, as he writes, the "common culture" that young people create and sustain. Willis, for example, celebrates the ways that young people subvert dominant music and fashion industries by taping music from the radio for free and buying secondhand clothes and using them in exciting and interesting ways. He also documents the ways in which an all-pervasive media culture has come to wholly saturate the rituals of everyday life,

> The omnipresent cultural media of the electronic age provide a wide range of symbolic resources for, and are a powerful stimulant of, the symbolic work and creativity of young people. . . . The media enter into virtually all of their very creative activities. But whilst the media invite certain interpretations, young people have not only learnt the codes, but have learnt to play with interpreting the codes, to reshape forms, to interrelate the media through their own grounded aesthetics. They add to and develop new meanings from given ones. (Willis, 1990, p. 30)

Willis does much to highlight the work that young people invest in popular culture and the ways in which popular culture is occluding contemporary school culture for many. If *Learning to Labor* focused largely on school life, *Common Culture* was a more fully contextualized look at young people's creative lives as they traverse a wider range of spaces. Indeed, one of the major implications of *Common Culture* was its impulse to decenter "school" as the most relevant node in young people's lives and open up a much wider range of texts and sites for study.

Willis's expansive engagement with the lives of young people, it's critical to note, is imperative to developing policy from below. Just as Willis challenges the official role that schools play in young people's lives, he also opens up a space for us to ask what kind of policies make sense from "the ground up." This was also a vital part of *The Youth Review* compendium he helped to put together. The study, undertaken in Wolverhampton and sponsored by the Labour party, was an effort to understand the effects of unemployment on local youth, asking one of the most persistent new questions about work and class: What happens to the working-class when work disappears? As Willis reflects, this study indexed the "new social condition" of youth, and, consistent with his commitments to youth's realities and agency, asserted that "policies could be derived from the actual existing condition of the youth, rather than from the view of the powerful as to how they should change or be formed" (Mills & Gibb, Appendix, this volume).

Willis in New Times

At the time of publication, and shortly thereafter, *Learning to Labor* was critiqued for privileging class analysis over the persistent dynamics of gender and race. Most notably, Angela McRobbie charged that Willis overlooked the lives of young girls, reinforcing the lads' own sexist stereotypes. She wrote:

> Questions around sexism and working-class youth and around sexual violence make it possible to see how class and patriarchal relations work together, sometimes with an astonishing brutality and at other times in the 'teeth gritting harmony' of romance, love and marriage. One of Willis's "lads" says of his girlfriend, "She loves doing fucking housework. Trousers I brought up yesterday, I took 'em up last night her turned 'em up for me. She's as good as gold and I wanna get married as soon as I can."
>
> Until we come to grips with such expressions as they appear across the subcultural field, our portrayal of girls' culture will remain one-sided and youth culture will continue to "mean" in uncritically masculine terms. Questions about girls, sexual relations and femininity in youth will continue to be defused or marginalized in the ghetto of women's studies. (McRobbie, 1991, p. 18)

McRobbie's critique was incisive, and one that resonated with then-growing interest in questions of "identity" and "recognition" in the academy. In the United States in particular, although the mantra of race, class, and gender was often evoked, it was questions of race and gender that moved to the center of academic analysis. Although there are varying perspectives on why class analysis slipped off of the agenda of the left in the 1980s and 1990s (see Peter McLaren & Valerie Scatamburlo-D'Annibale, chap. 3, this volume), one of the most certain realities is that the "working class" was harder to find and locate as a political movement and social force. Politically, the

Thatcher and Reagan "revolutions" of the late 1970s and 1980s largely articulated working-class concerns to a rightist agenda that appealed to White, nativist sentiments, at the same time that the clout of labor declined, and the structural conditions of the economy changed. The new social movements of the 1960s and 1970s sutured identities around gender, race, sexual orientation, and disability, displacing any sense of collective identities that were specifically linked to class location—despite the fact that movements based on social identities were often fractured and ultimately rendered powerless by latent class splits.

The late 1990s and the turn of the 21st century have bred a new set of realities, and a new set of contexts vis-à-vis class and capitalism and their relationship to schooling. Willis brilliantly documented a particular moment in the historical narrative of capitalism—a moment that has now evaporated, to be replaced with a story that is more complex and, in many respects, more troubling. First, it is clear that the structural conditions of capital have shifted dramatically since Willis's study of a small industrial town. Corporations in "First World" nations such as the United States, the United Kingdom, and Australia have largely closed domestic operations and industrial production, moving operations to free trade zones and "Third World" countries where they exploit a largely destitute, Black, nonunionized workforce that is desperate to simply stay alive. This literal relocation has been devastating to the economic health of the White working class, who may now look back on the lads' situation with nostalgic longing, for at least the lads had a job awaiting them. Today's working class in the industrialized world is largely employed in low-wage jobs with no possibility of advancement, overwhelmingly, Black, often immigrant, and largely female. Second, such changes also reflect the material changes in the constitution of capitalism, as "productive labor" fades as the real basis of the economic structure, to be replaced with an age where the economy is largely driven by the circulation of capital through the fluctuations of markets. As Benjamin Lee and Edward LiPuma (2002) argued, the shifts in the way that capital is imagined has material consequences for its function, changes that have rapidly accelerated in the 30 years since the Bretton Woods agreement, which created enormous transformations in international financial markets. Such changes have also had implications for the cultural imaginings of modernity (Appadurai, 1996), the relationship between culture and capital (Jameson & Miyoshi, 1998; Lowe & Loyd, 1997), and the constitution of human and economic communities (Castells, 2000; Ong, 1999; Sassen, 2001, 2002).

Of course, these global repositionings also have implications for the ways that scholars theorize about the relationship between school, work, class, and capital, and how we make sense of youth's school and work identities. For example, Lois Weis's (1990) study of a White working-class high school in a deindustrializing area of the United States examines what happens to working class identities when there is no work, a theme that is also probed in several of Stanley Aronowitz's latest books (Aronowitz, 2001; Aronowitz & Cutler, 1998). Although Willis's study assumed a close relationship between the state, the economy, and the schools, such linkages are no longer as strong, as economies and educational systems are increasingly positioned within global, not national, contexts (Apple, 2003; Burbules & Torres, 2000; Stromquist & Monkman, 2000). Despite these powerful and often overwhelming forces, Willis's work reminds us that sparks proliferate, and that we must continually look to youth and their creativity to understand the potentials that exist at any specific moment. For example, as Naomi Klein (2000) demonstrated, there is a growing anticorporate sentiment among young people today. Within the context of schooling, Willis (2003) recently argued that educational researchers must focus attention on what he terms the "third wave" of cultural modernization, in which commodities are central to creative processes of identity, and to the revamped terrain of social and political relations and power.

Willis's work matters because it taps into questions that are at the core of any contemporary research or practice that is concerned with (re)building what Michael Apple termed "thick democracy" in a historical era when citizenship has become conflated with consumption (2003, p. 12; Dolby, 2003). For example, how do we define and think about the working-class in the context of changed state power, new global formations, and empire; how do youth still "learn to labor" under these conditions; and how can schools, as sites of power and struggle, change these realities? As Paul Willis demonstrates through his work over the last 25 years, the everyday lives of ordinary people—the literal and metaphorical "streets" of the world—are at the center of the answers (Willis, 1990).

The Essays

The essays in this volume are divided into three sections. In the first section, Madeleine Arnot, Peter McLaren and Valerie Scatamburlo-D'Annibale, Michael Apple, and Fazal Rizvi engage with the complexities of *Learning to Labor*, taking up both its limitations and possibilities within its own historical moment, and as we reflect on it from the vantage point of 2004. In the second section, Jane Kenway and Anna Kraack, Lois Weis, Kathleen Nolan and Jean Anyon, and Cameron McCarthy probe *Learning to Labor*, and Willis's other works, for their relevance for "new times," how we might retain and reinvigorate Willis's insights about class into the remarkably different economic, cultural, political, and cultural landscape that we face, and the ways that Willis's work can motivate and inspire a new generation of educational scholars. The volume concludes with reflections from Paul Willis, and David Mills and Robert Gibb's 2001 interview with Paul Willis, "'Centre' and Periphery."

Section I: Reflecting on *Learning to Labor*

In Section I, authors focus their reflections and analysis on Willis's work. Although *Learning to Labor* provides the anchor for this section, other texts are also discussed, within a broad framework of assessing the impact of *Learning to Labor* for educational theory, analysis, and policy.

Madeleine Arnot's chapter, "Male Working-Class Identities and Social Justice: A Reconsideration of Paul Willis's *Learning to Labor* in Light of Contemporary Research," opens the volume with a discerning analysis of *Learning to Labor*, examining three different readings of the book, and then placing *Learning to Labor* within the context of contemporary research on male working class identities. Arnot's thorough essay carefully interrogates many of the historical and contemporary critiques of the book, specifically in regard to the intersection of gender and class in Willis's work.

Although Arnot's work explores the intersection of gender and class, the second chapter of the volume returns us to the "abiding centrality of class." In "Paul Willis, Class Consciousness, and Critical Pedagogy: Toward a Socialist Future," Peter McLaren and Valerie Scatamburlo-D'Annibale explore the political trajectories and possibilities that emanate from several of Willis's works, including *Learning to Labor, Common Culture,* and *The Ethnographic Imagination.* McLaren and Scatamburlo-D'Annibale argue for a politics that moves beyond the defetishizing of cultural practices into the development of the working-class consciousness that is evident in Willis's analysis. Drawing on Willis, McLaren and Scatamburlo-D'Annibale aim to resituate class as both a lived culture and an objective existence, and to use this positioning to move towards a socialist future.

The concluding two essays of this section analyze Willis's work for what can be understood about yet another intersection: this time, between class and race. In his contribution to this volume, "Between Good Sense and Bad Sense: Race, Class, and Learning from *Learning to Labor,*" Michael Apple begins by tracing the influence of Paul Willis's work on his own intellectual development, noting that Willis's theoretical insights have helped to shape Apple's notions of "good" and "bad" sense, and the contradictions inherent in various positionalities, such as race and class. In the essay, Apple develops this analysis through an extended critique of BAEO, the Black Alliance for Educational Options, an alliance of African American parents and teachers who are supporters of the neo-liberal policy of school vouchers. Apple concludes by observing that Willis's work provides a critical touchstone for educational research in the future, as scholars strive to critically engage the understandings provided by the last two decades of "post" analysis without sliding back into a reductive class analysis.

In the final chapter in this section, "The 'Lads' and the Cultural Topography of Race," Fazal Rizvi complicates *Learning to Labor* through questioning the relationship between the "lads" and the racial "others" who populated their lives. Reflecting on his own experience in England as a "racial other" at the time, Rizvi interrogates Britain's colonial history and postcolonial present, and uses Stuart Hall's idea of "new ethnicities" to theorize the impact of new, hybrid cultural forms on the subjectivities of Willis's lads—past, present, and future. Rizvi concludes by arguing that racial relations, in Britain and elsewhere, must be understood within a global framework, one that recognizes both the entrenched racial antagonisms of the present, and the spaces of hybrid, dynamic identities that simultaneously flourish.

As a group, these essays reflect on the multiple contributions of Paul Willis's work to educational research over the past 25 years, and the continued relevance of his analysis for understanding the dynamic and intricate intersections between class, education, and the economy.

Section II: Learning to Labor in New Times

In Section II, "Learning to Labor in New Times," authors collectively interrogate how global economic shifts—including the massive shift away from industrial economies toward service-based ones—have registered attendant cultural, gender, and racial dynamics on the quotidian lives of 21st century citizens. Indeed, one of Willis's central insights was to show how "the lads' " gendered and racialized identities were imbricated in their ideas about labor itself. The four chapters in this section ask what happens when the reality of work itself changes, what "identity work" happens and why.

Jane Kenway and Anna Kraack's chapter, "Reordering Work and Destabilizing Masculinity," looks at how young men have responded to the shift to deindustrialized economies in two Australian locales. According to Kenway and Kraack, generations of men have "earn[ed] respect and reputation by performing a job well and diligently and by working hard to earn a decent wage." The move to a service economy is often seen as a move to "feminized" labor, potentially destabilizing these notions of male selfhood. Kenway and Kraack interrogate the dynamics at two different sites in Australia, comparing and contrasting responses. In the first example, Putland, men largely hold onto their ever-antiquated ideas about the labor market, internalizing many of their failures. In the second example,

Paradise, younger generations of men look to a growing tourist industry, potentially redefining their notions of labor and gender.

In the following chapter, "Revisiting a 'Moment of Critique': Class, Gender, and the New Economy," Lois Weis revisits the participants in her earlier study, *Working-class Without Work*. In this earlier study, Weis famously discussed a "moment of critique" in her teen working-class female partici-pants—the burgeoning idea that they could not rely on men to take care of them, that they needed to achieve their own education and career. In this follow-up study, Weis reinterviewed these (now) young adults to see how this critique played out in their lives. She highlights the experiences of two young women, Judy and Suzanne. Although distinct in many ways, each young woman, in fact, actualized many of her earlier dreams and aspira-tions for an education and career. However, neither was able to fully disentangle themselves from the patriarchal gender relations they grew up with. In particular, neither was able to fully escape the brutality of male abuse, whether from husband or partner.

Both Kenway and Kraack and Weis show how changing economic contexts have reworked traditional notions of gender. In the next chapter, "Learning to Do Time: Willis's Model of Cultural Reproduction in an Era of Postindustrialism, Globalization, and Mass Incarceration," Kathleen Nolan and Jean Anyon move the discussion more explicitly to the terrain of race. Here, Nolan and Anyon extend Willis's discussion of school, work, and social reproduction for working-class White youth, to the terrain of contem-porary Black youth. For these youth, incarceration is an increasingly prevalent reality, largely supplanting the role and importance of school. The authors situate the rise of incarceration with multiple and varied pressures of globalization, including the rise of the prison industry, as well as the growth of a "surplus" population of underskilled youth. Drawing on compelling ethnographic data, they argue that young people are more and more embodying dispositions—echoes of Willis's lads' "having a laff"—that will prepare them for a lifetime of intermittent incarceration. They end, however, on a hopeful note, noting that the cultural manifestations of urban youth are being articulated to larger political movements.

Finally, Cameron McCarthy's chapter, "Thinking About the Cultural Studies of Education in a Time of Recession: *Learning to Labor* and the Work of Aesthetics in Modern Life," brings this section to a close. Here, McCarthy argues for the role and importance of aesthetics in everyday life. The kind of material reproduction that Willis assumed in his work has been supplanted for many marginalized youth. More and more, the imagination is a material fact, as is the complex self-fashioning that is linked to global popular culture. According to McCarthy, Willis's "nationally and geograph-ically inscribed lads" are largely being replaced by a more complex set of identifications and affiliations—"the new representational technologies are the centers of public instruction providing the forum for the work of the imagination of the great masses of the people to order their pasts and present and plot their futures."

Taken together, these chapters extend the implications of Willis's work to more context-specific treatments of social and cultural reproduction. These articles all affirm the importance of material realities while looking beyond them, to the variability of life for contemporary global subjects.

Section III: Critical Ethnography, Culture, and Schooling: Paul Willis Reflects on *Learning to Labor*

The book concludes, in Section III, with Paul Willis's reflections, "Twenty-Five Years On: Old Books, New Times." In his reflection, Willis calls for a new commitment to ethnographic research that ranges across a wide swath of cultural sites, restoring the primacy of the everyday in critical analysis of new times.

Notes

1. Note, for example, the significant interest in Michael Hardt and Antonio Negri's *Empire* (2000).

References

Appadurai, A. (1996). *Modernity at large: Cultural dimensions of globalization.* Chicago: University of Chicago Press.

Apple, M. (2001). *Educating the "right" way: Markets, standards, god, and inequality.* New York: RoutledgeFalmer.

Apple, M. (2003). *The state and the politics of knowledge.* New York: RoutledgeFalmer.

Aronowitz, S. (2001). *The last good job in America: Work and education in the new global techno-culture.* Lanham, MD: Rowman & Littlefield.

Aronowitz, S., & Cutler, J. (1998). *Post-work: The wages of cybernation.* New York: Routledge.

Bowles, S., & Gintis, H. (1976). *Schooling in capitalist America: Educational reform and the contradictions of economic life.* New York: Basic Books.

Burbules, N. & Torres, C. (2001). *Globalization and education: Critical perspectives.* New York: Routledge.

Castells, M. (2000). *The rise of the network society* (2nd ed.). Oxford, UK: Blackwell.

Dolby, N. (2003). Popular culture and democratic practice. *Harvard Educational Review 73*(3), 258–284.

Hardt, M., & Negri, A. (2000). *Empire.* Cambridge, MA: Harvard University Press.

Jameson, F., & Miyoshi, M. (Eds.). (1998). *The cultures of globalization.* Durham, NC: Duke University Press.

Klein, N. (2000). *No logo.* New York: Picador.

Lee, B., & LiPuma, E. (2002). Cultures of circulation: The imaginations of modernity. *Public Culture, 14*(1), 191–213.

Lowe, L., & Lloyd, D. (Eds.). (1997). *The politics of culture in the shadow of capital.* Durham, NC: Duke University Press.

McRobbie, A. (1991). *Feminism and youth culture: From Jackie to just seventeen.* Boston: Unwin Hyman.

Morrow, R., & Torres, C. (1995). *Social theory and education: A critique of theories of social and cultural reproduction.* Albany: State University of New York Press.

Ong, A. (1999). *Flexible citizenship: The cultural logics of transnationality.* Durham, NC: Duke University Press.

Sassen, S. (2001). *The global city: New York, London, Tokyo* (2nd ed.). Princeton, NJ: Princeton University Press.

Sassen, S. (Ed.). (2002). *Global networks, linked cities.* New York: Routledge.

Stromquist, N. (2003). *Education in a globalized world: The connectivity of economic power, technology, and knowledge.* Lanham, MD: Rowman and Littlefield.

Stromquist, N., & Monkman, K. (Eds.). (2000). *Globalization and education: Integration and contestation across cultures.* Lanham, MD: Rowman and Littlefield.

Weis, L. (1990). *Working class without work: High school students in a de-industrializing economy.* New York: Routledge.

Willis, P. (1981). *Learning to labor: How working class kids get working class jobs.* New York: Columbia University Press. (Original work published 1977)

Willis, P. (1978). *Profane culture.* London: Routledge & Kegan Paul.

Willis, P. (1990). *Common culture.* Milton Keynes, UK: Open University Press.

Willis, P. (2001). *The ethnographic imagination.* Cambridge, UK: Polity Press.

Willis, P. (2003). Foot soldiers of modernity. *Harvard Educational Review, 73*(3), 390–415.

Reflecting on *Learning to Labor*

Male Working-Class Identities and Social Justice

A Reconsideration of Paul Willis's Learning to Labor *in Light of Contemporary Research*

MADELEINE ARNOT

The publication of Paul Willis's *Learning to Labor* in 1977 represented a landmark in the study of social identities and social justice in education. When first published, Willis's seminal thesis about why working-class boys get working-class jobs was described on its back cover as "an uncompromising book which is certain to provoke considerable controversy." Twenty-five years later, the book is still one of the most cited sociology texts in the study of education. The fact that this text has been read and reread in the very different decades of the 1970s, 1980s, and 1990s and now in the new century is indicative of the power of its analysis. In an extraordinary way, Willis's text links the "problem" of working-class education, which has framed social democratic policy discourses since 1944, with contemporary concerns about identities, culture, and social change. Rereading Willis at this critical stage in the field of sociology, I want to argue, has significance beyond the immediate concerns of the book. The various rereadings of the book, only some of which I refer to in this chapter, exemplify some of the complex theoretical and methodological shifts in critical educational theory. I argue that, despite the numerous rigorous criticisms of Willis's theory of working-class culture and the social-cultural reproduction of working-class inequalities, the themes of his study still represent an important symbolic marker in the study of gender and social class identities and in the development of critical research methodologies associated with transformative politics. Arguably, the book also represents a more grounded and situated analysis of identity than is currently on offer. Rereading the text therefore proffers the chance to reflect critically on the current theoretical project on social identities, social justice, and schooling.

I begin that discussion by illustrating three rather different readings of the book, before exploring how male class identities are now being researched and related to issues of social justice.

Connecting Identity, Agency, and Structure

Willis's research was conducted with a group of 12 working-class boys attending Hammertown school in the huge industrial conurbation in the Midlands. At the time, the town was working class with only 8% classified as professional middle class. The population was around 60,000 with one of the highest activity rates in the country. Women were especially active in this town, and most members of the labor force (some 79%) were involved in manufacturing in metal and metal goods; the rest worked in food, drinks, and tobacco industries, mechanical engineering, vehicles, bricks, pottery and glass, and distribution. Unemployment in the early 1970s in this area was only 1% under the national average. As Willis noted, Hammertown was "something of an archetypal industrial town. It has all the classic industrial hallmarks as well as those of modern monopoly capitalism in conjunction with a proletariat which is just about the oldest in the world" (p. 6).

The Hammertown "lads" studied by Willis had developed their own strong "antischool" culture—a culture that they had developed creatively out of the materials, resources, and insights available to them. Their praxis—the creative development, transformation, and reproduction of aspects of the larger culture—paradoxically and critically led them to certain kinds of work. The effect was "the manual giving of their labor power" to the structures of Western capitalism. This giving, "a compact with the future" as Willis described it, took working-class destiny and reformed it into new purposes. Part of that process involved what he called the "partial penetration" of the "really determining conditions of existence of the working class" (p. 3), which belied official versions given to them by the school and society.

> The tragedy and the contradiction is that these forms of "penetra-
> tion" are limited, distorted and turned back on themselves, often

unintentionally, by complex processes ranging from both general ideological processes and those within the school and guidance agencies to the widespread influence of a form of patriarchal male domination and sexism within working class culture itself. (Willis, 1977, p. 3)

Using his data, Willis offered an explanation about the failure of the educational system to improve the chances of these lads. Central to his analysis was the role of labor power, and in Part 2 of the book, Willis explored the relationship of patriarchy (and to a lesser extent racialism) to capitalism. The meaning of laboring and labor power to these "young non–academic and disaffected males" was understood in the context of the logic of these other social divisions. Thus Willis demonstrated empirically how the working class cultural pattern of the educational failure of manual working-class children was different from other middle-class and working-class patterns found in schools—it had its own logic, experiences, relationships, choices, and decisions. In this analysis, the extraordinary conjunction of structural and subjective possibilities were brought together in the description of the experiences and identifications of one particular group of youth.

Learning to Labor therefore spoke to the concerns of social justice, which, at the time, were focused on male working class educational experiences and offered an analysis of class identities that resonated with the sociological discourses then current. Willis himself described how the book "hit a certain time in academic history, a certain time in Marxism, in cultural studies, educational sociology, a certain time in educational politics around an emerging disillusionment and disenchantment with the promises of comprehensive schooling" (Willis, quoted in Mills & Gibb, Appendix, this volume). The analysis went to the heart of the liberal democratic merito-cratic ideals of schooling which in the post war settlement offered schools a contradictory dual repertoire (CCCS, 1981)—the pursuit of economic growth coupled with the desire to encourage greater social equality and cohesion. This dual repertoire at the center of Labour's reform efforts brought together vocational and liberal discourses within the school. Economic rationalism was coupled the promotion of the individual skills and competencies with the tapping of working-class pools of talent and the promotion of a more educated society. In contrast, Willis's research exposed the injustice and forms of "institutional repression" (Willis, 2000, p. 38) associated with such a repertoire for manual working-class boys. Creden-tialism, the boys understood, could no more lead to the "dismantling of the whole class society" (p. 38) than it could improve the chances of the manual working class. According to Willis,

> Prevented from pursuing alternative flowerings of their capacities or subversive courses of growth, credentialism enslaves their ["the lads"] powers and seeks to trap them in the foothills of human development. . . . From the collective point of view, lived out in the culture of "the lads," the proliferation of qualifications is simply a worthless inflation of the currency of credentialism, and advance through it, a fraudulent offer to the majority of what can really mean something only to the few (pp. 38–39)

However, the consequences of revealing such "institutional repression" underlying the functioning of meritocracy through certification were not necessarily negative. Curiously, Willis's account of the transitions of the young working-class male into manual labor confirmed to teachers that not only could they not be held directly responsible for working-class failure but also that by hearing the collective voices of "the lads," teachers could begin to address the realities of the boys' lives and intervene on their behalf in transformative ways. Distancing himself from the more deterministic functionalism of social/cultural reproduction theory, Willis positioned himself within what he saw as the radical educational practice that was being nurtured by the Centre for Contemporary Cultural Studies at Birmingham University at that time. Reflecting on his work, he wrote:

> If we have nothing to say about what to do on Monday morning everything is yielded to a purist structuralist immobilising reductionist tautology: nothing can be done until the basic structures of society are changed but the structures prevent us making any changes. . . . To contract out of the messy business of day to day problems is to deny the active, contested nature of social and culture reproduction: to condemn real people to the status of passive zombies, and actually cancel the future by default. To refuse the challenge of the day to day . . . is to deny the continuance of life and society themselves. It is a theoretical as well as a political failure. (Willis, 1977, p. 186, quoted in Skeggs, 1992, p. 182)

Willis firmly believed that, by using ethnographic methods to explore in depth the forms of human creativity or "art" and their social consequences, the possibility existed of radicalizing teachers' practice and addressing the injustices associated with capitalism as a economic and social form. In his more recent book *The Ethnographic Imagination* (Willis, 2000) he described how the study of social "penetrations," such as those of the "lads," is a means of widening and deepening the "always contingent and reflexive body of knowledge about humankind" about "how humans use resources for meaning-making in context." "Cultural practices of meaning-making are intrinsically self-motivated as aspects of identity making and self-construction: in making our cultural worlds we make ourselves" (Willis, 2000, p. xiv). In *Learning to Labor*,

> the ethnographic study of culture therefore had a general role to play in pointing to injustice and in contributing to, maintaining and extending norms of social justice and human decency. There are specifically internal connections here for a perspective attuned to the lived penetrations of social agents, i.e. understanding what *in situ* practices themselves 'say' about social justice. (Willis, 2000, p. 120)

Collecting of voices of those who might otherwise be silent must be done, according to Willis, in the spirit of "respecting, recording, illuminating and learning from forms of sensuous subordinate meaning making and self-making, even as they may be distorted and constrained by their unpropitious conditions" (p. 120). The ethnographer, in Willis's eyes, may give those studied potential power through the politics of "naming," and might "open up the invisibility of symbolic work, and thereby offer opportunities for the redirection or limitation of the reproductive consequences of lived penetrations"[1] (p. 121). Other namings could thus be put into circulation in official discourses, thus "interrupting or denying the smooth functioning of expert government regulation and the legitimisation of inequality" (p. 121). Referring to contemporary worlds, such ethnographic studies can develop greater theoretical understandings of the impact of the structures, social relationships, and "behind back" social change that generate new kinds of desires and new kinds of survival and thus new kinds of identity expressed in new kinds of collectivity and new kinds of politics (p. 121).

Such ideals, however, were never likely to be achieved easily nor in a linear fashion. Indeed, through describing in such vivid detail the ways in working-class "lads" worked on and with material circumstances and their "objective possibilities," *Learning to Labor* suggested that the egalitarian efforts of school could be diverted and even negated by the self-reproduction of working class subordination. The pleasure with which the "lads" took in having "the laff," fun and the pisstake (Willis, 2000, p. 38), their "tumble out of (rather than transition from) school" (p. 41) their random selection of jobs and their "resistant dignity" (p. 39) were shown to prepare them for the logic of labor under capitalism—"an intended and conservative reproduction" of the social structure. Critical modernist and later postmodernist educators in the United Kingdom and abroad not surprisingly received the book with a certain amount of ambivalence.

Nevertheless, the power of Willis's text lay in the richness of his account of the survival of the "lads" and in the potency of his analysis of social inequality. Its sociological legacy in the fields of education and youth cultural studies can be found in the continuing focus on the extraordinary creativity of various groups of youth in responding to their positionality. Indeed, the analysis of creativity in identity construction, identifications, and alliances arguably has now become the major focus of sociological studies. At the same time, the relevance of *Learning to Labor* has been greatly affected by poststructuralist readings of such a "modernist" and politically committed agenda (Skeggs, 1992).

Methodological Agendas for Social Justice

In retrospect, it is easy to see why *Learning to Labor* was seen as methodological and theoretical turning point, paving the way not just for critical ethnographies but also later for poststructuralist readings of identity and identity work. It was described as a key marker in the development of social scientific epistemology integrating an analysis of structure and agency that was unprecedented. The critical ethnographic methods employed by Willis were interpreted, initially, as a significant epistemological break with the structures of positivism and rational theory (although arguably these had already been challenged by Hargreaves [1967] and by Lacey's [1970] studies of school life). As Wexler (2000) recently commented, Willis's analysis of the reproduction of inequality moved away from more "neutral, atheoretical" studies of boys, "adding empirical quality to a more general theoretical introduction of critical theory to education" (p. 98). This critical methodology could be taught to new generations of social researchers interested in the experiences and identities of young people, particularly during the transition between school and work.

Willis's political agenda, however, was later challenged by a number of methodological and political critiques. Beverley Skeggs's (1992) review of *Learning to Labor* commented on the extent to which Willis's political project had committed the reader to a highly romanticized celebratory view of the working-class "lads." She pointed to the "seductive" nature of the text—noticing its use of rhetorical devices such as the use of "we," its encouragement to evolve a personal response to the subjects before discussing the sociological theory about their situation (the division between the first and second parts of the book), the use of dramatic incidents that would "do a soap opera proud," the vicarious access to an unfamiliar world, the appeal of Willis's political commitment with its celebration of agency over structure and domination, his optimism and the sympathy he generates for "the lads" and their "having a laff." However, the consequences led to "a reconfirmation" for middle-class socialists "of the revolutionary potential of the working-class—if only they weren't so sexist and racist" (1992, p. 188).

Poststructuralist and postmodernist rereadings of the study went further and questioned the extent to which the book was a methodological turning point. Poststructuralist and postmodern feminists, in particular, pointed to the various ways in which Willis's project had left unresolved central questions about, for example, the role of theory, especially in relation to central questions about agency, identity, and praxis. From this approach, Willis was read as trapped within the narratives of critical theory in the mid 1970s. Using a postmodern yardstick, Patti Lather (1991), for example, criticized Willis for his a priori use of neo-Marxist theory. She argued that there was no sense of the ways in which Willis's perspective as researcher might have been altered by the data. The role of theory was therefore presented as "nondialectical, unidirectional, an imposition that disallows counter patterns and alternative explanations" (p. 67). The methodological stance of such critical Marxist theory was that it essentially privileged externality, created a unitary analysis of "the lads," and left the researcher paradoxically in a politically neutral position, distanced from his subject.

Ironically, Willis was taken to task for his failure to develop any further dialogue or praxis with the boys in his study. Gore argued that, although Willis pointed to "the productive aspects of power," he had concluded with "elucidation of the oppressive structures which kept the lads in their class position" (Gore, 1993, p. 96). She argued that concept of "partial penetration"—the ability of people to pierce through cultural contradictions in incomplete ways that did not lead to ideology critique—was itself incomplete because it did not offer insights into the possibilities for intervention. Thus, although the "language of possibility" had its beginnings in such a text, the move from an awareness of structural constraints to transformative work had not been made. Strong tensions still existed between the "'discursive foci on critique and possibility" (Gore, 1993, p. 96).

Thus, although Willis had identified the area of resistance to authority as an important corrective to the overly deterministic correspondence, he was seen as maintaining a quasi-positivist or scientific realist approach to research. Without problematizing the research process itself, the dangers of objectification, and the distanced relationship between subject and object (Lather, 1991), Willis had apparently reproduced "covert forms of positivism" or a "scientific realist approach to research" that had led in the final instance to the sustaining of an "essential male gaze of social subordination and domination as knowledge practice" (Wexler, 2000, p. 98).

The consequences of such readings of Learning to Labor were substantial. On the one hand, Willis's theory of class resistance through youth cultural forms took hold of the sociological and political imagination (Brown, 1988)—its emphasis on identity construction became the dominant socio-logical research paradigm. On the other hand, as a result of such criticisms, Willis's book was understood to represent a modernist text *par excellence* by a new generation of social scientists trained in post-Enlightenment thinking. The consequence arguably, as Beverley Skeggs noted, was that the political and theoretical integrity of Willis's analysis "has been lost in much of the game playing of postmodern discourse" (1992, p. 193).

Masculinity as Class Opposition

A different, more positive reading of *Learning to Labor* has been proffered by those concerned with the processes of gender identity formation. In the context particularly of the development of a sociology of masculinity, Willis's book represents a major break with past theories of gender socializa-tion. Willis had, in effect, shown how identity construction—the production and construction of gender identities—could be researched. Since the publi-cation of *Learning to Labor*, as Connell (1995) argued, few have doubted that the social construction of masculinities is a systematic socially negotiated process. Nor have they been able to avoid the complex interface between the social structure and culture. Paradoxically, in this context, *Learning to Labor* did not pave the way just for critical ethnographies but also for poststruc-tural readings of gender identity and gender identity work.

As Connell (1995) noted, Willis's contribution was to place the study of gender well within the analysis of working-class cultures in education, at the interface between schooling and the economy and shop floor culture and within the study of antischool cultures. Significantly, the book focused not just on class specificity but also on "a study of masculinity in practice." For Connell, Willis's study and Andrew Tolson's (1977) seminal text *The Limits of Masculinity* were the first of their kind. Both suggested that school was the site in which multiple masculinities were generated, often in opposition to school authority relations, curriculum structures, and forms of discipline. Since then, many studies have explored the range of subject positions inhab-ited by boys inside and outside schools (e.g., Brown, 1988; Mac an Ghaill, 1994; Sewell, 1997, 1998). Thus, even though the formal dichotomy of "lads" and ear'oles was soon challenged by Brown's (1987) ethnography of "ordinary" working-class boys—those who wanted to "get on" and "get out" of their destinies—his study and the many others that followed focus on the *relational* world of boys. Boys were shown to be actively shaping gender rela-tions as much as social class relations and to be constructing their masculinity within the fluid relations of gender, ethnicity, class, age, and sexuality. Rather uniquely, as early as the 1970s, Willis had brought together the study of class, gender and race relations, in a complex and sophisticated way. It is not without cause that almost every study of masculinity at some point uses Willis's research as a reference point.

Willis had also shown the ways in which different masculinities and indeed particular forms of (heterosexual/White) hegemonic masculinity were created, regulated and reproduced within the same school. According to Connell, Willis had effectively demonstrated

> the *relations* between the different kinds of masculinity: relations of alliance, dominance and subordination. These relationships are constructed through practices that exclude and include, that intimidate, exploit and so on. There is a gender politics within masculinity. (Connell, 1995, p. 37)

After Willis, school studies focused on patterns of hegemonic masculinities rather than socialization. Cultural differentiations rather than just economic differentiation, as Connell noted, became central to the study of working-class identity formation.

Ahead of its time, *Learning to Labor* explored the contradictory and negative consequences of gender and, to a lesser extent, race on White working-class boys' identities. Willis offered pivotal insights into how masculinity/sexuality could become the key to social class resistance to unjust systems. Willis described his work as "creative explorations and rearticulation of received dominant social codes and reproduction: working-class/middle-class, Black/White, male/female. Binaries can be played off against each other and miscegenated or ironically positioned to reveal third terms" (Willis, 2000, p. 37). The dualism of masculine and feminine, which contemporary poststructuralist writers such as Bronwyn Davies (1989) saw as central to the discursive framing of identities in modern society, was explored through Willis's analysis. In *Learning to Labor*, he considered how such dualisms work for working-class lads who are trapped within the objective structures of capitalism. His analysis of the "lads'" culture demonstrated that forms of social class (antischool) resistance that are based on the celebration of traditional sexual identities ultimately confirm the cycle of social class reproduction (MacDonald, 1981/2002, p. 153). It is this insight that arguably still has not been challenged. His research showed that boys were adopting, adapting, reworking, and fashioning gender dualism rather than being socialized into one or other category. The lads' "identity work" involved them critically in the inversion of the mental/manual divide associated with capitalist economies, and the matching of hard physical labor with what we would now call the "narrative superiority of masculinity."

The way in which such dualism worked in the school setting was config-ured by the realities of schooling for working-class male youth. Willis saw that "the lads" understood what was the price of conformism to the state educational agenda for the manual working classes. Conformism would entail collusion by the working classes in their own educational suppression. As Willis argued, the working-class "lad" "must overcome his inbuilt disad-vantage of possessing the wrong class culture and the wrong educational decoders to start with" (Willis, 1977, p. 128). To conform, however, would have meant the emasculation of the working-class youth. These English "lads" celebrated their masculinity against school norms of docile, conforming and diligent pupils. By labeling such pupils as effeminate and "cissies"—the ear'oles—"the lads" affirm their pugnacious and physical masculinity in an antischool culture. They thus confirm their respect for their masculine identity, derived from their families and peer group, and see its fulfillment in hard, physically demanding manual jobs. A critical aspect of *Learning to Labor* therefore is the discussion of what Willis called the "*cross-valorization* of manual labor with the social superiority of masculinity" (p. 148). In an account that has many resonances with contem-porary poststructuralist discussions of identifications, disidentifications, and subject positionings (e.g., Skeggs, 1997), Willis describes the identity work of "the lads." He commented that not all divisions should be viewed as oppressive:

> For "the lads," a division in which they take themselves to be favoured (the sexual) overlies, becomes part of, and finally, partially changes the valency of a division in which they are disadvantaged (mental/manual power). (Willis, 1977, p. 148)

According to Willis, "the lads" invert the mental–manual hierarchy and transpose it onto the gender dualism and male–female hierarchy. In effect, the mode of production and class oppression are reproduced in part through the equivalence established between the mental/manual division of labor and between masculinity and femininity. This also paves the way for the reproduction of male manual labor power on the factory floor:

> The important inversion however is not achieved within the proper logic of capitalist production. Nor is it produced in the concrete articulation of the site of social classes of two structures which in capitalism can only be separated in abstraction and whose forms have now become part of it. These are patriarchy and the distinc-tion between mental and manual labour. *The form of the articulation is of the cross-valorisation and association of the two key*

terms in the two sets of structures. The polarisation of the two structures become crossed. Manual labour is associated with the social superiority of masculinity and mental labour with the social inferiority of femininity. In particular manual labour is imbued with a masculine tone and nature which rends it positively expressive of more than its intrinsic focus in work. (p. 148)

Willis's analysis of the struggle of the working class male in the context of a dominant class culture resonated well with that of Bourdieu (1977), who argued at that time that working-class men have much to lose through educational success in such a culture.[2] Protecting themselves from social mobility and indeed from emasculation, working-class men find ways of expressing their sexuality. Bourdieu argued that biological (male/female) and gender (masculine/feminine) determinations "exert their influence on linguistic (or sexual) practices and imagery through the structure of homologous oppositions which organise the images of the sexes and classes" (Bourdieu, 1977, p. 51, quoted in MacDonald, 1981/2002; Arnot, 2002). What is at stake in acquiring dominant linguistic and cultural forms is not just the accusation of class disloyalty, but also the negation or repudiation of masculine sexuality defined in terms of virility, pugnacity, and self-assertion. Taking on bourgeois culture (a way of speaking, self-presentation through gesture, dress, and so forth) also implies a particular relation to one's body—hence, the different names for part of the body (the femininity and daintiness of *la bouche* against the roughness and violence of *la gueule*) in bourgeois and working-class speech. By inverting the classification between class cultures, Bourdieu argued, working-class men celebrate their masculine sexuality and their physical (manual) culture by punctuating their language with "coarse" and "crude" words and "broad and spicy stories"—a theme that also emerges strongly in *Learning to Labor* and, interestingly, in contemporary poststructuralist research on boys' laddish behavior in schools.

In ways that resonate well with contemporary concerns about localized social identities, Willis argues that the interconnections he uncovered between gender and class were specific to particular positionings of youth. In an interview, he demonstrated his awareness of the formation of multiple identities and multiple articulations of these binary categorizations. He commented thus:

I wasn't arguing that a certain working class male masculinity was forever linking manualism and masculinity, but that these were different binary systems with their own histories, and that in other situations, you might have different articulations of gender, patriarchal and capitalist categories. There is a real instability in the way that gender systems and capital systems or capital relations are articulated with each other. (Willis, quoted in Mills & Gibb, in this volume)

Gender Relations, Identities, and Family Life

Although Willis's classic had exposed the "brutality of capitalist productive relations" (McRobbie, 1980, p. 41), its social justice agenda arguably had failed to address the extent of male power over women and White oppression of Black groups within the working-class. Thus although setting a new agenda around concepts of masculinity, Willis had neglected to explore more fully those empirical data that demonstrated precisely the complex interaction between masculinity and femininity and its harsh consequences for working-class women. Angela McRobbie, for example, paid homage to the extraordinary creativity of Willis's study of male adolescents. At the same time she also saw that, through the language of adolescent male sexuality embedded in these texts, Willis had illustrated (but had not sufficiently analyzed) the ways in which class and patriarchal relations work together, "sometimes with an astonishing brutality and at other times in the teeth-gritting harmony of romance, love and marriage" (p. 38). McRobbie argued, like other cultural theorists of the time, that Willis failed to come to grips with working-class male cultures. She commented that

> "the lads" may get by with—and get off on—each other alone on the streets but they did not eat, sleep or make love there. Their peer group consciousness and pleasure frequently seem to hinge on a collective disregard for women and the sexual exploitation of girls. (McRobbie, 1980, p. 40)

What McRobbie found striking was how "unambiguously degrading to women is the language of aggressive masculinity through which "the lads" kick against the oppressive structures they inhabit" (p. 38). Willis was taken to task for his failure to comment critically on, for example, the way a female teacher's authority was undermined by being labeled a "cunt," the way "the lads" mime masturbating of a giant penis for amusement, their litany of sexual obscenities, and the way they publicly expressed their disgust for menstruation (jam rags) at every opportunity. The violence of the imagery, the cruelty of the lads' sexual double standard, the images of sexual power and domination become the lads' last defensive resort. By dignifying these racist, sexist, and homophobic "lads" in their degradation, McRobbie and later Skeggs (1992) argued that Willis's project failed to understand the articulation of male power and domination.

Feminist critics also pointed to the impression gained in *Learning to Labor* that male manual work depended solely on the cultural reproduction of machismo from father to son,[3] the male pride in physical labor and contempt for pen pushing. Willis had thus failed to integrate these aspects of working-class culture into a full account of the working-class family. Like most cultural theorists of the time, the family was outside the sphere of analysis. It was represented in some ways as a "softer sphere in which fathers, sons and boyfriends expect to be, and are, emotionally serviced" (McRobbie, 1980, p. 41). The private experiences (relations with parents, siblings, and girlfriends) behind "the lads' " hard outer image, and their immersion in working-class culture outside the public sphere, were largely ignored. As McRobbie noted, working-class culture "happens as much around the breakfast table and in the bedroom as in the school and in the workplace" (p. 44).

This debate still resonates with current writing on masculinity. Recently, Willis (quoted in Mills & Gibb, Appendix, this volume) recognized the strength of this feminist critique about the reduction of patriarchal relations to class, the underestimating of the importance of the home and domestic relations, and the uncritical reproduction or celebration of "sexist conventions, forms and prejudices." Yet, 25 years after this analysis of *Learning to Labor*, the internal dynamics of family life still tend not to be seen by social and cultural theorists as significant as economic factors in framing youth identities. The more the family takes center stage, the more likely it is that gender identities are located not just within the division of labor, but also within two other axes of gender power identified by Connell (1987)—that of *power relations* and what he called *cathexis* (emotional/sexual selves and attachments). These latter two axes are beginning to emerge in accounts of gender identities (in particular studies of masculinity), although unfortunately the connection to social justice is often not made explicit.

A more fully *sexed* notion of working-class culture that Angela McRobbie so powerfully called for is only now the subject of most contemporary social justice research on identities and education. Christine Heward (1996), for example, challenged contemporary scholarly work on masculinity which still tends to relate masculinity, to particular "normative understandings of family relations." These normative models tend to take up the theme of father–son relations as critical to the development of male gender identity and mother–daughter relations as critical to female gender identity. Freudian psychoanalysis and Parsonian sex-role theory, she argued, have legitimated this view of the sexual division of labor in the family. As a result, there is still little analysis of how masculinities are negotiated, experienced, and worked on in relation to more holistic notions of the psychosocial gendered power dynamics of family life.

As Heward pointed out, a boy's identification with his father (even if the father was absent most of the time) was seen as central to the construction of masculinity, which was understood in the context of "the world of work and power." Willis, like Tolson (1977), had built his theory of the "lads" using the father's position in the labor market and class culture as "an important differentiator in the construction of masculinities" (Heward, 1996, p. 36). Using seven male biographies, Heward demonstrated how "the ambivalence and alienation which characterise father–son relations" are in fact rooted in the "vast range of complexities of power, emotion and sexuality nexus *within* families." Each biographical example illustrates how the dynamics between mothers and fathers and the son's negotiations of those dynamics are problematic, contested, and unpredictable. Thus young men's experiences of family life are deeply shaped by both parents. Heward argued:

> The importance of mothers in the process of identity formation should be acknowledged rather than dismissed as anti-models who have performed their initial nurturing function. (Heward, 1996, p. 48)

The relations of self to structure in this analysis become far more complex than just the gender and generational transmission of working-class work cultures. Gender regimes and power relations, particularly in the family and workplaces, are being transformed for example by women "turning away from exploitative male heterosexuals." Intimate relations have been transformed, child-care regimes have changed, and female and male patterns of employment and work cultures have shifted. As Heward argued, "women and relations between men and women are a potent source of change in intimate relations" (p. 48)—thus, it would seem essential today that in order to understand today's "lads" we must look to the third of Connell's elements— that of emotional life and to explore "intra and inter family gender relations within structural contexts." "This would permit a wide variety of outcomes to be envisaged and make mothers integral rather than peripheral to the process of constructing masculinities" (Heward, 1996, p. 48).

Other recent research of working-class boys in English secondary schools has highlighted the centering of mothers in boys' lives. For example, in their analysis of the contemporary practice of masculinity in schools, Nayak and Kehily (2001) highlighted the contradictory role of mothers in working-class boys' humor. Like Willis's findings, "having a laff" for these boys represents one of the means by which different positions of domination and subordination among boys are established and regulated, allowing some boys to exert power over others. Humor is used as an "unofficial resource" in the culture of manhood. In Willis's analysis such humor had significance as preparation for the styles and rituals of male shop floor culture, or a form of class cultural resistance. However, today such humor has become the means by which White working-class heterosexuality is affirmed. "Wind ups, joke telling, funny stories, spontaneous gags, mimicry," Nayak and Kehily found, become the "unseen forms of communication, validating or rejecting male forms of behaviour" (p. 111). Young men are "hardly learning to labor." Having a laugh today is "every bit as dedicated to counter culture of humour as 'lads' in Willis's study, but it is less about gaining power and more about feeling entitled to it."

> We contend that heavy industrial humour may become a means of recuperating masculinity in a post industrial economy. The values embedded in schoolboy pranks, jokes and funny stories then act as symbolic codes which young men may learnt to 'be masculine' *in the absence of secure manual work.* [my emphasis added] (Nayak & Kehily, 2001, p. 112)

Where Willis observed the *class significance* of such humor, Nayak & Kehily saw cussing, blowing matches, ritualized insults, and funny/spicy stories as the undercurrents at work behind English *heterosexual masculinity.* Significantly such behavior reinforces hypermasculine egos by exploring the deepest sexual taboos about sons' relationship with their mothers. The ritualized insults play with the idea of their mothers as slags, sluts, and whores. These highly personal comments are a source of great distress for some boys, some of whom are reduced to tears in public. However, by mobilizing sexist discourses of power such as mother cussing, boys achieve superior positions in the group. They could even collude with male teachers' jokes about their mothers being "slags."

Arguably, contemporary sociological research has taken Willis's acknowledgement of working-class family culture further and has queried the powerful association between fathers and son as the only influence on the construction of working class male identity. Clearly, fathers play a major role in representations of working class masculinity, but the construction of male heterosexuality is also played out within the emotional relationships of parents and other family members. Recent poststructuralist research on masculinity has therefore developed even further the insights Willis introduced into the study of gender identities, although not necessarily within the same discourse of social justice.

Contemporary "Lads" in a Performance Discourse

Willis's ethnographic study of the response of working class youth to their schooling and their social and economic positioning exposed the social contradictions of postwar illusions of meritocracy. From a policy perspective, *Learning to Labor* offers a unique platform from which to consider the nature and extent of contemporary sociocultural and economic inequalities. Following Willis, we can now ask: Does the school with all its performance and standardizing cultures now include rather than exclude such working-class youth? Has the individualizing of educational achievement led to the transformation of such young men who had previously prepared themselves, in resistance, for their destinies as unskilled manual labor?

The book, it seems, has greater, not less, relevance in the current school climate in the United Kingdom when the processes of social exclusion have become even more acute than in the more lenient times of full employment and social democratic philosophies. Today, young men in the manual working-classes (those who are variously called "status zero" or the "under-wolves," Wilkinson & Mulgan, 1995) have even less investment in the economic future, even less prospect of making the transition into continuous work of the sort described by Willis in the late 1970s. Paradoxically, with the heightened pressure on young people today through competitive, tightly regulated, and divisive performance driven school systems, research in the United Kingdom suggests that today's "lads" appear to be pushed to even more extreme alternative cultures, and there appears to be a spread of a laddish behavior (although not working-class culture) among other groups of boys.

Willis's theory of class reproduction was challenged, as he himself recognized (Willis, 1979; Willis, Bekenn, Ellis, & Whitt; 1988),[4] by the loss of male labor in manufacturing industry in the United Kingdom. By 1989, the three great industrial sectors made up only 25% of jobs in the country, whereas the service sector accounted for 15 million jobs—almost 70% of employment. Such economic restructuring and the contraction of manufacturing industry in the United Kingdom had the greatest impact on those boys whose fathers worked in factory or other industrial jobs. The loss of their fathers' jobs was to reduce young men's expectations of finding "real work" (Haywood & Mac an Ghaill, 2001; Mac an Ghaill, 2001). The collapse of the youth labor market, the replacement of factory work with new technologies, and the expansion of the service industries all fundamentally affected the opportunities for these young men's employment after school. Willis's lads could no longer expect the conventional transitions from school to work through traditional apprenticeships and familial contacts.

Evidence from more recent studies of working-class masculinities (Mac an Ghaill, 1994; Sewell, 1997, 1998) suggests that the reforms of schooling from the late 1980s to the mid 1990s exacerbated rather than reduced school resistance. By increasing emphasis on performance and on competition within and between schools, and by raising the stakes in terms of compliance to a school culture that was class oriented, schools were more rather than less likely to be viewed as hostile institutions, especially because the sorting and selecting functions of schools were made more visible. The new school ethos bore little relationship to the realities of economic dysfunction and community breakdown. As Haywood and Mac an Ghaill (1996, 2001) argued, in areas in which working-class youth are already marginalized, surveilled, and excluded from the productive life of the society, the reconstruction of schooling according to market principles was most likely to force confrontations between young Black and White working-class boys and their teachers. It was these confrontations that created and sustained counterhegemonic masculinities among such youth that were both antiacademic and antischool.

Mac an Ghaill's (1994) ethnographic research in Parnell Comprehensive School in a predominantly working-class inner-city industrial area also in the Midlands confirmed the presence of a group of what he called "Macho Lads" who celebrate a powerful version of heterosexual machismo not dissimilar to that of "the lads" in Willis's study. As Haywood and Mac an Ghaill argued, deindustrialization creates "a crisis in White working-class forms of masculinity." The responses of the macho lads to the new ethos of schooling involves celebrating alternative sources of gender power. Gender power based on what Mac an Ghaill called *hyper-masculinity* is not so much the mechanism through which they could celebrate manual labor, but appeared to be the main source of their identity (Mac an Ghaill, 1994, p. 71). Still inverting the values of the school system, still retaining highly traditional gender values, today's "lads" now choose to celebrate the three Fs—*fighting, football, and fucking* (see also Connell's [1989] account of unemployed White working class men in Australia and Canaan's [1996] study of predominantly White working-class youth in the Midlands). In short, these "lads" cope with the multiple uncertainties of their position by promoting an exaggerated concept of heterosexual masculinity. By "behaving badly," they regain control of their lives.

Contemporary White and Black "lads" thus appear to find ways of celebrating manhood without relying on a work identity. The generational connections between hard male physical labor and working-class masculinity described by Willis are not always possible, although as Mac an Ghaill argued, White working-class lads in Parnell School still held onto outdated modes of masculinity that centered around traditional manual waged labor. In contrast, the Afro-Caribbean and Asian Macho Lads in Parnell School appeared to have less commitment to work in the locality and were more used to unemployment and economic insecurity. In Mac an Ghaill's analysis the major difference between "the lads" of the 1970s and "the lads" of the 1990s appeared to be in terms of the purposes/significance of their counterschool culture.

Male heterosexuality was found to have played a major role in shaping the responses of a group of African Caribbean boys to school (Sewell, 1997, 1998). In order to succeed, aspiring Black youth had to assume a form of "racelessness" and lose their community and ethnic identity to avoid the wrath of their teachers. The reaction to this racelessness was the counter-promotion of a new Black identity, which took the form of what bell hooks (1993) called "phallocentric masculinity" among those who found comfort from exclusion in hedonism and an antischool Black machismo. Yet these African Caribbean "lads" who were in "retreatism or rebellion" were not necessarily less positive about learning than girls. However, teachers in this case study had not only gendered these boys, but were obsessed with the dangers of Black male sexuality.

What has therefore become a major issue in current research on social justice issues is *the norm of male heterosexuality*. Today, a much preferred theoretical position for most masculinity researchers is that of poststructuralism, which offers insights into "a certain game of truth" (Martino, 1999, p. 240). From such a Foucauldian perspective, researchers can think about the various ways boys are inserted into the "game of truth" in which they learn about what it is to be "man" (p. 240). In this context, masculinity becomes a range of practices, a form of performativity that can shift in different locales, occasions, moments, and sites. There is no a priori theory of the subject. Instead, the focus is in how boys constitute themselves as male subjects. The emphasis is on the cultural techniques of boys, the "polymorphous techniques of power" (Foucault, 1978, quoted in Martino, 1999, p. 240), which they experience and sometimes own. From a Foucauldian perspective, the analysis has shifted away from the class significances of working-class masculinity to the various statuses given to masculinity in a particular school culture, an analysis of how the desires of adolescent boys are channeled and relayed, and how the hierarchy of valorized and subordinated masculinities come into being (Martino, 1999, p. 242).

Increasing interest in this aspect of male power has led to a multitude of projects on white and Black male heterosexuality among working-class youth in school (see Frosh, Phoenix, & Pattman, 2002; O'Donnell & Sharpe, 2000; Arnot, et al., 1999). The argument now put forward is that this dominant hegemonic form of masculinity has been encouraged by schools, promoted extensively by the media (*Men Behaving Badly, Loaded*) and taken up now by a variety of different boys. Displaying styles of behavior and modes of identification that ape "the lads'" culture of the 1970s, all sorts of other schoolboys have been found to exploit similar aggressive forms of heterosexual and racist masculinity as that found among Willis's manual working-class "lads." Politicians since the 1990s have publicly declared *laddism* to be the cause of male working-class educational failure and the reason for all boys' alleged underachievement (Francis, 1999; Raphael Reed, 1999). What was understood in Willis's analysis to be a class cultural response to the conditions of material existence of the working classes and of the nature of schooling within capitalism is now being represented as a characteristic of masculinity itself, irrespective of social class.

For some, the explanation for this extension of laddishness from the working classes to other social groups including even middle-class children is found (paradoxically) in the *remasculinization* of schooling, with its new cultures of competition, standards, performance, and exclusions (Mac an Ghaill, 1999). Jackson (2002), for example, argued the adoption of laddish behavior is much stronger because of the changes in the educational system, which are generating increased insecurity and pressure. Although boys appear to be using sexist and heterosexist discourses to frame their masculinity vis-à-vis femininity, she argued that from a social-psychological perspective, laddishness is also about coping with the fear of academic failure in a dominant culture of performavitity. Middle-class boys might appropriate the culture of Willis's "lads" because of the advantages of adopting the styles of disengagement and indifference of White working-class boys in such a heightened competitive environment. Some of the strategies that Becky Francis (1999) found boys now associate with "laddish-ness" involve procrastination, intentional withdrawal of effort and rejection of academic work, the appearance of effortless achievement, and disruptive behavior. The presence of a competitive performance-oriented culture generates anxiety especially among boys whose gender identity needs to be based on achieving power, status and superiority.

Heywood and Mac an Ghaill (2001) argued that the shift from "soft welfare" to harder market economies has lead to the restructuring of teaching, which, in turn, has emphasized hierarchies of domination and subordination. They suggested that the restructured authority system, intensified surveillance, disciplinary codes, curriculum and testing, stratifi-cation technologies, and the allocation and knowledge selection processes have resulted in a range of new, hierarchically ordered masculinities. New discourses of entrepreneurialism and new masculine authoritarianism are being replaced by modern forms of "technical bureaucratic knowledge." In this context, there is less socialiability between teacher and taught, and chil-dren "are now conceptualised as value added knowledge containers." The play of masculinities in school in this contemporary context therefore repre-sents a complex dynamic that appears to have less oppositional and thus has less transformative political potential. However, as Reay (2002) recently argued, there is little evidence to suggest that traditional working-class masculinities and such performance cultures in schools can in the end be reconciled politically. One cannot easily transform the other. For that to happen, those promoting working-class male educational success would need to address the centrality of masculinity as an identity forged out of deep traditional patterns of socialization.

Conclusions

The debate about family life, cathexis, and also "Laddishness" in schools, to some extent, has shifted away from Willis's account of working-class boys preparing to go into working-class jobs in their locality. The concept of "the lads" has been extended in the media, in politics, and even in boys' popular worlds to represent "all boys." As a result it is difficult to retrieve the touch-stone of critical engagement signified by the class cultural studies of the 1970s. The transformative project developed in the critique of social democracy is not clearly reflected within the critical analyses of the global-ized economy and performance-based choice cultures of schooling in the current decade. The relationship of young people's meaning making and official discourses of education, between critique and possibility, is not as clearly expressed; it is often implicit.

Paradoxically, although Willis's seminal text became a symbolic marker of modernist methodologies and narratives, at the same time arguably it antic-ipated, through the wealth of its description and theoretical insight, the development of poststructuralist tradition of studies of masculinities. As I have shown, many of the themes of contemporary poststructuralist work on masculinities were originally represented in *Learning to Labor*—most notably the working through of social classifications and dualisms, the nature of meaning making and identity construction, the situated relational worlds of identity formation, and the complex cross-articulations of class, race, sexuality and gender. The epistemological break therefore was not necessarily as strong as it has been represented. At the same time, I want to argue that some of the strengths of Willis's analysis are precisely the weak-nesses of contemporary accounts of gender.

Contemporary research on masculinities might suggest that Willis's analysis is less relevant in today's more fluid society. The argument would be that monocausal analysis of power such as the social reproduction model with its concerns about rational subjects and predictable power relations and the "romance" of working-class male creativity in the face of degrada-tion could not adequately cope with the complexity of experience among contemporary boys. Can such a theory really account for the responses of boys to the restructured globalizing economy? Poststructural research on school based masculinities, on public discourses around masculinity, and on male narratives and biographies suggests that we need more a more dense, complex, and social psychological analysis of power plays in schools, families, and communities. As we have seen, since the publication of *Learning to Labor*, there has been what has been called a "biographical turn" (Coffey, 2001) among those interested in social identities. There is now a greater interest in how an individual's "self-identity is constructed and negotiated through complex social processes" (p. 53). More attention is being paid to the creation of "choice" biographies, away from normative biographies.

This new phase, which Stanley and Morgan (1993) call the "bio-graphising of social structure and the structuralising of biography," can, however, also lead to romanticizing the individual, the personal, and their stories. Although schools are now seen as key sites for the "active construction, production and reproduction of biographies and identities," only some studies are good at ensuring that "personal narratives, individual lives and experiences are located within the situated, political and local contexts of education and schools" (p. 57). Indeed, as leading masculinity scholars such as Mac an Ghaill (1999) admit, the poststructuralist approach, although immensely valuable, cannot easily read the significance of the collective forms that masculinity take within new economies.

Willis's insights should be at the center of our thinking about a society in which qualifications matter even more than before and the social exclusion of the manual working classes is even harsher. Willis's critical ethnography was never just an ethnography, nor just an example of social-cultural reproduction theory. His work causes us to reflect on how far society has changed since the 1970s, how much we, as social scientists, have developed our analysis of the meaning of education for different groups of youth, how much we have gained and lost methodologically. But *Learning to Labor* also asks us to consider how we too might develop what Bernstein (1996) called "a generative theory" about the relationship between schooling and the economy—research questions that can be, as we have seen addressed and readdressed time and again. I would like to conclude by quoting from *Learning to Labor*. In today's context, the following observations about the relationship between identities and the social justice "impulse" are especially meaningful.

> Masculinity must not . . . be too simply posed. It has many dimensions and edges. In one way it is a half-blind, regressive machismo which brings self-destructive violence, aggression and division to relationships within the working class. In another way imparting something of what lies behind it, masculinity expresses impulses which can be progressive.
>
> Behind the expression of masculinity lies an affirmation of manual labour power and behind that (though mediated and distorted) a sense of the uniqueness of the commodity of labor

power and of the way in which the general abstract labour unites and connects all kinds of concrete labour.

The masculine disdain for qualification, for all its prejudice, carries still a kind of "insight" into the divisive nature of certification, and into the way in which mental work and technicism are mobilised ideologically primarily to maintain class relations rather than to select the most efficient or to increase productive efficiency. (Willis, 1977, p. 152)

Acknowledgments

The first draft of this chapter was presented at the American Educational Research Association, New Orleans, April 1–6, 2002, at the session celebrating 25 years since the publication of *Learning to Labor*. I would like to thank Nadine Dolby and Greg Dimitriadis for their invitation to participate in this symposium. I am also very grateful to Paul Willis for his comments on the first draft and for sending me the interview with Mills and Gibb and *The Ethnographic Imagination*. My thanks to Carol Vincent for giving permission to reprint large sections of this article, which was first published in her edited collection *Identities & Social Justice* (London: RoutledgeFalmer, 2003).

Notes

1. More than consciousness raising which Willis considered to be potentially vacuous.
2. Willis argued in an interview with Mills and Gibb (Appendix, this volume) that he was much influenced by Bourdieu, although interestingly he was not familiar with this particular article by Bourdieu, which coincidentally explored the same ground (personal communication).
3. It is relevant to note that Willis's childhood was shaped by the father–son relationship. He was brought up by his father alone after his mother's death when he was 9. Willis described his father as having played a vital role in transforming a working-class culture into a process of social and intellectual growth (Willis, quoted in interview with Mills and Gibb, in this volume).
4. See Willis's own studies of male unemployment (Willis et al., 1988).

References

Arnot, M. (2002). *Reproducing gender? Essays on educational theory and feminist politics*. London: RoutledgeFalmer Press.

Arnot, M., David, M. & Weiner, G. (1999). *Closing the gender gap: Postwar education and social change*. Cambridge: Polity Press.

Bernstein, B. (1996). *Pedagogy, symbolic control and identity: Theory, research, critique*. London: Taylor & Francis.

Bourdieu, P. (1977). The economics of linguistic exchange. *Social Science Information*, 16(6), 661.

Brown, P. (1987). *Schooling ordinary kids: inequality, unemployment and the new vocationalism*. London: Tavistock.

Brown, P. (1988). Education and the working class: A cause for concern. In H. Lauder & P. Brown (Eds.), *Education in search of a future* (pp. 1–19). Barcombe, Lewes: The Falmer Press.

Canaan, J. E. (1996). "One thing leads to another": Drinking, fighting and working-class masculinities. In M. Mac an Ghaill (Ed.), *Understanding masculinities* (pp. 114–125). Buckingham: Open University Press.

Centre for Contemporary Cultural Studies. (1981). *Unpopular education: Schooling for social democracy in England since 1944.* London: Hutchinson.

Coffey, A. (2001). *Education and social change.* Buckingham: Open University Press.

Connell, R. W. (1987). *Gender and power.* Cambridge: Polity Press.

Connell, R. W. (1989). Cool guys, swots and wimps: The interplay of masculinity and education. *Oxford Review of Education,* 15(3), 291–303.

Connell, R. W. (1995). *Masculinities.* Cambridge: Polity.

Davies, B. (1989). The discursive production of male/female dualism. *Oxford Review of Education,* 15(3), 229–241.

Foucault, E. (1978). *The history of sexuality, Vol. 1* (R. Hurley, Trans.). New York: Vintage.

Francis, B. (1999). Lads, lasses and (new) Labour: 14–16-Year-old students' responses to the "laddish behaviour and boys" underachievement debate. *British Journal of Sociology of Education,* 20(3), 355–371.

Frosh, S., Pheonix, A., & Pattman, R. (2002). *Young masculinities.* London: Palgrave.

Gore, J. (1993). *The struggle for pedagogies.* New York: Routledge.

Hargreaves, D. (1967). *Social relations in a secondary school.* London: Routledge and Kegan Paul.

Haywood, C. & Mac an Ghaill, M. (1996). What about the boys? Regendered local labour markets and the recomposition of working class masculinities. *British Journal of Education and Work,* 9(1), 19–30.

Haywood, C., & Mac an Ghaill, M. (2001). The significance of teaching English boys: Exploring social change, modern schooling and the making of masculinities. In W. Martino & B. Meyenn (Eds.), *What about the boys* (pp. 234–237). Buckingham: Open University Press.

Heward, C. (1996). Masculinities and families. In M. Mac an Ghaill (Ed.), *Understanding masculinities* (pp. 35–49). Buckingham: Open University Press.

Hooks, B. (1993, August 15). Hard Core rap lyrics stir backlash. *New York Times.*

Jackson, C. (2002). "Laddishness" as a self-worth protection strategy. *Gender and Education,* 14(1), 37–51.

Lacey, C. (1970). *Hightown grammar: The school as a social system.* Manchester: Manchester University Press.

Lather, P. (1991). *Getting smart: Feminist psychology and pedagogy in the postmodern.* London: Routledge.

Mac an Ghaill, M. (1994). *The making of men: Masculinities, sexualities and schooling.* Buckingham: Open University Press.

Mac an Ghaill, M. (1999). New cultures of training: Emerging male (hetero) sexual identities. *British Education Research Journal,* 25(4), 427–443.

MacDonald, M. (2002). *Schooling and the reproduction of class and gender relations.* Reprinted in M. Arnot. Reproducing gender? Essays on educational theory and feminist politics. London: RoutledgeFalmer. (Original work published 1981.)

Martino, W. (1999). "Cool boys," "party animals," "squids" and "poofters": Interrogating the dynamics and politics of adolescent masculinities in school. *British Journal of Sociology of Education,* 20(2), 239–263.

McRobbie, A. (1980). Settling accounts with sub–culture. *Screen Education,* 34, 37–50.

Nayak, A. & Kehily, M. J. (2001). "Learning to laugh": A study of schoolboy humour in the English secondary school. In W. Martino and B. Meyenn (Eds.) *What about the boys? Issues in masculinity in schools* (pp. 110–123). Buckingham: Open University Press.

O'Donnell, M., & Sharpe, S. (2000). *Uncertain Masculinities.* London: Routledge.

Raphael Red, L. (1999). Troubling boys and disturbing discourses on masculinity and schooling: A feminist exploration of current debates and interventions concerning boys in school. *Gender and Education,* 11(1), 93–110.

Reay, D. (2002). Shaun's story: Troubling discourses of white working class masculinities. *Gender and Education,* 14(3), 221–234.

Sewell, T. (1997). *Black masculinities and schooling: How Black boys survive modern schooling.* London: Trentham Books, (pp. 111–127).

Sewell, T. (1998). Loose canons: Exploding the myth of the "Black macho" lad. In D. Epstein, J. Elwood, V. Hey, & J. Maw (Eds.), *Failing boys: Issues in gender and achievement.* Buckingham: Open University Press.

Skeggs, B. (1992). Paul Willis, *Learning to Labour*. In M. Barker & A. Beezer (Eds.), *Reading into cultural studies* (pp. 181–196). London: Routledge.

Skeggs, B. (1997). *Formations of class and gender*. London: Sage.

Stanley, L. & Morgan, D. (1993). Editorial. *Sociology*, 27(1), 1–4.

Tolson, A. (1977). *The limits of masculinity*. London: Tavistock.

Wexler, P. (2000). *Mystical society: An emerging social vision*. Boulder, CO: Westview Press.

Wilkinson, H., & Mulgan, G. (1995). *Freedom's children: Work, relationships and politics for 18–34 year olds in Britain Today*. London: Demos.

Willis, P. (1977). *Learning to labour: How working-class kids get working-class jobs*. Farnborough, Hants: Saxon House, Teakfield.

Willis, P. (1979). Shop floor culture, masculinity and the wage form. In J. Clarke, C. Critcher, & R. Johnson (Eds.), *Working class culture* (pp. 185–198). London: Hutchinson.

Willis, P., Bekenn, A., Ellis, T., & Whitt, D. (1988). *The youth review: Social conditions of young people in Wolverhampton*. Aldershot: Avebury.

Willis, P. (2000). *The ethnographic imagination*. Cambridge: Polity Press.

CHAPTER 3

Paul Willis, Class Consciousness, and Critical Pedagogy
Toward a Socialist Future

PETER McLAREN AND VALERIE SCATAMBURLO-D'ANNIBALE

Paul Willis's *Learning To Labor*, published in 1977, marked a pivotal moment in the history of educational criticism.[1] As Stanley Aronowitz acknowledged in his introduction to the book, Willis's work represented a significant contribution to radical and Marxian-inspired analyses of the function of schools while nonetheless challenging some of their basic presuppositions. In what was to be acknowledged as one of the most significant ethnographies of working-class youth culture, a pathfinding work that connected a humanistic study of everyday life with a sophisticated macropolitical analysis of the workings of ideology and social power, Willis sought to understand how ordinary, everyday mainstream cultures were produced and to explore the expressions of resistance that were aimed at dominant social forms. *Learning to Labor* uncoils in compelling detail the ideological tensions between an oppressed group (working-class "lads") and the status quo (middle-class, white-collar "ear'oles") in order to demonstrate the dynamic processes involved in the production, reproduction, and transformation of cultural meanings that constitute class-based ideology. Scuppering much of the ethnographic conventions of the time, Willis's ethnographic study, both in theory and method, demonstrated how lived culture and the rituals of everyday school life among primarily nonelite

41

groups contributed to the shaping of capitalist structures and social relations of power and privilege. One of the most noteworthy aspects of Willis's work was its implacable openness to "experience" as well as its attempt to explore a theoretical basis for activist struggle (see Willis, 1978).

Willis argued that the lads' culture drew on the broader working-class and factory cultures and social heritage to which these young men had been introduced and exposed in their homes, neighborhoods, and communities. Their resistance to, and contempt for, the "official" knowledges presented to them in school were derived from and influenced by the features of Hammertown's broader working-class tradition. Contrary to the many myths ensconced in the rhetoric of "meritocracy," the lads were consciously but uncritically aware that their own cultural and economic location in the larger social totality was the best guide to their futures—they realized, in short, that they would probably not get "good" jobs. The lads' culture, therefore, led them to "reject, ignore, invert, make fun of, or transform most of what they [were] given in careers lessons" (Willis, 1977, p. 92). Rather than treating the lads as passive subjects deprived of agency, Willis contended that the lads were not simply channeled into jobs but rather were actively (if not defiantly) embracing their future in the realm of "unskilled" labor. Paradoxically, their resistance to the conformity encouraged within the educational setting also functioned to reproduce them as laborers in the workforce—in other words, the cultural practices that were interpreted as expressions of resistance in school situations were concomitantly serving as forms of accommodation to working-class futures. The pioneering aspect of Willis's work, however, was that he insisted that the processes by which working-class youths ended up with working-class jobs were far more complex than previous theorists had suggested. But more than this, Willis argued that the ability and eagerness of the lads to resist demonstrated at least a partial (if not sufficient) recognition of their social locatedness and the way in which they were economically situated as members of an oppressed class. This, of course, created at least the possibility of attaining the kind of class consciousness that would refuse to capitulate to at least the most orthodox features of capitalism's requirements.

Willis's *Learning to Labor* was, of course, one of several projects conducted under the auspices of the Birmingham Centre for Contemporary Cultural Studies during the 1970s. At the time, the work of the center as a whole was undoubtedly influenced by various strands of Marxism. In virtually all of its work, class was a central concept that was considered and analyzed not only in terms of its cultural aspects (i.e., people's beliefs, values, practices) but also *in relation to economic realities*. The earliest manifestations of cultural studies were, therefore, shaped substantially by social class and its attendant issues/concerns. Since then, as contemporary cultural studies have assumed an increasingly postmodern coloration, class (along with Marxism) has been generally consigned to the "discard tray labeled 'modernity'" (Milner, 1999, p. 114). Although the conflation of Marxism with modernity is, in and of itself, problematic enough given that Marx was one of the sharpest critics of liberal modernity (cf. Wallerstein, 1995), the dismissal of class as a so-called "modernist" category is even more disturbing because class as a category was never really dissolved in the bubbling vat of postmodern theory, despite claims to the contrary. Nonetheless, the category of class has been marginalized not only within the prevailing precincts of cultural studies but also in what routinely passes for "radical" social theory. Talking about class is "unpopular" and presumably not "sexy enough for the intelligentsia," whose members seem more enthralled by the "intellectual eroticism" of studying difference (Munt, 2000, pp. 3, 7). As Collini (1994, p. 3) aptly noted, in the "frequently incanted quartet of race, class, gender and sexual orientation, there is no doubt that class has been the least fashionable ... despite the fact that all the evidence suggests that class remains the single most powerful determinant of life-chances."

Discussions of the working class, so central to Willis and other founding figures of cultural studies, now tend to "stick in the throat like a large chunk of stale Hovis" (Anthony, cited in Munt, 2000, p. 3), and academics seem particularly squeamish when the subject is raised. To speak of the working class and/or working class culture at a time when the topic of social class has been deemed defunct by the sentinels of intellectual fashion is often viewed as somewhat naive, nostalgic, even perverse. Issues of class and explorations of class consciousness belong, or so we have been told, to an earlier era; notions of class are no longer "central to the current fashion in cultural studies" (Lave, Duguid, & Fernandez, 1992, p. 258). In a presumably "post"-everything society, the "problem" of class has been supplanted by "new" concerns with identity and difference—categories that are considered more appropriate to the "postmodern" condition. Today, a rather uncritical and ahistorical postmodern "pluralism" reigns supreme.

As a partial result of the conceptual shift within social theory, and cultural studies in particular, it is not surprising that Willis's study subsequently became a target of criticism. *Learning to Labor* was critiqued for its class reductionism and its almost exclusive focus on working-class males, their experiences and their forms of resistance. It has also been the object of unsupple accusations by positivists for not constituting an adequate sample for making generalizations across wider communities and groups, and feminists have charged that the study ignored cultural forms of patriarchy. Additionally, Willis's classic study has been plagued by charges of romanticizing working-class culture. The alleged structural functionalism (or functional structuralism, take your pick) of his theorizing has been traced to an epistemic essentialism and dualism. His sweeping dialectic of freedom/determination has been chastised for its presumed ahistoricism and utopianism. Yet despite these criticisms—and possibly, in part, because of them—*Learning to Labor* continues to be his most influential text—one that (a) represented a landmark in the annals of critical educational discourse; (b) created a seismic shift in the tectonic plates of educational ethnography; and (c) foregrounded the centrality of class issues/relations in the analysis of school cultures, pedagogical practices, and material conditions. We are not, however, interested in rehashing the critiques of Willis's work with the intent of defending it or contributing to the governing themes of his critics. Rather, we are concerned with identifying some political trajectories that emanate from Willis's work, for he has provided some interesting fodder for radical educationalists committed to engaging (rather than cavalierly dismissing) the legacy of Marxism at a time in U.S. history when Marxism has all but disappeared as a legitimate problematic out of which analysis and social action can proceed.

The Abiding Centrality of Class

Despite the lack of attention accorded to the category of class in contemporary scholarly narratives, everyday life is saturated with class relations. Class never went "away," and its marginalization in the academy and in realm of educational and cultural studies "merely alludes to the success of entrenched beliefs in liberal pluralism" (Munt, 2000, p. 10). This marginalization is, of course, a symptom of the larger tendency—namely, the suppression of Marxism—by erstwhile "post" and "ex" Marxists. Indeed, for years, Marxism has been maligned by the prevailing centers of intellectual power, which tend to reject it in what San Juan (2003) calls "reflex epithets" as "totalizing," "reductionist," and even "repressive." Today, the critique of Marxism by cultural studies has "become a series of unthinking reflexes and slogans that are mobilized to dismiss historical materialist critique as quickly as possible" (Katz, 2000, p. 51). In many respects, class has actually been hidden from analytic and political view by the "postmodern" turn in cultural studies. Although we would not dispute that cultural studies has made great inroads in addressing the previous dearth of cultural investigation into gender, sexuality, "race," and ethnicity, it has come at a considerable cost and has led to an evacuation of the key concern that gave birth to cultural studies in the first place—namely, a profound commitment to overcoming capitalist exploitation. Recently, Andrew Milner (1999, pp. 10–13) addressed the abandonment of class in academic and political discourses, despite the array of empirical data that provides ample evidence of the continued existence of class and people's identification with it (in both a positive and negative sense), where the daily realities of inequality in society speak not only to deep structural divides but also to economic and cultural exploitation and oppression. Milner (1999) in fact argued that the more class has become theoretically abstract and/or dealt with in a metatheoretical sense, the more it has been marginalized and, in some instances, completely obliterated from the theoretical and political canvas. The vogue is toward textual readings of class at the expense of grounded, ethnographic investigations.

We view this as a disturbing theoretical and political development, for it seems to domesticate the radicalism that informed the earliest manifestations of the cultural studies project. Rather than posing a challenge to dominant ideological formations and indeed to capitalism, post-Marxist, postmodern cultural studies (at least in the American academy) have become "an Establishment organon" (San Juan, 2002, p. 222) and have evolved into an apologetic narrative that reinscribes the banality of liberal pluralism. Our own work in recent years has attempted to redress this tendency (McLaren, 1998, 2000; McLaren & Farahmandpur, 1999, 2000; Scatamburlo-D'Annibale & McLaren, 2003). Our approach has not been one of defeatism nor triumphalism but one of emphasizing the strategic centrality of class in theorizing the "social." We argue that given the entrenchment of neo-liberal globalization practices and the global dominance of U.S. military and economic power, class is as important a category and explanatory instrument as it ever was, perhaps even more so. We believe that the ongoing significance of Willis's work can point us in the direction of a more sustained emphasis on class consciousness and class struggle within educational research. In this context, Palmer's comments could not be more apposite:

> Class, as both a category of potential and becoming and an agency of activism has thus reasserted its fundamental importance. More and more of humanity now faces the ravages of capitalism's highly totalizing, essentializing, and homogenizing impulses. . . . There are no answers separate from those of class struggle, however much this metanarrative of materially structured resistance intersects with special oppressions. Class has not so much fallen as it has returned. It had never, of course, gone anywhere. *Identified* as simply one of many plural subjectivities, class has actually been obscured from analytic and political view by poststructuralism's analytic edifice, erected at just the moment that the left is in dire need of the clarity and direction that class, as a category and an agency, a structure and a politics, can provide. The legacy of Marxism in general, and of historical materialism in particular, is to challenge and oppose this obfuscation, providing an alternative to such material misreadings, building an oppositional worldview that can play some role in reversing the class struggle defeats. (Palmer, 1997, p. 72)

We reject the notion put forward by postmodernists and poststructuralists that class is simply about habits and behavior, cultural status, or social prestige, or that is primarily a language sign whose meaning is overpopulated with referents and therefore "undecidable." Class is both a lived culture and an objective entity. It has an objective existence as an empirical category and a subjective existence in terms of the way in which it is lived.[2] The progenitors of cultural studies well understood this, even though they tended to emphasize (and in some cases, overemphasize) the subjective dimensions of class in response to the perceived economism of certain versions of Marxist theory. Yet in their rush to avoid the "capital" sin of "economism," many contemporary cultural and educational theorists have fallen prey to an uncritical and ahistorical "culturalism" that has severed the links between culture and class in a profoundly problematic manner. Unlike earlier theorizations that bridged a cultural approach and the Marxist concept of class struggle, the very notion of class struggle and the very idea that Marxism still has something to teach us is considered passé. In the contemporary postMarxist climate, those who dare speak of class tend to be Weberians who "ignore discussions of capital and labour"; as such, there has been a "tendency to depoliticize class analysis so that it naturalizes social divisions" and replaces the "engine of protest" with a "resigned, imperceptible social organism" (Munt, 2000, p. 3). Because there is no evidence that class has withered away in either the United States or Britain, there is no convincing argument that class analysis can be consigned to the proverbial dustbin of history. On the contrary, at a time when we are in the midst of returning to the "most fundamental form of class struggle" (Jameson, 1998, p. 136) in light of global conditions, class analysis must be foregrounded. This can and must be done at different levels. On the one hand, there is a need to return to concrete sites of class experience and to theorize out of them, for they represent forms of situated knowledges that may provoke the forms of class consciousness necessary in the struggle against capitalist exploitation. On the other hand, we cannot discard the notion of class as an objective phenomenon. Dominant postmodernist formulations tend to view class as one among a diversity of semiotically constructed identities and just another form of "difference." In other instances, class is associated with the process of consuming commodities as a "lifestyle event" or focuses on their circulation. Against such puerile conceptualizations, we believe it is imperative to acknowledge that class is directly connected to where a person is located within the capitalist division of labor and that it is labor that is the source of value (Allman, McLaren, and Rikowski, 2003). Capitalism is a system based on the imposition of "universal commodification, including, centrally, the buying and selling of human life-time" (Dyer-Witheford, 1999, p. 9). Furthermore, class is not simply another ideology that serves to legitimate oppression. Rather, class denotes "exploitative relations between people mediated by their relations to the means of production" (Gimenez, 2001, p. 24). Although all categories are social, "class is the quintessence of the social"; unlike other categories, class cannot be determined "except by the position of the individual in society, and cannot be reproduced except through participation in the functioning of the economic system. . . . Class . . . was created by capitalism and is reproduced together with it, and for this reason poses a real danger to it" (Kagarlitsky, 2000, p. 95).

Such an understanding of class has largely been marginalized in excessively "culturalist" narratives that confuse class (which has an objective status) with class consciousness, which is undoubtedly shaped and conditioned by social and cultural factors. Acknowledging this dimension of class does not undermine the subjective aspects of class as lived culture and lived experience, but it does point out that classes do not simply come into being by subjective fiat. Furthermore, the "objectivity of capitalist exploitation" cannot be relativized by "treating it as a mere reflex of hermeneutic self-understanding" (Harvey, 1998, p. 9) or as a mere discursively articulated subject position.[3] Unfortunately, educational discourse on the "left" has been awash in "postmodern" platitudes that sublimate class and valorize uncritical and fetishized notions of "difference" while marginalizing socialist alternatives to the social universe of capital. In an effort to counteract what we perceive to be politically domesticating and depotentiating tendencies in North American educational criticism, we argue elsewhere (Scatamburlo-D'Annibale & McLaren, 2003; McLaren & Farahmandpur, 2001) for the increasing relevance of Marxist analysis by locating the struggle for educational reform within current struggles against the globalization of capitalism and the conditions that produce the material armature of the imperial state. In doing so, we foreground the importance of working toward the socialization of productive property. Despite post-Marxist claims to the contrary, Marxist theory still has a key role to play in generating ideas that challenge intellectual orthodoxies and rationalizations for educational inequalities.

Expressive Practices and a Grounded Marxist Aesthetics

Throughout Paul Willis's innovative and expansive *oeuvre*, not only has he demonstrated an abiding interest in class consciousness and its potential role as a weapon against capital, but he has also revealed an unyielding conviction that Marxist criticism can bring about a world less populated by economic exploitation and social injustice. These features of Willis's work operate dialectically within his overall project as a Marxist scholar: Working-class consciousness can be "educated" by Marxist theory, while Marxist theory can, at the same time, be both bodied forth and conceptually deep-ened by those emboldened in their daily praxis by working-class consciousness. For Willis, understanding human action stipulates grasping its dialectical relation to social and symbolic structures. He has been espe-cially attentive to how systems of intelligibility are produced within cultural formations and how ideological hegemony is maintained internally to specific group cultures within identifiable historical moments, such as the present era of disaggregated and fragmented identities. Of course, he is most concerned with ways of challenging existing ideologies, hegemonic relations, and institutional orthodoxies through the creative operations of nondominant cultural formations.

To engage in a systematic and detailed examination of the production and reproduction of conflictual and contradictory cultural formations exer-cised by various social classes at specific historical moments, and to preoccupy oneself with how these formations contribute to the reproduc-tion of and resistance to existing capitalist social relations, is a lifelong research endeavor, and it is no surprise that Willis often takes pains to clarify and revise his work when the occasion demands. Few theorists comprehend as well as Willis what is at stake politically when, at the metropolitan heart of the capitalist empire, the commodity reigns supreme. Willis understands only too well that commodities are always produced in excess of human need, and this poses a specific problem for the reproduction of cultural life and for the reproduction of capitalist social relations in particular. Specifi-cally, Willis is interested in the dynamism constitutive of cultural production resulting in what he calls "sensuous meaningfulness" or "the bodily oil of lived presence" (Willis, 2000, p. 31). He is concerned most of all with what he terms "expressive practices" linked to "living cultures." Although these cannot be apodictically linked to the immanent and histor-ically produced situations and logics of economic production, it is, nevertheless, highly likely that such practices are connected to these logics. His work has led him to formulate moments of resistance as forms of "embedded logics in rebellious impulses or social counter-forces" (1990, p. x). It is within these impulses and forces that capitalism as a living dynamic, rife with contradictions, can best be understood.

Willis comprehends the contradictions of capitalism as both sites for cultural struggles as well as other types of nondiscursive struggles, and also as "sources for change and expansion" (1990, p. x). Here Willis sees the prickly processes of cultural reproduction tied up in the development and maintenance of "the 'teeth-gritting' harmony of capitalist formations" while at the same time, paradoxically, operating as "critical resistant or rebellious forces" (1990, p. xi). Willis reveals how working-class students produce living critiques of their identity formation within capitalist culture and in doing so explains how their "penetrations" cannot always be understood as a form of critical reflexivity. In fact, they most often take expressive forms communicated in and through their bodies. As Willis argued:

> I would never argue that the lads' culture in *Learning to Labor* is socialist though I would argue that it contains materials that must be dealt with in any socialist reconstruction. The point of my ethnography was precisely to show the profane complexity of cultural experience, only a small part of which—partially, selectively, differently at different moments of the argument—is explicable in our theoretical forays. For me culture is a very commodious and profane conceptual bag. It is much, much broader than ideology. I would never equate the two. My notions of cultural practices and cultural production ... produce *living* critiques and penetrations of dominant ideology only as a small (though critical) part of their total effective presence. They often do so in eccentric, collectively unspoken rather than individually verbal ways, and almost as the byproduct of the application of sensuous human capacities to immediate ends. I hesitate to use the word "cognition" at all to describe such processes. Furthermore, the in-built limiting structures here embedded as they are in sensuous, concrete forms are not in any conceivable sense a question of "false consciousness." It is not a mistaken or false perception, for instance, to experience class exploitation as concretely mediated and mitigated (for white men) and changed through gender and race power. These things are "real," too. (1990, p. x)

Central to cultural reproduction of the social relations of capitalist societies is the process of cultural production, a process that undergoes various stages of transformation. Cultural formations and expressive modalities are the shape-shifters of the postindustrial era, although not in a metaphysical sense; rather, they are continually transforming themselves into something else, only to return again, like the proverbial rag-and-bone shop of the repressed, in an expanded and enlarged aspect of their original state, refleshed, resignified, recathected, often with a vengeance. Willis is keenly interested in the internal relations of expressive practices—enacted while on the dole, in dance clubs, in the mall, in the classroom, or in the local pub— focusing on their critical content, their cultural production, and how cultural production is implicated in the larger process social reproduction. His center of inquiry can be said to revolve around the following axis: How do cultural commodities relate to the creative capacities and practices of the individuals who create them, and to the process of commodification in general?

In *Common Culture*, Willis discusses "symbolic work" (work that rests on the development of expressive labor power) to draw attention to the active and productive nature of cultural consumption, the "making whole" through binding fragments together, thereby defetishizing (remaking) commodities. We engage in symbolic work through our cultural practices of purchasing commodities. Our identification with the object appears to be the product of the commodity-in-itself that is purchased, but in reality it is the social effects of the purchase that we mistake for the magical attributes of the commodity. In other words, we often confuse the effects of the purchase of a commodity for the identity that we believe the commodity bestows upon us. We mistake our self-identity achieved through our purchase of the commodity for the effects of our expressive labor power. What people often confuse with the act of purchasing is, in reality, a purchasing effect, which is not a quality of their own symbolic labor. Symbolic work, as theorized by Willis, involves the transformation of commodities through the process of productive consumption; this involves the expenditure of expressive human labor to produce expanded value. In this process, alienated and fetishized meanings are converted into new contextual meanings and embodied satisfactions that were not previously available to the consumer. This process functions to expand the use value of the commodity over its exchange value through a form of defetishization. When we are faced with the production of expanded expressive labor power through the productive consumption of cultural commodities that is at odds with the repressive disciplines of the labor process, we have, according to Willis, participated in an act of resistance.

Willis has always been interested in communicative action, in the culturalization of the body, but it is in his later works, *Common Culture* (1990), and *The Ethnographic Imagination* (2000), that these interests are most fully explored. Willis begins with the assumption that no commodity is ever completely fetishized. If this were the case, communication would be impossible. He ends with the conviction that communication is only truly possible when fetishization breaks down. In other words, a given commodity must be defetishized in order to offer communicative and cultural use values. Cultural commodities, observes Willis, possess an in-built stability; there is a "double naturing" or self-repairing quality about them; they are continually extinguished and renewed, never escaping the process of fetishization, but never being reduced to that process, either. Cultural commodities are for use, not for ownership. They seduce, they offer the promise of community but never deliver on that promise. As consumers, we become addicted to the failure of the commodity, by its fraudulent claims, by its enticing promises. You can't get commodities to sign a contract, but you still take them up on their offer. What makes them creative is that they remain unfettered by historical norms of consumption and they are preloaded with expressivity. Words are never eaten the same way, and they taste differently depending on the combinations that are put in the mouth; but the best part is that they can be spit out and stripped of their dominating power before they arrive at their final destination in the stomach. Commodities are linked to the logic of capitalist production in terms of their availability within contexts of prior communicative meaning and symbolic appropriation—that is, in relation to their specific human role within communicative and cultural meaning systems which are inherently social.

Willis achieves a theoretical dynamism in *The Ethnographic Imagination* that surpasses much of his previous work. His writing appears less turgid and is crafted in a more self-consciously poetical style. On the one hand, his writing still betrays a textual heavy-handedness and arcane theorizing and trumpery that has become the signature of many postmodern writers, with ideas and concepts laboriously troweled onto the surface of his text until it appears to collapse under the weight of its own ideas; on the other hand, there are moments when his own expressive style is refreshingly probing, resembling the wordplay of a loutish Leavisite hanging out with fellow wordsmiths in the local pub, playing the theoretical dozens with the street-wise deftness of a homeboy from South Central LA. *The Ethnographic Imagination* is a work that stalks the meaning of cultural objects and arti-facts from the dark alleys of cultural criticism, cautiously approaching its subject matter from various theoretical angles and trajectories, yet never veering from the central question: How does human "praxis" rearrange the "objective possibilities" of a cultural object or material form? Carefully fash-ioning a transgressive aesthetic sensibility, Willis traverses the lost territory between particular signifiers and emotional expressivity with the hard-scrabble earnestness of a shop steward. This is especially evident, for instance, in his discussion of working-class speech codes as a process of making words into fists, a process that is populated by a politics of subver-sion and freighted with creative alternatives to official representations and naturalized ideological accounts.

In *The Ethnographic Imagination* Willis nominates resistance as a "grounded aesthetics." Grounded aesthetics is simply a modality of living through a creative defetishization of cultural commodities, and the reloca-tion of their social meaning. Grounded aesthetics highlights how "vertical" structures within capitalism that employ abstract reason and mentalized communication and that treat human beings as objects to control can be detached for "lateral" use and circulation for expressive resistance. Willis is able to boast an optimism of the will precisely because he is absolutely sold on the fecundating power of human creativity and on ethnography as a means of understanding how such creativity works in commercialized human culture. Willis sees ideological and institutional processes as producing the alienated individual of postmodern culture from above but symbolic work as producing the subject from below. He also sees the expanding and creative nature of expressive labor power as a basis for critiquing instrumental labor power, thereby challenging the capitalist labor processes and forming a basis for collective organization and a struggle on behalf of common interests. This can only occur when symbolic work is made less invisible. Because cultural production is not self-conscious enough of its own constitutive processes, informal meaning-making can help strengthen mental/manual divisions characteristic of capitalist societies.

A Critical Pedagogy of Class Consciousness

Willis undoubtedly ranks among the most prominent Marxist cultural theorists, especially in terms of the relevance of his work for education. Nonetheless, we would be remiss if we did not share some reservations we have concerning the overall trajectory of his work. In attempting to examine social life from the inside out, Willis is, at times, overly preoccupied with the expressive nature of meaning-making, particularly within the semiautonomous spaces of mediated cultural formations, or structures of mediation. There often tends to be an undialectical overemphasis on abstract labor and the production of fetishized social relations (both mediated aspects of communicative activity and resistance to reified or alienated aspects of the same activity). These fetishized social relations are tied up with the alienation produced between the worker and the commodity he or she produces but also, as Marx pointed out in his labor theory of value, with those that enable individuals to misperceive everyday social intercourse as a relation between things. This, in our view, provokes Willis at times to elevate cultural formations responsible for "alienation effects" over and above material relations of production. Although Willis is clearly aware that such cultural formations are "structured" by capitalism as a specific system of social/production relations, these relations appear much less central to his work. We don't believe that capital can be defeated through fighting within and against its mediated forms. Resistance requires more than the defetishization of commodities. It requires the very overturning of the generalization of commodity production itself and the dereification of capital and the nation state; that is, it requires overturning the historical and material conditions that shape bourgeois ideology and our imprisonment within it (see Allman, McLaren, Cole & Rikowski, 2003). It requires creating the social and material conditions that can help to shape and educate class consciousness in the pursuit of socialist futures. Especially at a time of deepening social and economic crisis, punctuated by imperialist wars of aggression and conquest, resistance requires a democratic and centralized class struggle in order to transform state power and abolish the very value form of labor that not only gives class society its ballast, anchoring it in the process of commodification, but also its conditions of possibility.

We believe that Willis's grounded aesthetics needs to be complimented by a larger strategy for socialist transformation, one that proceeds from an assessment of the objective factors and capabilities latent in the current conditions of class struggle (see McLaren 2003). The worldwide social movement against anti–corporate globalization and the anti-imperialist/ antiwar movements preceding and following the U.S. invasion of Iraq, have provided new contexts (mostly through left-wing independent publications and resources on the internet) for enabling various publics (and nonpublics beyond the institutions that serve majority groups) to become more critically literate about the relationship between current world events and global capitalism (see Pozo, 2003 and Moraes, 2003). Following an engagement in these new opportunities for analysis, it is possible to forge a vision of possible futures for humanity and the development of an understanding of what, exactly, stands between us and the realization of that vision. It is likely that the changes that we seek will not be possible without a massive social revolution consolidated around the wider struggle against imperialism, in support of human rights, and a search for a socialist alternative to capital. This will require a socialist "education" of working-class consciousness. And this, in turn, means challenging the mediated social forms in which we live and learn to labor.

One way of scrutinizing the production of everyday meanings so that they are less likely to provide ballast to capitalist social relations is to study working-class consciousness. It is here that Willis's work can be especially productive. Bertell Ollman (1993) noted that more systematic and effectively theorized studies of working-class consciousness remains to be done, given that most current studies of working-class consciousness have been derived from non-Marxist approaches. A key point to remember, according to Ollman, is that class consciousness is much more than individual consciousness writ large. The subject of class consciousness is, after all, class. Viewing class consciousness from the perspective of the labor theory of value and the materialist conception of history, as in Ollman's account, stipulates that we view class in the context of the overall integrated functions of capital and wage labor. And although people can certainly be seen from the functionalist perspective as embodiments of social-economic functions, we need to expand this view and understand the subjective dimensions of class and class consciousness. Ollman follows Marx's advice in recommending that in defining "class" or any other important notions, we begin from the whole and proceed to the part (see also the writings of Ilyenkov, 1977, 1982a, 1982b).

Class must be conceived as a complex social relation in the context of Marx's dialectical approach to social life. It is important in this regard to see class as a function (from the perspective of the place of a function within the system), as a group (qualities that are attributed to people such as race and gender), and as a complex relation (i.e., as the abstracted common element in the social relationship of alienated individuals). A class involves, therefore, the alienated quality of the social life of individuals who function in a certain way within the system. The salient features of class—alienated social relation, place/function, and group—are all mutually dependent.

Class as function relates to the objective interests of workers; class as group relates to their subjective interests. Subjective interests refer to what workers actually believe to be in their own best interests. Those practices that serve the workers in their function as wage laborers refer to their objective interests. Ollman summarized class consciousness as "one's identity and interests (subjective and objective) as members of a class, something of the dynamics of capitalism uncovered by Marx (at least enough to grasp objective interests), the broad outlines of the class struggle and where one fits into it, feelings of solidarity toward one's own class and of rational hostility toward opposition classes (in contrast to the feelings of mutual indifference and inner-class competition that accompany alienation), and the vision of a more democratic and egalitarian society that is not only possible but that one can help bring about" (Ollman, 1993, p. 155). Ollman underscored (correctly in our view) the notion that explaining class consciousness stipulates seeking what is not present in the thinking of workers and what is present. It is an understanding that is "appropriate to the objective character of a class and its objective interests" (1993, p. 155). But in addition to the objective aspect of class consciousness we must include the subjective aspect of class consciousness, which Ollman described as "the consciousness of the group of people in a class in so far as their understanding of who they are and what must be done develops from its economistic beginnings toward the consciousness that is appropriate to their class situation" (1993, p. 155). But what is different between this subjective consciousness and the actual consciousness of each individual in the group? Ollman wrote that subjective consciousness is different from the actual consciousness of the individual in the group in the following three ways:

> (1) It is a group consciousness, a way of thinking and a thought content, that develops through the individuals in the group interacting with each other and with opposing groups in situations that are peculiar to the class; (2) it is a consciousness that has its main point of reference in the situation and objective interests of a class, viewed functionally, and not in the declared subjective interests of

class members (the imputed class consciousness referred to above has been given a role here in the thinking of real people); and (3) it is in its essence a process, a movement from wherever a group begins in its consciousness of itself to the consciousness appropriate to its situation. In other words, the process of becoming class conscious is not external to what it is but rather at the center of what it is all about. (Ollman, 1993, p. 155)

Class conscious is therefore something that Ollman described as "a kind of 'group think,' a collective, interactive approach to recognizing, labeling, coming to understand, and acting on the particular world class members have in common" (1993, p. 156). Class consciousness is different from individual consciousness in the sense of "having its main point of reference in the situation of the class and not in the already recognized interests of individuals" (1993, p. 157). Class consciousness is something that exists "in potential" in the sense that it represents "the appropriate consciousness of people in that position, the consciousness that maximizes their chances of realizing class interests, including structural change where such change is required to secure other interests" (1993, p. 157). Ollman stresses that class consciousness "exists in potential," that is, "class consciousness is a consciousness waiting to happen" (1993, p. 187). It is important here not to mistake class consciousness as some kind of "abstract potential" because, in contrast, it is "rooted in a situation unfolding before our very eyes, long before understanding of real people catches up with it" (1993, p. 157). Class consciousness, then, is not something that is fixed or permanent but is always in motion. The very situatedness of the class establishes its goal—it is always in the process of becoming itself, if we understand the notion of process dialectically. Consequently, we need to examine class from the perspective of Marx's philosophy of internal relations, as that "which treats the relations in which anything stands as essential parts of what it is, so that a significant change in any of these relations registers as a qualitative change in the system of which it is a part" (Ollman, 2003, p. 85).

Willis captures this dynamics of class when he writes:

Non-class categories may tell you more empirically about a person, but they do not "move" or develop by themselves. To understand principles of change or how those categories combine or develop over time, to make sense of the picture, to historicize it we need the dynamism of economic relations. To be crude, class explains more about them than they can explain about it. Socially received and atavistic, often still unnamed or analyzed, categories provide the sea, class the currents. Class and productive relations and commodity production provide nodal points of influence, confluence, and change that allow us to organize and see the empirical "wholes" in more ordered and interlinking ways. (2000, p. 112)

It is precisely in mapping out and explaining these "nodal points" that Willis's work can offer us a deeper understanding of the formation and education of class consciousness. Although the former nodal points Willis describes as "manual wage labor and masculinity, spatial concentration, white-collar/blue-collar, work/leisure, collectivity" have not deserted Willis's work, the new nodal points that interest him include the conditions of cultural practices such as their "different relations to language and to embedded forms of sensuous meaning; different access to and different types of relationships, with resources available for symbolic work and for the development of the expressive self" (2000, p. 112). But again, too often Willis's focus on how capital is "lived" in the sensuous domain of the fetishized cultural object and its dialectical relation to individual and group identity and fails to account sufficiently for the role of production in generating the value form in which labor is produced. It is here that Willis's work could benefit from a more dialectical approach like the one pioneered by Ollman. Willis's work as it stands could be more effectively deployed as a strategic weapon in the struggle against capital if it assumed a more world-historical, international, multicultural, and anti-imperialist perspective. Such a perspective would still be grounded in the social dimension of meaning-making but within the context of a wider counteroffensive against economic and environmental degradation brought about by globalized capitalism's imperial blitzkrieg. The glimmerings of what a postcapitalist socialist society might look like are as yet unbirthed in Willis's overall political project.

Having said this, we agree that where Willis's work can provide an especially significant contribution to the existing work on class consciousness resides in the challenge of according "sufficient weight to the social relations in which people produce and reproduce the means of material life without reducing everything to these" (McNally, 2001, p. 113). Here Willis's empirical and theoretical work can help to establish what David McNally called "the dialectical determination among the internally related elements that constitute a social whole" (2001, p. 113). Willis's contributions to our understanding of commodity fetishism can be especially fruitful in helping us fathom the dialectical relationship that obtains between ideological class divisions and the forces of production and between the inner laws of capital and cultural and subjective processes. In the broadest sense, it can enable us to situate with more analytic precision the struggle over the meaning and the inner dialectical quality of the commodity within wider social, cultural, and historical processes and formations (keeping in mind that there are aspects of Willis's work that could themselves be improved with a more directed focus on the totality of capitalist social relations). In this regard, Willis emphasizes the importance of linguistic translation in helping to undress the hidden processes of symbolic work both as a means to resist the deleterious aspects of ideological fetishism and as a way of creating new inroads to political self-fashioning. Here we recognize in Willis's work a suggestive strategy for taking received meanings from bourgeois commodity culture and, as Volosinov (1986) would put it, contesting their "tenure." In this context, Willis's work provides a crucial avenue for exploring the formation and functioning of the conflicting ensembles of social and cultural relations, moral assumptions and obligations, and forms of social activity and discourse that make up the contemporary "moral economy" among working-class groups (see Thompson, 1963, 1991). We suggest that much of the contemporary work on commodity culture and class consciousness could be deepened if undertaken with an eye to exploring the connections between Willis's work and those of the Bakhtin School of the 1920s that includes V. N. Volosinov (1986), M. M. Bakhtin (1981, 1984), and P. N. Medvedev (Medvedev & Bakhtin, 1985). We also discern a fruitful complementarity between Willis's use of aesthetics as a form of resistance and the work of Walter Benjamin (1968, 1999), especially in light of Benjamin's materialist theory of language and his understanding of how, in the words of McNally (2001, p. 224), "bourgeois society tries to efface the human body, beginning with the fetishism of the commodity." Like Benjamin, Willis believes that degraded bodies in our society can trouble significantly the formation of capitalist commodification and become sites for resistance and revolt. McNally noted appositely, after Benjamin, that "a precondition of emancipation is that repressed desires must enter into the language of everyday life and that the latter must recover the language of the body and of things" (2001, p. 225). If it is true that the pathways to liberation must make their way through the language of the body, then surely these bodies, and the way they are enfleshed with the capacity to recall memories long repressed and dreams long forgotten, constitute the most important resource in forming the larger collective body of class-conscious workers necessary for class struggle to achieve its goal.

Because Marx lays bare "relations among what is, what could be, what shouldn't be, and what can be done about it" (Ollman, 2003, p. 82), Ollman argued that Marxism constitutes "science, critique, vision and recipe for revolution" simultaneously "with each of these qualities contributing to and feeding off the others" (2003, p. 82). It is by approaching Marxism with this description in mind that one can best assist educators in exploring the causeways of revolutionary consciousness and praxis (Allman, McLaren, & Rikowski, 2003). It is precisely by utilizing Marx in this fashion that Willis's work can be strategically employed by radical educators bent on developing cultural strategies within forms of lived culture that can move defetishization into new creative contexts for sundry ad hoc struggles alongside, within, and against commodity culture (see Ollman, 1971). The key objective for critical educators is not only to become involved in making the process of cultural commodification less invisible to those whose subjectivities are formed within it, but to become involved in creating the kinds of social, political, and educational conditions that not only can assist in the defetishization of cultural practices but can shape the development of working-class consciousness (McLaren, 2000).

So much that we have learned about the ethnographic imagination from Willis's work can be brought to bear in new and productive ways on the study of class consciousness and its transformation into new forms of socialist resistance. Such an engagement can afford educators new ways of broadening the struggle for new resources of meaning-making and self-making, extending the norms for social transformation, and advancing the struggle for a socialist future.

Notes

1. Many of us have viewed ourselves as fellow-travelers of Willis, on the bumpy and uncharted road to liberation—what Raymond Williams called *The Long Revolution*—which can most effectively be brought about by socialist renewal. Willis had been riding the rails of socialist research for years while many of us were still cutting our graduate school teeth on his *Profane Culture*, delighting ourselves in his theoretical renditions of the Teddy Boys, Mods, and Rastas, and debating the strengths and weaknesses of indexical, homological, and integral levels of cultural relations among motor bike boy culture (not to mention integral circuiting). During the British invasion of graduate schools of education in the 1980s, commandeered by the Birmingham School of Contemporary Cultural Studies, any radical doctoral student worth her (or his) salt who was not familiar with the works of Paul Willis, Phil Corrigan or his brother, Paul, Stuart Hall, Richard Johnson, Angela McRobbie, or Dick Hebdige was unable to participate with any credibility in the weekly brown-bag seminars or lunchtime conversations in the graduate student lounge. Those of us who were lucky enough to have our doctoral work read and encouraged by Willis, or other visitors from the United Kingdom to the radical campuses of the day, felt more than lucky: We were blessed.

2. In *The 18th Brumaire of Louis Bonaparte*, Marx proposed a clear distinction between the objective fact of class position and the subjective fact of class consciousness. In this discussion of the French peasantry, Marx (1984, p. 124) argued that:

   In so far as millions of families live under economic conditions of existence that separate their mode of life, their interests and their culture from those of the other classes, and put them in hostile opposition to the latter, they form a class. In so far as there is merely a local interconnection among these small-holding peasants, and the identity of their interests begets no community, no national bond and no political organization among them, they do not form a class.

3. For a lengthier exposition of our approach, see Scatamburlo-D'Annibale and McLaren (2003).

References

Allman, P., McLaren, P., & Rikowski, G. (2003). After the box people: The labour–capital relation as class constitution and its consequences of Marxist educational theory and human resistance." In J., Freeman-Moir and A. Scott (Eds.), *Yesterday's dreams: International and critical perspectives on education and social class* (pp. 149–179). Christchurch, New Zealand: Canterbury University Press.

Bakhtin, M. M. (1981). *The dialogic imagination: Four essays* (M. Holquist, Ed.; C. Emerson & M. Holquist, Trans.). Austin: University of Texas Press.

Bakhtin, M. (1984). *Problems of Dostoevky's poetics* (C. Emerson, Ed. & Trans.). Minneapolis: University of Minnesota Press.

Benjamin, W. (1968). *Illuminations* (H. Arendt, Ed.). New York: Schocken Books.

Benjamin, W. (1999). *Selected writings, Volume 2: 1927–1935* (M. Jennings, H. Eiland, & G. Smith, Eds.). Cambridge, MA: Belknap Press of Harvard University Press.

Collini, S. (1994). Escape from DWEMsville. *Times Literary Supplement*, 4756 (May 27), 3–4.

Dyer-Witheford, N. (1999). *Cyber-Marx: Cycles and circuits of struggle in high-technology capitalism*. Urbana and Chicago: University of Illinois Press.

Gimenez, M. (2001). Marxism, and class, gender and race: Rethinking the trilogy. *Race, Gender & Class, 8*(2), 23–33.

Harvey, D. (1998). The practical contradictions of Marxism. *Critical Sociology, 24*(1, 2), 1–36.

Hill, D., McLaren, P., Cole, M. & Rikowski, G. (2002). *Marxism Against Postmodernism in Educational Theory*. Landham, MD: Lexington Books.

Ilyenkov, E. V. (1977). *Dialectical logic: Essays on its history and theory*. Moscow: Progress.

Ilyenkov, E. V. (1982a). *Leninist dialectics and the metaphysics of positivism*. London: New Park.

Ilyenkov, E. V. (1982b). *The dialectics of the abstract and the concrete in Marx's Capital*. Moscow: Progress.

Jameson, F. (1998). *The cultural turn*. London: Verso.

Kagarlitsky, B. (2000) *The return of radicalism*. London: Pluto Press.

Katz, A. (2000). *Postmodernism and the politics of "culture."* Boulder, CO: Westview Press.

Lave, J., Duguid, P., Fernandez, N. & Axel, E. (1992). Coming of age in Birmingham: Cultural studies and conceptions of subjectivity. *Annual Review of Anthropology, 21*, 231–249.

Marx, K. (1984). *The 18th Brumaire of Louis Bonaparte*. New York: International. (Original work published 1869.)

McLaren, P. (1998). Revolutionary pedagogy in post-revolutionary times: Rethinking the political economy of critical education. *Educational Theory, 48*(4), 431–462.

McLaren, P. (2000). *Che Guevara, Paulo Freire, and the pedagogy of revolution*. Boulder, CO: Rowman & Littlefield.

McLaren, P., & Farahmandpur, R. (1999). Critical pedagogy, postmodernism, and the retreat from class: Towards a contraband pedagogy. *Theoria, 93*, 83–115.

McLaren, P. & Farahmandpur, R. (2000). Reconsidering Marx in post-Marxist times: A requiem for postmodernism? *Educational Researcher, 29*(3), 25–33.

McLaren, P., & Farahmandpur, R. (2001). The globalization of capitalism and the new imperialism: Notes towards a revolutionary critical pedagogy. *The Review of Education, Pedagogy & Cultural Studies, 23*(3), 271–315.

McLaren, P. (2003). Critical pedagogy in the age of neoliberal globalization: Notes from history's underside. *Democracy and Nature, 9*(1), 65–90.

McNally, D. (2001). *Bodies of meaning: Studies on language, labor, and liberation*. Albany: State University of New York Press.

Medvedev, P. N., & Bakhtin, M. (1985). *The Formal method in literary scholarship: A critical introduction to sociological poetics* (A. J. Wherle, Trans.). Cambridge, MA: Harvard University Press. (Original work published 1928.)

Milner, A. (1999). *Class: Core conceptual concepts*. London: Sage.

Moraes, M. (2003). The path of dissent: An interview with Peter McLaren. *Journal of Transformative Education, 1*(2), 117–134.

Munt, S. (Ed.). (2000). *Cultural studies and the working class*. New York: Cassell.

Ollman, B. (1971). *Alienation: Marx's conception of man in capitalist society*. New York: Cambridge University Press.

Ollman, B. (1993). *Dialectical investigations*. New York: Routledge.

Ollman, B. (2003). Marxism, this tale of two cities. *Science & Society, 67*(1), 80–86.

Palmer, B. (1997). Old positions/new necessities: History, class, and Marxist metanarrative. In E. M. Wood & J. B. Poster (Eds.), *In defense of history: Marxism and the postmodern agenda* (pp. 65–73). New York: Monthly Review Press.

Pozo, M. (2003). Toward a critical revolutionary pedagogy: An interview with Peter McLaren. *St. John's University Humanities Review*, 58–77.

San Juan, E., Jr. (2002). *Racism and cultural studies: Critiques of multiculturalist ideology and the politics of difference.* Durham, NC: Duke University Press.

San Juan, E. (2003). Marxism and the race/class problematic: A re-articulation. *Cultural Logic.* http://eserver.org/clogic/2003/sanjuan.html.

Scatamburlo-D'Annibale, V., & McLaren, P. (2003). The strategic centrality of class in the politics of "race" and "difference." *Cultural Studies/Critical Methodologies, 3*(2), 148–175.

Thompson, E. P. (1963). *The making of the English working class.* London: Gollancz.

Thompson, E. P. (1991). *Customs in common.* London: Merlin.

Volosinov, V. N. (1986). *Marxism and the philosophy of language* (L. Matejka & I. R. Titunik, Trans.). Cambridge, MA: Harvard University Press.

Wallerstein, I. (1995). *After liberalism.* New York: New Press.

Willis, P. (1977). *Learning to labor.* New York: Columbia University Press.

Willis, P. (1978). *Profane culture.* London: Routledge and Kegan Paul.

Willis, P. (1990). Foreword. In D. E. Foley (Ed.), *Learning capitalist culture: Deep in the heart of Tejas* (pp. vii–xii). Philadelphia: University of Pennsylvania Press.

Willis, P. et. al. (1990). *Common culture.* Milton Keynes: Open University Press.

Willis, P. (2000). *The ethnographic imagination.* Cambridge: Polity.

CHAPTER 4

Between Good Sense and Bad Sense
Race, Class, and Learning from Learning to Labor

MICHAEL W. APPLE

In *Models and Mystery* (Ramsey, 1964), Ian Ramsey made a distinction between two kinds of models. The first, "pictorial models," seek to show the world "as it really is." Such models, although useful, are usually relatively undynamic and risk becoming reified representations of reified people and processes. The second, "disclosure models," enable us to see the people and processes in wholly new and considerably more dynamic ways. In the (often overused) Kuhnian sense of the word, they provide for and signify paradigm shifts (Kuhn, 1970). Only a very few works in the fields of sociology, cultural studies, and education can be said to have provided powerful disclosure models. But if I were asked to nominate truly lasting contributions, ones that continue to deserve to be read today, within that select few would be *Learning to Labor* (Willis, 1977, published in the United Kingdom as *Learning to Labour*). Indeed, along with, say, the scholarship of Bourdieu and Bernstein, Paul Willis's work stands as an achievement that has not only stood the test of time but remains among the most compelling analyses of how class can be understood. Indeed, I would want to claim that its basic approach provides some of the essential building blocks for a critical analysis of many of the dynamics of differential power and experience with which all of us are concerned.

Paul Willis has been a friend and colleague for over 20 years. Because of this, some of what I say must be partly autobiographical, not because my

61

perspectives should be privileged above others', but because like many others in the field my own work was changed in fundamental ways by *Learning to Labor*.

I need to return us to the intellectual/political world within critical educational studies of the mid-1970s in order to restore our sense of Paul Willis's unique contribution. In the United States, as in many other nations, critical sociological work on schooling was dominated either by the reductive and economistic readings of the relationship between schools and society of Bowles and Gintis (1976) or by the somewhat more critical culturalist readings of people such as myself and Jean Anyon (Anyon, 1979; Apple, 1979). With varying degrees of complexity, the emphasis was on the schools' role in economic and cultural reproduction and on the debates over base and superstructure and structure and agency (Apple, 1982a, 1982b). As the tradition grew in sophistication, such reproduction was seen as contested and not always successful (Apple, 1982b; Apple & Weis, 1983), and more attention began to be paid not only to content but to the form and organization of knowledge, pedagogy, and evaluation and the principles that underpinned them, and to the ways all of this was actually experienced by students and teachers (Apple, 1982b). *Learning to Labor* became crucial in this project. Even when it was not overtly cited (which by and large it almost always was), it provided the conceptual door for others to go through. Certainly this was true in my case.

The first edition of my book *Ideology and Curriculum* was published in 1979, although the manuscript had been completed in 1977. In the final chapter, after the entire book was spent on analyzing the structures of cultural domination in the curriculum and in schooling in general, I argued—correctly, but in a conceptually and politically underdeveloped and somewhat naive manner when I look back on it now—that "ideological reproduction" was not all that was going on. Students and teachers were not puppets. Culture was neither epiphenomenal, nor unimportant; it counted in crucial ways and provided significant resources in hegemonic and counterhegemonic struggles.

During the period of time in which I was completing the final draft of the manuscript, I was lecturing in England. Colleagues there spoke to me about *Learning to Labor*. I bought it and read it immediately. Over the following months, it became increasingly clear to me that each time I wanted to more fully understand the relationship between culture and economy in education, to more fully grasp the materiality of cultural form and content and the political dynamics in which it played such a constitutive part, I was using a set of lenses that in large part were influenced by my reading and rereading of Paul's work. I sensed that, at the time, his analyses had a relatively underdeveloped theory of the role of the state in structuring the very arena in which the schools and their definitions of "official knowledge" and "legitimate" social and pedagogic relations played a large part (see, e.g., Apple, 2000; Apple et al., 2003) and that it romanticized the possibility of using the lived culture of youth in developing a political response to oppressive realities, in "disarticulating" them from one set of positions and "rearticulating" them to a more progressive set of positions and collective actions. But these issues seemed minor compared both to the things that his work disclosed and to the doors that it opened to the entire realm of cultural studies inside and outside of education, such as the influential tradition of critical cultural analysis that came out of the Centre for Contemporary Cultural Studies at Birmingham. Anyone looking at the books of mine that immediately followed (Apple, 1982b, 1986)—with their focus on lived culture, on the contradictory meanings and results of resistance, on the realities of cultural production that, while influenced by political economy, could not be reduced to it, on the ways in which gender, race, and class were linked in fully contradictory ways—couldn't fail to see the influences on me that were embodied in both Willis and the CCCS.

Yet, thinking back on Paul's work and its influences on me then has also made me recognize the continuity of such influence. It is not simply "in the past." His analyses provided me with the epistemological and conceptual tools that formed the basis of a considerable portion of the work I do *now*. I can trace the development of a number of my own projects to the rather Gramscian understanding of the contradictory formations involved in "common sense" that has played such an important role in Willis's own work over the years. Whether one calls them "penetrations" (a concept that proved to be troublesome because of its masculinist tendencies) and "limitations" as Paul did, or elements of "good" and "bad" sense in tension as I have done, our modes of being in and understanding the world are seen as contradictory. Habitus and body hexis are constitutively contradictory, filled with elements of real understandings that both help and hurt at one and the same time. Thus, concepts that have such a long history in, say, Marxist (and other) perspectives, such as "false consciousness," are to be rejected both as simplistic and as ungrounded in lived and embodied culture of identifiable people and movements as they go about their daily lives.[1]

Let me say more about this. For example, it would not be possible to understand my work over the entire past decade—in, for example, *Cultural Politics and Education* (1996), *Official Knowledge* (2000), and *Educating the "Right" Way* (2001)—without understanding its historic genesis in parts of *Learning to Labor* and *Common Culture*. My agenda has been to demonstrate how the formation of hegemonic (and later counterhegemonic) alliances has been accomplished, how people can be "hailed" or pulled under the leadership of a new hegemonic bloc, what I have called "conservative modernization" (Apple, 2001; see also Dale, 1989/1990). This creative process of disarticulation and rearticulation can *only* be accomplished if dominant groups work off of and on the elements of real understanding of social and educational problems that are already there within social groups and movements. The formation of ideological umbrellas cannot be done without this process. And a critical understanding of the creative work that neo-liberals and neo-conservatives have been engaged in so successfully in education, in the economy, in the political sphere, and elsewhere can best be gotten at by analyzing the ways in which there have been discursive connections made with the elements of good sense that people have.

In reflecting on this, I recognize then that in many ways, at the very core of the critical research I have done both on rightist social movements and on how to interrupt them is the perspective I first encountered in *Learning to Labor*. Perhaps the best way of documenting how these influences continue to have an impact on my work and that of my students is to give a elaborated example. The example has to do with the current move to the right in education and so much else in our societies. It concerns the intersection of race and class and the politics of educational policy and how identities can be constructed and reconstructed so that they are connected to social movements that wish to transform society.

Mapping Conservative Modernization

This is both a good and bad time in the world of educational policy. On the one hand, there have been very few periods when education has taken such a central place in public debates about our present and future. On the other hand, an increasingly limited range of ideological and discursive resources dominates the conceptual and political forms in which this debate is carried out. These debates are occurring on an uneven playing field, one on which what were formerly seen as rightist policies have now become "common sense" (Apple, 2000, 2001). Yet such conservative policies have a different kind of cachet today. There is a sense that these are not only things that will protect a romantic past; these policies are now often seen as "radical" but necessary solutions to an educational system that is out of control and is no longer responsive to the needs of "the people."

Thus, a new kind of conservatism has evolved and has taken center stage in many nations. "Conservative modernization" is decidedly not simply a mirror of previous rightist movements. Although parts of these positions may have originated within the New Right, they are now not limited to what has traditionally been called the Right. They have been taken up by a much larger segment of government and policymakers and, as shown in this section of this chapter, have even been appropriated by groups one would least expect to do so, such as African American activists. How are we to understand this? In answering this question, although my focus here is largely on the United States, the tendencies I describe have implications well beyond one nation.

The concepts we use to try to understand and act on the world in which we live do not by themselves determine the answers we may find. Answers are not determined by words, but by the power relations that impose their interpretations of these concepts. Yet there are key words that continually surface in the debates over education. These key words have complicated histories, histories that are connected to the social movements out of which they arose and in which they are struggled over today. These words have their own histories, but they are increasingly interrelated. The concepts are simple to list: markets, standards, accountability, tradition, God, and a number of others. Behind each of these topics is an assemblage of other words that have an emotional valence and that provide the support for the ways in which differential power works in our daily lives. These concepts include democracy, freedom, choice, morality, family, culture, and a number of other key concepts. And each of these in turn is intertextual. Each and every one of these is connected to an entire set of assumptions about "appropriate" institutions, values, social relationships, and policies.

Think of this situation as something of a road map. Using one key word—markets—sends you onto a highway that is going in one direction and that has exits in some places but not others. If you are on a highway labeled *market,* your general direction is toward a section of the country named *the economy.* You take the exit named *individualism* that goes by way of another road called *consumer choice.* Exits with words such as *unions, collective freedom, the common good, politics,* and similar destinations are to be avoided if they are on the map at all. The first road is a simple route with one goal—deciding where one wants to go without a lot of time-wasting discussion and getting there by the fastest and cheapest method possible. There is a second route, however, and this one involves a good deal of collective deliberation about where we might want to go. It assumes that there may be some continuing deliberation about not only the goal, but also even the route itself. Its exits are the ones that were avoided on the first route.

There are powerful interests that have made the road map and the roads. Some want only the road labeled *market,* because this supposedly leads to individual choice. Others will go down that road, but only if the exits are those that have a long history of "real culture" and "real knowledge." Still others will take the market road because for them God has said that this is "his" road. And finally, another group will sign on to this tour because they have skills in mapmaking and in determining how far we are from our goal. There's some discussion and some compromise—and perhaps even some lingering tension—among these various groups about which exits will ulti-mately be stopped at, but by and large they all head off in that direction.

This exercise in storytelling maps onto reality in important ways. The first group is what is appropriately called *neo-liberals*. They are deeply committed to markets and to freedom as "individual choice." The second group, *neo-conservatives*, has a vision of an Edenic past and wants a return to discipline and traditional knowledge. The third, one that is increasingly powerful in the United States and elsewhere, is what I call *authoritarian populists*—religious fundamentalists and conservative evangelicals who want a return to (their) God in all of our institutions.[2] And finally, the mapmakers and experts on whether we got there are members of a partic-ular fraction of the managerial and professional *new middle class*.

In analyzing this complex configuration of interests around conservative modernization, we need to act on what Eric Hobsbawm described as the historian's and social critic's duty. For Hobsbawm, the task is to be the "professional remembrancers of what [our] fellow citizens wish to forget" (Hobsbawm, 1994, p. 3). That is, it requires us to detail the absent presences, the there that is not there, in most rightist policies in education. How does their language work to highlight certain things as "real" problems, while marginalizing others? What are the effects of the policies that they have promoted? How do the seemingly contradictory policies that have emerged from the various fractions of the Right, aspects of which have now taken on a life of their own at times—such as the marketization of education through voucher plans, the pressure to "return" to the Western tradition and to a supposedly common culture, the commitment to get God back into the schools and classrooms of America, and the growth of national and state curriculum and reductive national and state (and often "high stakes") testing—actually get put together in creative ways to push many of the aspects of these rightist agendas forward?

In a number of recent books, I have critically analyzed why and how this has occurred. Along with others (see, e.g., Whitty, Power, & Halpin, 1998; Gillborn & Youdell, 2000), I have examined a range of proposals for educa-tional "reform" such as marketization, standards, national/statewide curricula, and national/statewide testing. This critical examination has demonstrated that, even with the often good intentions of the proponents of many of these kinds of proposals, in the long run they may actually exacer-bate inequalities, especially around class and race. Furthermore, they may paradoxically cause us both to misrecognize what actually causes difficult social and educational problems and to miss some important democratic alternatives that may offer more hope in the long run (see, e.g., Apple, 2000, 2001; Apple & Beane, 1999; Apple et al., 2003).

It is helpful to think of this as having been accomplished through the use of a vast socio/pedagogic project, a project that has actively—and in large part successfully—sought to transform our very ideas about democracy. Democracy is no longer a political concept; rather, it is wholly an economic concept in which unattached individuals—supposedly making "rational" choices on an unfettered market—will ultimately lead to a better society. As Foner (1998) reminded us, it has taken decades of creative ideological work to change our commonsense ideas about democracy. Not only does this change fly in the face of a very long tradition of collective understandings of democracy in the United States, but it has also led to the destruction of many communities, jobs, health care, and so many other institutions not only in the United States but also throughout the world (Greider, 1997; Katz, 2001). Hidden assumptions about class and a goodly portion of the politics of whiteness may make it hard for us to face this honestly (see Fine, Weis, Powell, & Wong, 1997).

But let me stop myself here. I should have put two words in the last sentences of the preceding paragraph—*us* and *we*—in quotation marks. Who is the "we"? Does it include all those who have been hurt by that combination of neo-liberal and neo-conservative polices that now play such an important role in our discourse in education? If these policies have a disproportionate and negative effect on, say, the working class and on people of color—as they seem to do—should we assume that, for example, all persons of color will recognize this and will reject both the policies and their underlying ideologies? That this is not the case is the subject of the rest of this chapter as I employ models strongly influenced by Willis's approach to understand how and why this may not be the case.

Strange Allies

Given the history of their struggles both for redistribution and recognition, it would be very difficult to integrate historically disenfranchised social groups, especially people of color, under the umbrella of conservative modernization (Apple, 2000; Fraser, 1997). However, this does not make it impossible. As I noted in the introduction to this chapter, one of the ways in which hegemonic alliances are built is through a process in which dominant groups creatively use the elements of "good sense" (what Willis had called "penetrations") that disenfranchised groups possess and then attach their neo-liberal and neo-conservative agendas to these elements (Apple, 2001). Unfortunately, the partial success of such a strategy among those groups who are often counted as "despised others" (Fraser, 1997) in our societies is a subject that many progressives would like to forget. Yet there is increasing evidence that there are growing numbers of members of "minority" groups, conservative women, and gays and lesbians who are activists in neo-liberal and neo-conservative movements, and to a lesser extent in authoritarian populist religious movements. (Of course, given the crucial role that Black churches have played in the historical struggles for justice [West, 1982], it would be surprising if there were not elements of such sentiments within African American communities.)

There have been exceptions to this relative neglect. In a recent book, Dillard (2001), for example, critically examined a number of the key actors within conservative circles who themselves are members of historically oppressed groups, but who—for a variety of personal and political reasons—give vocal support to neo-liberal and neo-conservative causes. Aggressively "free" market policies, a rejection of affirmative action and the use of race and/or gender as a category in public decisions, mobilizing for public funding for religiously based schooling, welfare "reform," and a host of similar issues provide the centers of gravity for these individuals. Many of the figures on which she focuses will be familiar to those on the United States side of the Atlantic: Dinesh D'Sousa, Thomas Sowell, Clarence Thomas, Linda Chavez, Glenn Loury, Richard Rodriguez, and similar national spokespersons of conservative causes. Each of these figures is a person of color. Among them are well-known academics, journalists, government officials, and a justice of the Supreme Court. Other figures may be familiar only to those readers who have closely followed the cultural and political debates on the Right in the United States over such things as educational policy, sexuality, affirmative action, and welfare reform: Star Parker, George Schuyler, Andrew Sullivan, Elizabeth Wright, Bruce Bawer, and Susan Au Allen, among others.[3]

There is of course a history of dominant groups using—or at least giving visibility to—"minority" voices to "say the unsayable" in the United States and elsewhere (Lewis, 1993, 2000). Thus, for example, Ward Connerly, a prominent conservative African American businessman and a vocal member of the Board of Regents of the University of California, has taken a very visible stand against affirmative action. For him, government involvement is actually harmful to Black Americans. "While others are assimilating, Blacks are getting further and further away from one nation indivisible" (quoted in Dillard, 2001, p. 50). His insistence on "individual merit" and his rejection of state intervention for the cause of equality has clearly been employed by the larger, and mostly White, conservative movement to legitimate its own policies. As a prominent conservative spokeswoman put it, "You can't have white guys saying you don't need affirmative action" (Dillard, 2001, p. 15). Powerful neo-liberal and neo-conservative movements both inside and outside government circles, hence, can steadily expand the realm of what is in fact sayable by prefacing what would otherwise be seen as consistently racist positions with a quote from a well-known

Black spokesperson. One of the most articulate critics of such moves states that this enables dominant economic, cultural, and racial groups "to cannibalize the moral authority of minority voices by skirting responsibility" (Dillard, 2001, p. 20).

Because of this very history of dominant groups employing the selective voice of the "other" to legitimize its actions, there has been a concomitant history of regarding those members of minority communities who openly affiliate with conservative movements as "pariahs." They have been dismissed as either "traitors" or "sell-outs," and even seen as "self-loathing reactionaries who are little more than dupes of powerful white ... conservatives" (Dillard, 2001, p. 4). Although these labels are powerful indeed, many conservative persons of color see themselves very differently. In their self-perception, they are "crusading rebels" against a state and a liberal elite within the ranks of their own communities whose own self-understanding as "helping the people" actually mystifies policies that work to destroy the very moral and social foundations of their communities. Here they can also turn to a rich history of nationalist, self-help, and conservative moral principles within these communities as a source of "authenticity" and legitimacy (Dillard, 2001, p. 13).

Of course, there *are* internally developed conservative traditions within, say, communities of color, many of which have made lasting contributions to the very existence and continuity of the cultures within these communities (see, e.g., Lewis, 1993, 2000). However, given the fact that so much of the conservative tradition in the United States was explicitly shaped by racist and racializing discourses and practices,[4] and by a strongly anti-immigrant heritage as well, and given the fact that much of the current neo-liberal and neo-conservative attacks on the public sphere have had disproportionate effects on the gains of poor communities and on communities of color, the current existence and growth of such movements among dispossessed groups is more than a little striking. This makes their current iterations all the more interesting.[5] As I show later, neo-liberal and neo-conservative economic, political, and cultural movements *and* some of the African American groups that have been connected to them are both seeking to redefine the relations of power in particular social fields, with education being a prime site where these relations of power are being worked through (Bourdieu, 1984). A complex process of discursive and positional disarticulation and rearticulation is going here, as dominant groups attempt to pull dispossessed collectivities under their own leadership and dispossessed groups themselves attempt to employ the social, economic, and cultural capital usually possessed by dominant groups to gain collective power for themselves. As will be evident, the label "conservative" cannot be employed easily in understanding the actions of all of the dispossessed groups who do ally themselves with conservative causes without at the same time reducing the complexity of the particular social fields of power on which they operate.

Perhaps the most interesting example of the processes of discursive and social disarticulation and rearticulation that one could find today involves the growing African American support for neo-liberal policies such as voucher plans (see, e.g., Moe, 2001). A key instance is the Black Alliance for Educational Options (BAEO), a group of African American parents and activists that is chaired by Howard Fuller, the former superintendent of Milwaukee public schools, one of the most racially segregated school systems in the United States. BAEO provides vocal support for voucher plans, "choice" (a sliding signifier whose meaning has increasingly become fixed around issues of vouchers in the United States when it is used in political discourse), and similar conservative proposals. It has generated considerable support within Black communities throughout the nation, particularly within poor inner-city areas, and has an identifiable presence in 27 cities within the United States.[6] The fact that the Supreme Court of Wisconsin has ruled that the Milwaukee voucher plan is constitutional and the U.S. Supreme Court recently ruled that the Cleveland voucher plan is also constitutional gives more legal and political legitimacy to BAEO's efforts, since both plans were officially aimed at providing the "right to exit" for inner-city and largely "minority" residents.

A sense of the language that underpins BAEO's commitment can be seen in the following quote:

> Our children are our most precious resource. It is our responsibility to love them, nurture them and protect them. It is also our responsibility to ensure that they are properly educated. Without a good education, they will [not] have a real chance to engage in the practice of freedom: the process of engaging in the fight to transform their world. (BAEO web site)

BAEO's mission is clear. "The Black Alliance for Educational Options is a national, nonpartisan member organization whose mission is to actively support parental choice to empower families and increase educational options for Black children" (BAEO web site). Its position is even clearer in its manifesto:

BAEO Manifesto
Current systems of K–12 education work well for many of America's children. But, for far too many children, the current systems do not work well at all. A high percentage of these children are poor children of color living in urban areas. For these children, the old

educational strategies and institutional arrangements are not preparing them to be productive and socially responsible citizens. This requires that we dramatically change our teaching and learning strategies and create new governance and financial structures.

BAEO believes we must develop new systems of learning opportunities to complement and expand existing systems. We need systems that truly empower parents, that allow dollars to follow students, that hold adults as well as students accountable for academic achievement, and that alter the power arrangements that are the foundation for existing systems.

BAEO understands that there are no "silver bullets" or "magic wands" which will instantly make things better for our children. BAEO is also not anti-public school. However, we do believe that parent choice must be the centerpiece of strategies and tactics aimed at improving education for our children. We must empower parents, particularly low-income parents, to make the best choices for their children's education.

Consider the potential impact of this power in the hands of families who previously have had little or no control over the flow and distribution of the money that drives the policies and procedures of the educational systems of this country. Consider how the absence of this power means that their children will remain trapped in schools that more affluent parents, some of whom oppose parental choice, would never tolerate for their own children. Consider how this power shift may change the shape of the future for their children.

BAEO will bring together the ideas, aspirations, energies, and experiences of all generations in this struggle. (BAEO web site)

The use of language here is striking. The language of neo-liberalism (choice, parental empowerment, accountability, individual freedom) is reappropriated and sutured together with ideas of collective Black freedom and a deep concern for the community's children. This creates something of a "hybrid" discourse that blends together meanings from multiple political sources and agendas. In some ways, this is similar to the long history of critical cultural analyses that demonstrate that people form bricolages in their daily lives and can employ language and commodities in ways undreamed of by the original producers of the language and products (see, e.g., Willis, 1990, 2000).

Although this process of rearticulation and use is important to note, it is equally essential to recognize something that makes the creative bricolage in which BAEO is engaged somewhat more problematic. A very large portion of the group's funding comes directly from conservative sources such as the Bradley Foundation. The Bradley Foundation, a well-known sponsor of conservative causes, has not only been in the forefront of providing support for vouchers and privatization initiatives, but also is one of the groups that provided significant support for Herrnstein and Murray's book *The Bell Curve* (1994), a volume that argued that African Americans were on average less intelligent than Whites and that this was genetic in nature. Thus, it would be important to ask about the nature and effects of the connections being made between rightist ideological and financial sources and BAEO itself. It is not inconsequential that neo-liberal and neo-conservative foundations provide not only funding but media visibility for "minority" groups who support—even critically—their agendas.

The genesis of such funding is not inconsequential. Many of the strongest proponents of vouchers and similar plans may claim that their positions are based on a belief in the efficiency of markets, on the fear of a secularization of the sacred, or on the dangers of losing the values and beliefs that give meaning to their lives. However, historically, neither the economic nor the moral elements of this critique can be totally set apart from their partial genesis in the struggles over racial segregation, over busing to achieve integration, and in the loss of a federal tax exemption by conservative—and usually White only—religious academies. In short, the fear of the "racial other" has played a significant role in this discursive construction of the "problem of the public school" (Apple, 2001). Does this mean that groups such as BAEO are simply being manipulated by neo-liberal and neo-conservative foundations and movements? An answer to this question is not easy, but even with my cautions just stated it is certainly not a simple "yes."

Strategic Compromises?

It is important not to engage in reductive analyses here, ones for example that assume that simply because a group's funding comes from a specific source, therefore all of its own agendas will be fundamentally determined by where it gets its money. This is certainly not always the case. Indeed, in public forums and in discussions that my colleague Tom Pedroni and I have had with some of leaders of BAEO, these leaders have argued that they will use any funding sources available so that they can follow their own specific program of action. They would accept money from more liberal sources, but Bradley and other conservative foundations have come forward much more readily.[7] In the minds of the leaders of BAEO, the African American activists are in control, not the conservative foundations. Thus, for BAEO, they see themselves as strategically positioning themselves in order to get funding from conservative sources. What they do with this funding, such as their strong (and well advertised in the media) support for voucher plans (although this support too is contingent and sometimes depends on local power relations), is wholly their decision. For them, the space provided by educational markets can be reoccupied for Black cultural and/or nationalist politics and can be employed to stop what seems to them (more than a little accurately in my opinion) to be the strikingly ineffective, and even damaging, education of Black children.[8]

However, although I have a good deal of respect for a number of the leaders of BAEO, it is important to remember that they are not the only ones strategically organizing on this social field of power. Like BAEO, groups affiliated with, say, the Bradley Foundation also know exactly what they are doing and know very well how to employ the agendas of BAEO for their own purposes, purposes that in the long term often may run directly counter to the interests of the majority of those with less power at both the national and regional levels. Is it really in the long-term interests of people of color to be affiliated with the same groups who provided funding and support for books such as Herrnstein and Murray's (1994) *The Bell Curve*? I think not, although once again we need to recognize the complexities involved here.

I am certain that this kind of question is constantly raised about the conservative stances taken by the people of color who have made alliances with, say, neo-liberals and neo-conservatives—and by the activists within BAEO itself. When members of groups who are consistently "othered" in this society strategically take on identities that support dominant groups, such questioning is natural and I believe essential. However, it is also crucial to remember that members of historically oppressed and marginalized groups have *always* had to act on a terrain that is not of their choosing, have always had to act strategically and creatively to gain some measure of support from dominant groups to advance their causes (Lewis, 1993, 2000; Omi & Winant, 1994). It is also the case that more recently national and local leaders of the Democratic Party in the United States have too often assumed that Black support is simply *there*, that it doesn't need to be worked for. Because of this, we may see the further development of "unusual alliances" over specific issues such as educational policies. When this is coupled with some of the tacit and/or overt support within some communities of color not only for voucher plans but for antigay, antiabortion, pro-school-prayer, and similar initiatives, the suturing together of some Black groups with larger conservative movements on particular issues is not totally surprising (see Dillard, 2001).

The existence and growing power of committed movements such as BAEO, though, do point out that we need to be careful about stereotyping groups who may publicly support neo-liberal and neo-conservative policies.

Their perspectives need to be examined carefully and taken seriously, not simply dismissed as totally misguided, as people who have been duped into unthinking acceptance of a harmful set of ideologies. There are complicated strategic moves being made on an equally complex social field of power. I may—and do—strongly disagree with a number of the positions that groups such as BAEO take. However, to assume that they are simply puppets of conservative forces is not only to be too dismissive of their own attempts at social maneuvering, but I also believe that it may be tacitly racist as well.

Saying this doesn't mean that we need to weaken our arguments against marketization and privatization of schooling. Voucher and tax credit plans (the later ultimately may actually be more dangerous) will still have some extremely problematic effects in the long term. One of the most important effects could be a *demobilization* of social movements within communities of color. Schools have played central roles in the creation of movements for justice. In essence, rather than being peripheral reflections of larger battles and dynamics, struggles over schooling—over what should be taught, over the relationship between schools and local communities, over the very ends and means of the institution itself—have provided a crucible for the *formation* of larger social movements toward equality (Apple et al., 2003; Hogan, 1983). These collective movements have transformed our definitions of rights, of who should have them, and of the role of the government in guaranteeing these rights. Absent organized, community-wide mobilizations, these transformations would not have occurred.

This is under threat currently. Definitions of democracy based on possessive individualism, on the citizen as only a "consumer," are inherently grounded in a process of deracing, declassing, and degendering (Ball, 1994). These are the very groups who have employed struggles over educational access and outcomes to form themselves as self-conscious actors. If it is the case, as I strongly believe it is, that it is the organized efforts of social movements that ultimately have led to the transformation of our educational system in more democratic directions (Apple, 2000), the long-term effects of neo-liberal definitions of democracy may be truly tragic for communities of color, not "only" in increasing inequalities in schools (see, e.g., Apple, 2001; Gillborn & Youdell, 2000; McNeil 2000), but in leading to a very real loss of the impetus for *collective* solutions to pressing social problems. If all problems are simply "solved" by individual choices on a market, then collective mobilizations tend to wither and perhaps even disappear. If history is any guide here, the results will not be pleasant. Thus, although short term support for neo-liberal and neo-conservative policies may seem strategically wise to some members of less powerful groups, and may in fact generate short-term mobilizations, I remain deeply worried about what will happen over time.[9] It is the long-term implications of individuating processes and ideologies, and their effects on the necessity of larger and constantly growing social mobilizations that aim toward substantive transformations within the public sphere, that need to be of concern as well. For we need to remember that—although in *Learning to Labor* Paul Willis focuses on the possibility of working on "penetrations," on the elements of "good sense" that people have, to form progressive movements—given the unequal balance of forces and the conservative discourses that now circulate so widely in society, progressives may *not* be the movements that will be the most successful in the process of disarticulation and rearticulation.

A concern over the effects of individuation that such "choice" programs may ultimately bring is unfortunately actually mirrored in the (already limited) literature on Black support for neo-liberal and neo-conservative policies. All too much of the critical literature on such "strategic alliances," even such work as Dillard's compelling book (2001), tends to focus on individuals, rather than on larger social movements. As I noted earlier, it is social movements that historically have had the power to transform social and educational policy and practice. An emphasis on individuals does humanize the issues that are in contention and it does allow us to see the people behind the Rightist presence within marginalized communities. However, this very focus causes us to miss the dynamics that have led to the growth of groups such as BAEO and to the strategic moves that are being self-consciously made on the unequal social fields of power in which educational policy operates. This doesn't vitiate the strength of what such analyses of the growing conservative tendencies among some "othered" communities have given us. However, the question is not whether it is possible to build a Rightist-led coalition that will include elements of "multiculturalism." Indeed, as I have shown in this part of the chapter, such a process is in part already being successfully attempted. Instead, the questions we must constantly ask are the following: At what cost? At whose expense? We do know, for example, that the integration of some elements of communities that have historically been seen as "the other" has occurred, that certain elements have been brought under the umbrella of conservative modernization. For instance, some Latino/as, Asian Americans, gays and lesbians, and others have given their support to what are surprisingly conservative causes. Although perhaps overstating her arguments for political reasons, Dillard, for example, is at her most perceptive when she sees that the roots of the support of conservative positions among some members of oppressed groups may often be based in not wanting to "be Black." It is worth quoting her at length here.

> [One] point on which Latino, Asian-American, women, and homo-
> sexual conservatives seem to agree is the desire, to restate the matter

> bluntly, not to be like blacks—members of a group that persists in pressing for collective redress from the government rather than pursuing the path of individualism, upward mobility, and assimilation. That some Latino and Asian-American conservatives have engaged in this narrative is troubling. If Toni Morrison is even partially correct in asserting that previous waves of immigrants have embraced (white, middle-class) American identity "on the back of blacks," then there is reason to fear that new immigrants will seek to replicate this pattern. In the process, the already tense relationships among African-Americans, Latinos, and Asian-Americans could degenerate. That some African-American conservatives, a contingent that remains predominantly middle and upper-middle-class, appear content to follow suit—to assimilate on the backs of the black poor—is doubly disturbing (Dillard, 2001, p. 182).

Although I do not think that her arguments are as applicable to groups such as BAEO, for many other persons and organizations with which she does deal Dillard's points need to be taken very seriously. For the implication of such arguments is that the major losers in the shifting discursive terrain surrounding race and identity may very well prove once again to be poor Blacks. Once more, they will be pathologized. Their voices will be silenced. And they will continue to be "everybody's convenient and favorite scapegoat" (p. 182). Given the central place that race has played in the development of the neo-conservative movement of "return" and the neo-liberal movement of "choice" (Apple, 2001), we should not be surprised if rightist multiculturalism promises more of the same, but covered in a new and seemingly more diverse discourse.

"Not wanting to be Black" does not explain the support of vouchers by groups such as BAEO, however. Instead, it is the very fact of *being Black*, of recognizing and fighting against their social and cultural positioning as the ultimate "other," that has caused them to seek out strategic—some might say heretical—alliances with some of the main tendencies that, paradoxically, have been in the forefront historically in supporting such positioning. In *Educating the "Right" Way* (Apple, 2001), I called for thinking heretically about possible alliances that might subvert parts of the agendas involved in conservative modernization. Whether BAEO's "heretical actions" actually do subvert such agendas and the racial stratification of schools remains to be seen. I fear that they may not. But one must also ask what choices they in fact do have, given the structures of inequality that currently exist. Not recognizing the strong elements of good sense in their persistent struggles to understand and act on a world organized around a politics of racialization is simply inadequate.

Conclusion

In this chapter, I have documented the ways in which Paul Willis's work has had a continuing influence on my own, especially his recognition of the crucial importance of the contradictory tensions between "good" and "bad" sense in people's common sense and his recognition of the problem of employing the elements of good sense of oppressed people to disarticulate them from previous alliances and rearticulate them to new collective movements. I gladly recognize this publicly, in his role both as a friend and as someone who has helped to teach me a way of understanding the world and the politics of lived culture that, once one understands the world this way, one cannot easily return to previous models. For me and for many others, this kind of "disclosure model" is lasting.

At the same time, I have instantiated this understanding in a concrete example. I have examined a growing phenomenon—the growth of seemingly conservative sentiments among "despised others." At the core of my analysis is not only an interest, shared with Willis, in seeing the rich complexity of the politics of lived action, however. My arguments also center on a deep concern about what is at stake for all of us if rightist multiculturalism succeeds in redefining what and whose knowledge is of most worth and what our social and educational policies are meant to do. No matter what one's position is on the wisdom of BAEO's strategic actions, the entire case provides a crucial example of the politics of disarticulation and rearticulation, on the ways in which social movements and alliances are formed and re-formed out of the material and ideological conditions of daily life, and of the politics of discursive reappropriation (Apple, 2001; Hall, 1996).[10] Thus, an analysis of such movements is important both in terms of the balance of forces and power involved in specific educational reforms, but also in terms of more general issues concerning the processes of social transformation and agency. A critical but sympathetic understanding of groups such as BAEO may enable us to avoid the essentialism and reductionism that enters into critical sociological work on the role of struggles over the state and over the connections between culture and power (Apple et al., 2003). It can provide a more nuanced sense of social actors and the possibilities and limits of strategic alliances in a time of conservative modernization (see Apple and Pedroni, in press).

Although I support the struggles of groups such as BAEO and have a good deal of sympathy with their critique of the current functioning of public (state supported) schools, I have very real worries about whether they can control the uses to which their support of neo-liberal policies will be put. Yet, having said this, there may be some salutary effects of their efforts to mobilize around vouchers.

If the common school loses its legitimacy among significant numbers of people within communities of color—and there is some evidence that this may be happening within some communities (Moe, 2001)—this may force a reexamination of the unequal ways schools are currently financed in the United States, where a school's funding is dependent on the local tax base and its very real inequalities. It also may create the conditions in which teachers and their unions may have to work much more closely with local communities than is the case now simply in order for teachers to maintain their legitimacy in the eyes of people of color. I say this knowing that, oddly enough, this might provide evidence for parts of the neo-liberal case about school markets. Fear of competition among teachers and other educators then may have hidden effects that may, finally, lead to even more support among them for needed changes in schools.

Having said this, however, I predict the opposite. Although these changes may occur, it is unfortunately just as likely that the effects will be ones less positive in their long-term consequences. Less funding will be given to public (state supported) schools. A politics of blame will evolve in which parents who have no choice but to keep their children in underfunded and highly policed inner-city schools will be seen as the source of the problem of the common school. Much depends on the balance of forces at the time. Given what I and others have shown about the often-negative results of the combination of neo-conservative and neo-liberal reforms in schools, I am not sanguine about what will happen. At the very least, though, we need to be aware that the complicated politics and strategic maneuverings that are occurring on the terrain of educational policy will have complicated, contradictory, and unforeseen results. The example of BAEO signifies the beginning, not the end, of this story.

Although I have focused on the growth of strategic alliances between "despised others" and conservative forces in the United States, I predict that such alliances may not be limited to this one nation.[11] This may be disturbing to many progressively inclined educators, and this leads to my final point. Any groups that disagree with BAEO about the wisdom of supporting vouchers and of making tactical alliances with the Right have a task that goes well beyond simply criticizing their position or their strategy. Critics of their positions and strategies must have a detailed and in depth understanding both of what generates their anger at public (state supported) schools and at the lack of responsiveness that all too many school systems have shown to communities of color and the poor and working class for decades. The conditions to which groups like BAEO are responding are *real* and immensely destructive on real children in real communities (see, e.g., Kozol, 1991). Thus, those who worry about BAEO must ask what they themselves are for. They need to redouble their own efforts to end the racial contract that underpins "our" economic and political institutions (Mills, 1997), to work even harder to provide the economic and cultural conditions that would make African American parents have faith in their schools, and to challenge the ways in which a politics of "whiteness" underpins so much of the daily life of this society. Simply saying no to BAEO, then, is not enough. Indeed, I would claim that it is a racializing act itself unless it is accompanied by powerful antiracist actions.

A Final Word on Paul Willis

In recognizing my (and our) debt to Paul Willis, I have focused my attention on the ways in which race and class intersect in complex ways here, with the primary attention being given to race. Yet I cannot end this chapter without noting that there are other equally crucial reasons for us to continue to return to *Learning to Labor*. This has to do with the turn to the "post" in much of the current critical scholarship in education today. As I have argued at much greater length elsewhere, such a turn has proven to be immensely productive (see, e.g., Apple, 1996, 1999). Indeed, the reader will undoubtedly have noticed my own debt to selective parts of post positions in this chapter—a focus on identity, on discourse, on an anti-essentializing problematic, for example. However, the often unreflective turn to the post also has had some unfortunate effects. Today, for instance, when there often is either an evacuation of class in all too much critical educational and cultural research or a return to the reductive and economistic readings of class so reminiscent of Bowles and Gintis, critical work could be revitalized by returning—critically—to *Learning to Labor*. Class, not only as a set of structural positions and locations, but profoundly as a vital and lived *project*, can return in its most sophisticated forms. Granted we will need to recognize that "it" is filled with contradictions and intersected by a multitude of dynamics surrounding gender, sexuality, "race," "ability," age, region, religion, and colonial and postcolonial relations and histories—but class analysis needs to be returned. Some of us may like to think of class as a "text," as a discursive construct that is by its very nature reductive and essentializing, and that it simply speaks to one more instance of a power/ knowledge nexus. I believe that this is itself a dangerously essentializing position to take. It may be a bit reductive for me to say that class can only be considered this way by those who do not recognize the materialities of their own class positions, who have the luxury of not having to deal with the "worlds of pain" involved in being excluded from the supposed benefits of "our" postmodern universe of hybridity and "choice." But it would be salutary to consider what it means—analytically and personably/politically—to take such a position on class.

In the meantime, returning to *Learning to Labor*, with its silences acknowledged, would be a fine first step in how one creatively understands the ways in which elements of good and bad sense operate in people's daily lives. The act of going back to Paul Willis's work would also enable us to recapture our sense of what class means and how it works—and of how it is connected to other constitutive dynamics over and through which we struggle to create an education that is worthy of its name. That too would be one way of demonstrating our continuing respect for what Paul Willis accomplished.

Acknowledgments

I thank David Gillborn, Steven Selden, and in particular Tom Pedroni for their perceptive comments on the issues raised in this essay. Tom Pedroni has offered important conceptual, historical, and empirical suggestions and criticisms. A number of my arguments are indebted to his own ongoing investigation of BAEO and the complexities of African American educational politics (see Pedroni, 2003). Sections of this chapter have appeared in the *London Review of Education*.

Notes

1. See Willis's reflections on these issues in Willis (2000).
2. The term "authoritarian populism" originally comes from the compelling work of Stuart Hall. Unlike Hall, however, I would prefer to limit its use to a particular group of people who make up the "religious right." For more on this, see Hall (1980) and Apple (2001).
3. Although her analysis could be more detailed and subtle in certain places, Dillard (2001) does a good job of detailing the "structures of feeling" of conservative affiliations among a number of people who usually are not expected to take such position. She deals with a wide range of different forms of conservative leanings: from the economy, the legitimacy of activist government, the politics of the body, and the role of religion in public affairs on the one hand, to questions dealing with what knowledge should and should not be taught as "legitimate" and, say, the place of race in university admissions on the other.
4. "Progressive" traditions in the United States were not free of such racializing and racist logics. See, for example, Selden (1999).
5. That, say, a number of African American groups, ones that are making alliances with distinctly conservative movements, exist and are growing says something very important about the fascination with identity politics among many progressive scholars and activists in education and elsewhere. Too often writing on identity (wrongly) assumes that identity politics is a "good thing," that people inexorably move in progressive directions as they pursue what Nancy Fraser would call a politics of recognition (Fraser, 1997). Yet any serious study of rightist movements demonstrates that identity politics is just as apt to take, say, angry and retrogressive forms—antigay, racist nativism, antiwomen, etc. For many such people, "we" are the new oppressed, with that "we" not including most people of color, feminists, "sexual deviants," immigrants, and so on (see, e.g., Kintz, 1997, and Blee, 2002). Yet, as I noted earlier, even people within these "despised" groups themselves may take on such retrogressive identities.
6. BAEO is a heterogeneous organization. Much, though not all, of BAEO's leadership is from the middle class, but it does have a good deal of grass-roots support. Where it specifically meets and intersects with Rightist organizations, those who interact with such organizations tend not to be among the poor and working class. However, a class analysis is not sufficient

here. Racial solidarity may come first; race fundamentally mediates class relations. Thus, the issue of the class position of BAEO's leadership needs to be thought about in complex and subtle ways. I thank Tom Pedroni for this point.

7. In this regard, Tom Pedroni's ongoing research on BAEO is of considerable importance (see Pedroni, 2003).

8. In this regard, the political issue they are facing is in some ways similar to the debates over "market socialism." Can economic and political forms developed under the auspices of less progressive tendencies and power relations be employed to further goals that are organized around a very different set of ideological sentiments? See, for example, Bardhan and Roemer (1993) and Ollman (1998).

9. Dillard (2001) herself is very fair in her assessment of what the implications of such support may be. She nicely shows the contradictions of the arguments and logic of the people she focuses on. In doing so, she draws on some of the more cogent analyses of the relationship between democracy and the maintenance of the public sphere on the one hand and an expansive and rich understanding of what it means to be a citizen on the other. Readers of her discussion would also be well served to connect her arguments to the historical struggles over the very meanings of our concepts of democracy, freedom, and citizenship such as that found in Eric Foner's illuminating book, *The Story of American Freedom* (1998), but Dillard's discussion is substantive and useful. It also serves as a reminder of the continuing importance of a number of democratic and critical writers such as Hannah Arendt (1973, 1990), whose work, although not perfect by any means, unfortunately is no longer read as often as it should be.

10. An analysis of groups such as BAEO could enable us to extend the range of Basil Bernstein's work on *recontextualization* as well (see Bernstein, 1990).

11. Heidi Safia Mirza's ongoing work on the role of schooling in communities of color in England is very interesting in this regard.

References

Anyon, J. (1979). Ideology and U.S. history textbooks. *Harvard Educational Review, 49,* 361–386.

Apple, M. W. (1979). *Ideology and curriculum.* Boston: Routledge and Kegan Paul.

Apple, M. W. (Ed.). (1982a). *Cultural and economic reproduction in education.* Boston: Routledge and Kegan Paul.

Apple, M. W. (1982b). *Education and power.* Boston: Routledge and Kegan Paul.

Apple, M. W. (1986). *Teachers and texts.* New York: Routledge.

Apple, M. W. (1996). *Cultural politics and education.* New York: Teachers College Press.

Apple, M. W. (1999). *Power, meaning, and identity.* New York: Peter Lang.

Apple, M. W. (2000). *Official knowledge* (2nd ed.). New York: Routledge.

Apple, M. W. (2001). *Educating the "right" way: Markets, standards, God, and inequality.* New York: Routledge.

Apple, M. W., & Beane, J. A. (1999). *Democratic schools: Lessons from the chalk face.* Buckingham: Open University Press.

Apple, M. W., et al. (2003). *The state and the politics of knowledge.* New York: Routledge.

Apple, M. W., & Weis, L. (Eds.). (1983). *Ideology and practice in schooling.* Philadelphia: Temple University Press.

Apple, M. W., & Pedroni, T. (in press). Do vouchers make strange bedfellows? Conservative alliance building among the dispossessed. *Teacher College Record.*

Arendt, H. (1973). *The human condition.* Chicago: University of Chicago Press.

Arendt, H. (1990). *On revolution.* New York: Penguin Books.

Ball, S. (1994). *Education reform.* Buckingham: Open University Press.

Bardhan, P., & Roemer, J. (Eds.). (1993). *Market socialism: The current debate.* New York: Oxford University Press.

Bernstein, B. (1990). *The structuring of pedagogic discourse.* New York: Routledge.

Blee, K. (2002). *Inside organized racism: Women in the hate movement.* Berkeley: University of California Press.

Bourdieu, P. (1984). *Distinction.* Cambridge: Harvard University Press.

Bowles, S., & Gintis, H. (1976). *Schooling in capitalist America.* New York: Basic Books.

Dale, R. (1989/1990). The Thatcherite project in education. *Critical Social Policy, 9*(1), 4–19.

Dillard, A. D. (2001). *Guess who's coming to dinner now: Multicultural conservatism in America.* New York: New York University Press.

Fine, M., Weis, L., Powell, L., & Wong, L. M. (Eds.). (1997). *Off White.* New York: Routledge.

Foner, E. (1998). *The story of American freedom.* New York: Norton.

Fraser, N. (1997). *Justice interruptus.* New York: Routledge.

Gillborn, D., & Youdell, D. (2000). *Rationing education.* Philadelphia: Open University Press.

Greider, W. (1997). *One world, ready or not.* New York: Simon and Schuster.

Hall, S. (1980). Popular democratic vs. authoritarian populism. In A. Hunt (Ed.), *Marxism and democracy* (pp. 150–170). London: Lawrence and Wishart.

Hall, S. (1996). On postmodernism and articulation. In D. Morley & K-H Chen (Eds.), *Stuart Hall: Critical dialogues in cultural studies* (pp. 131–150). New York: Routledge.

Herrnstein, R., & Murray, C. (1994). *The bell curve.* New York: Free Press.

Hobsbawm, E. (1994). *The age of extremes.* New York: Pantheon.

Hogan, D. (1982). Education and class formation. In M. W. Apple (Ed.), *Cultural and economic reproduction in education* (pp. 32–78). Boston: Routledge and Kegan Paul.

Katz, M. B. (2001). *The price of citizenship.* New York: Metropolitan Books.

Kintz, L. (1997). *Between Jesus and the market.* Durham, NC: Duke University Press.

Kozol, J. (1991). *Savage inequalities.* New York: Crown.

Kuhn, T. (1970). *The structure of scientific revolutions.* Chicago: University of Chicago Press.

Lewis, D. L. (1993). *W. E. B. DuBois: Biography of a race, 1868–1919.* New York: Henry Holt.

Lewis, D. L. (2000). *W. E. B. DuBois: The fight for equality and the American century. 1919–1963.* New York: Henry Holt.

McNeil, L. (2000). *Contradictions of school reform.* New York: Routledge.

Mills, C. (1997). *The racial contract.* Ithaca, NY: Cornell University Press.

Moe, T. (2001). *Schools, vouchers, and the American public.* Washington, DC: Brookings Institution.

Ollman, B. (Ed.). (1998). *Market socialism: The debate among socialists.* New York: Routledge.

Omi, M., & Winant, H. (1994). *Racial formation in the United States* (2nd ed.). New York: Routledge.

Pedroni, T. (2003). *Strange bedfellows: African American participation in the Milwaukee school choice coalition.* Unpublished PhD dissertation, University of Wisconsin, Madison.

Ramsey, I. (1964). *Models and mystery.* London: Oxford University Press.

Selden, S. (1999). *Inheriting shame.* New York: Teachers College Press.

West, C. (1982). *Prophesy deliverance!* Philadelphia: Westminster Press.

Whitty, G., Power, S., & Halpin, D. (1998). *Devolution and choice in education.* Buckingham: Open University Press.

Willis, P. (1977). *Learning to labour.* Westmead: Saxon House.

Willis, P. (1990). *Common culture,* Boulder, Westview.

Willis, P. (2000). *The ethnographic imagination.* Cambridge: Polity Press.

CHAPTER 5

The "Lads" and the Cultural Topography of Race

FAZAL RIZVI

Twenty-five years after its publication I can still recall my first encounter with Paul Willis's landmark book, *Learning to Labor* (first published as *Learning to Labour*, 1977). It made a huge impression on me: Not only did it challenge some of my deeply held neo-Marxist assumptions about social reproduction and education, it also helped me to think through some of the experiences I had teaching mathematics in the mid 1970s, in a high school at the northern outskirts of Manchester, England—in a town not unlike Hammertown, depicted so powerfully by Willis from the perspective of the "lads." Willis provided a powerful ethnographic account of the lads as they sought to make sense of their experiences at school, located within a community in England's declining industrial heartland, and their futures in and out of employment.

The school in Manchester where I taught was also located in an urban community, which was characterized by declining employment opportunities for the White working-class youth, on the one hand, and increasing levels of postcolonial immigration, leading to a great deal of racial unrest, on the other. I found myself within this complex "cultural topography of race," to use a term used by Willis to describe the social dynamics of race relations at Hammertown. However, the problem in my case was that the "the lads" at my school found it difficult to place me within their preexisting cultural topography of race—mostly because I was the only non-White teacher at the school. They had been told that I had come to their school from Australia but that I was born in India. Yet as far as they were concerned, I looked like a South Asian and therefore the racist term "Paki" clearly applied to me. Somewhat problematically, however, I did not readily fit the stereotypes the lads had of "the Pakis." There was something different about me—to begin with, I was their teacher. Within a few weeks of my being at that school the lads found a way out of their dilemma. Because I was no ordinary "Paki," I acquired a nickname: "Super Paki." As a young teacher who had only recently arrived in England, I found this name both personally disturbing and deeply contradictory. On the one hand, I viewed it as overtly racist and offensive. Yet, on the other hand, I could not but be flattered by the affection the term was meant to express toward me. I was also somewhat amused by the lads' sense of humor.

It was within the context of this experience that I first read *Learning to Labor*. Willis's rich analysis provided me with some of the resources I needed to theorize about the nickname I had been given, along with a number of other racist encounters I had at the school. It helped me to understand that, as a teacher, I embodied the school's authority, which although it was recognized by the lads was simultaneously resisted and opposed, although not in any direct fashion, but always through "having a laff," "taking the piss," and "dossing." This opposition, as Willis (1977, p. 12) put it, was "expressed mainly as a style." Just as the lads were creative in the ways in which they differentiated themselves from the norms of the school, they also sought to define me as different from the other "Pakis," who were subjected to more ridicule than I. I was admired for not being like the other "Pakis" but was also disliked for the way I had embodied the received English cultural norms that were expressed through my authority at the school.

The lads' relationship to me was characterized by a deep ambivalence that expressed a degree of respect but also involved a substantial measure of cultural disdain, especially when I asserted my authority and insisted that lads perform the learning tasks to which they were mostly hostile. On these occasions, they did not hesitate to apply the stereotypes to me. As Willis (1977, p. 152) suggested, these stereotypes involved a "clear demarcation between groups and a derogatory view of other racial types." These stereotypes were "simply assumed [by the lads] as the basis of this or other action: it is a daily form of knowledge in use." This knowledge discursively cast people within a cultural topography of race that defined everyone as either "us" or "them," with relatively clear sets of social characteristics, expectations, and entitlements applying differentially to each group.

This topography applied as much to the labor market as it did to interracial relations within the school. Thus, the lads understood the labor market to be fundamentally divided along class, gender, and race lines. As Willis (1977, p. 152) argued, racial division provided the lads with "an ideological object for feelings about the degeneracy of others and superiority of the self." The West Indian males were entitled to jobs that were dirty, messy, and unsocial, requiring masculine assertiveness, whereas Asians were placed at the opposite end of the cultural scale, in jobs that required them to be "cissy," passive, and lack aggression. This racist differentiation clearly served to divide the working class both materially and ideologically. This constituted one of the ways in which the lads were complicit in reproducing the logic of "the complex social definition of labor power under capitalism," despite their oppositional culture and "partial penetration" (Willis, 1977, p. 126).

Perhaps the most important of Willis's many insights in *Learning to Labor* is his theorization of this complicity. The lads understood perfectly how their oppositional practices at school condemned them to poorly paid jobs and perhaps even to unemployment; they nonetheless rejected the middle-class values and the academic practices of school as irrelevant to their lives. The complicity did not arise out of a false consciousness, involving a simple reproduction of their class position within the grand narrative of capitalism. The lads were not dupes, lacking any agency: quite the contrary. In their everyday lives they had a reasonably good understanding of the prevailing structures of power, and a working knowledge of how to live with it, even if this helped produce unfavorable social outcomes for them. The lads examined and solved everyday problems with deftness and dexterity, often with a great deal of creative imagination.

In *Learning to Labor*, Willis used the term *penetration* to account for the ways in which counterschool culture saw through the meritocracy and individualism of schooling, allowing and helping the lads to develop realistic assessments of the pessimistic futures they confronted in manual labor. They lived with this realization with a great deal of reflexivity about the structural forces that affected their lives. These forces were seen not only as determinants but also "as sources of what is to be known and discovered in the possibilities of experience" (Willis, 2000, p. 35). In his recent book *The Ethnographic Imagination*, Willis argued that fun and pleasure, "the laff," are powerful creative resources for, and mechanisms of, penetration, through which the lads confronted "the power of institutional command, drawing out, developing and reproducing powers and abilities and a cultural world of reference not defined by institutional roles." Thus, the cultural topography of race included having fun at the expense of those who were considered racially different. Both collectively and individually, the lads extended a great deal of creative effort to making sense of the consequences for them of patterns of immigration that changed their social milieu and life chances. However, they did this thinking within the cultural topography of race the defined the racial order in Britain at that time, but not unreflexively.

And so it was with my nickname. The term "Super Paki" enabled them to attach a new social identifier to me without disturbing their existing cultural topography of race. In a sense, it demonstrated their narratives of race to be reasonably flexible, even if it remained trapped within the dominant stereotypes. It showed their interpretive frameworks to be dynamic, capable of modification and change in the face of new social conditions, personal interactions, and political circumstances. In *The Ethnographic Imagination* (2000), Willis reflected further on this interpretative process in an effort to elucidate his larger notion of cultural production by focusing on the active and productive nature of cultural practices that are seldom passive but are located within the flows of the broader cultural topography and are intended to make situated personal and collective meanings.

In this way, Willis avoids the dangers of essentialism in the earlier reproduction theories of education and culture (Bowles & Gintis, 1975, for example), by viewing the cultural topography of race as continually changing, being challenged, interrupted, and reconstructed, involving, often in ways that are contradictory, complex structural processes on the one hand and the processes of imagination and creativity on the other.

The cultural topography of race is thus historically specific. The discourses and cultural practices inherited from the past and the broader culture are reconstituted and rearticulated in processes through which people struggle to make sense of their everyday lives, both seriously and cynically—in the case of the lads, with a great deal of joviality and fun. The racial categories that people use are thus not homogeneous and static but are given concrete form by the specific social relations and the historical context in which they are embedded. They are continuously changing, often through processes of resistance and contestation as people attempt to understand their social circumstances differently. On occasions, they construct new patterns of social relations, whereas in other circumstances particular practices persist, often through the use of new code words and new ideological forms that obscure old discriminatory behavior.

If cultural topographies of race represent distinctive spatio-temporal modalities of racial discourse and practices, with their own history and structures of meaning, then Willis's ethnography in *Leaning to Labor* is a historically specific one, located within a particular social and economic context, involving a range of key assumptions about the production of meaning, identity and social outcomes. Indeed, Willis (2000, p. 86) himself acknowledged that he "caught 'the lads' in *Learning to Labor* at the end of what was perhaps the last golden period of working-class cultural coherence and power in a fully employed Britain." Implicit in Willis's analysis in *Learning to Labor* is the view that this cultural coherence and power was racially organized, and was much threatened by large-scale immigration during the 1970s. The "lads" expressed this anxiety through various overt and covert practices of racism.

The cultural topography of race Willis described in *Learning to Labor* is thus specific to Britain's colonial history, postcolonial immigration, and the strength of its working-class traditions. In the last 25 years Britain has become transformed into another kind of society. It has experienced massive losses of manual industrial work available to the working classes. Over 4 million manufacturing jobs have been lost. The new jobs that have emerged for the working classes are largely lower paid service jobs—casual, part-time, low-paid, and insecure, especially for young people, older workers and ethnic minorities. This structural feature of society has had major implications for the cultural topography not only of class but also of gender and race. Fundamental economic and social changes since the mid 1970s, Willis (2000, p. 85) argued "have certainly made the reproductive balances of British society more jagged, cynical and unstable." They have had important implications for gender forms, identities, and relations. For the working class, masculinity has become disconnected from particular forms of labor.

Similarly, the racial signifiers that were once assumed by the lads have become destabilized and highly contradictory. The "lads" had assumed that it was "natural" that people belonged to supposedly different "races," which constituted distinct and separate communities. For them, the boundaries of inclusion and exclusion were based on the imagined community of Britain as a nation. But this interpretive framework for the signification of race is no longer as clear-cut, changed perhaps irredeemably not only by economic and social changes but also by highly localized antiracist activism in Britain, on the one hand, and the contemporary processes of globalization, on the other.

In what follows, I examine some of these changes in order to determine the ways in which the transformed cultural topographies of race now require new ethnographic practices, which do not describe a particular locality within its own terms, but also investigate its relationship to the broader global processes, as has been argued by a range of recent authors, including Doreen Massey (1994), Michael Burawoy et al. (1999), and Michael Smith (2001).

As a geographer, Massey attempted to show how concepts of space and place are relevant to any ethnographic examination of social relations and cultural practices. She argued that changes in the world economy can be characterized in a number of ways, from modernism to postmodernism, from industrial to postindustrial manufacturing to services, and from Fordist to post-Fordist. However, each of these characterizations indicate the "prevailing uncertainly about the shape of the new"—the uneven extension of the boundaries of economic relations in both intensity and scope (Massey, 1994, pp. 157–158)—which is one of the key processes at the heart of globalization of capital. This has resulted in "the stretching out of different kinds of social relationships over space," creating new relations of power: relations imbued with meaning and symbolism. These new global relations of power, argued Massey, have implications for the ethnographic study of localities, which can no longer avoid taking into account global processes.

As sociologists, Burawoy and his colleagues (1999) similarly argued for the need to understand identities and relations in global terms. Making a distinction between "global imperialism" and "global postmodern," Burawoy suggested that under the former, class, gender, race, and nation constituted "relatively stable and enduring subjects," possessing "a certain insularity and essentialist character" (p. 346). Under global postmodernism, on the other hand, boundaries have broken down and identities proliferated. Gender and class relations are no longer "given" but have to be negotiated. The experiences of migration and the rebellion of the second- and third-generation ethnic experiences challenge and break through conventional boundaries. Buroway et al. (1999, p. 347) added that "these experiences become more common as migration cuts national identity adrift from states, building new diasporas within fluid boundaries." The children, born and raised in Britain, of immigrant parents and grandparents have a radically different kind of relationship to their local communities, and to the global diasporic networks that play an increasingly significant role in their lives. Globalization has not only transformed the nature of work and labor markets but has also created new conditions for intergroup relations and for thinking about social identities (Castells, 1997). In such a context, ethnographic practice requires globalization to be grounded in specific locations, and localities need to be globally articulated.

In *Learning to Labor*, the lads viewed "Jamaicans" and "Pakis" as relatively homogeneous groups, culturally apart from themselves. There was little evidence of social mixing, except in ways that were antagonistic. Assumed was a context of immigrants as newly arrived without a significant voice of their own. Interethnic friendships were almost nonexistent. The nature of interethnic relations in Britain has now changed markedly. Ethnic groups are no longer see themselves or are mostly treated as racially homogeneous, as was the case in Hammertown. Close friendships across cultures now exist widely, as does a substantial degree of alignment between White and immigrant oppositional youth cultures. It is therefore impossible now to understand the cultural orientation of the White working class without also theorizing its complex relationship with changing dynamics of race relations in Britain. I agree with Angela McRobbie (1996), who argued that we cannot fully understand contemporary youth cultures without looking critically at the issue of how these cultures are constituted *relationally*. To do this, we cannot simply focus on the White working-class youth without also determining how other cultural groups relate to them—how subjectivities with different cultural histories intersect with each other to produce new subjectivities, more so now than ever before, in contexts created by global flows of ideas and people and a postcolonial cultural politics that rejects the idea of an authentic racial subject.

Stuart Hall used the notion of "new ethnicities" to capture the cultural transformations now taking place in Britain wrought by migration. Hall (1996, p. 441) considered the ways in which immigrant communities have represented themselves in response to their "common experience of racism and marginalization in Britain." Especially through arts and writing, they have contested the stereotypical and derogatory representations of Black people at large with positive images of the Black community. They have resisted unifying modes of representation by highlighting the "extraordinary diversity of subjective positions, social experiences and cultural identities." Cultural identities are presented as multiple and mobile, with their own inner tensions. This has inevitably entailed "a weakening or fading of the notion that 'race' or some composite notion of race around the term Black will either guarantee the effectivity of any cultural practice or determine in any final sense it aesthetic value" (Hall, 1996, p. 443). Hall suggested that this creates a challenge for the Black communities, of how to construct a radical politics that works with and through difference, which is able to build those forms of solidarity and identification that makes common struggle possible but which does not presuppose any homogeneity of identities. Black communities have had to think about the dynamic nature of their identity under the new conditions of fluidity, hybridity, and mobility.

However, these conditions pose a challenge, equally, to the White working-class youth—of how to engage politically with the increasingly confident ethnic communities who reject totalizing systems of representation but nonetheless work collectively to contest racial inequalities. As John McLeod (2000, p. 225) pointed out, the emergence of "new ethnicities" in Britain has "altered the ways *all* people in one location, not just those constructed as 'diasporic communities'" have to consider questions of difference. Indeed, all oppositional divides between "native inhabitants" and "diasporic peoples," "majority" and "minority" are threatened with dissolution. This does not suggest the demise of traditional social categories, but rather the need to reconsider how the processes of racialization now occur and how racialization of particular groups of people is converted into the discursive and institutional practices of racism.

The communities that the lads had once assumed as their own, in which immigrants were uniformly regarded as outsiders, now have to be renegotiated and rearticulated. As Massey (1994) noted, communities acquire their particularity not from some long-internalized history or culturally embedded character, but from the specific interactions and articulations of contemporary social relations, social processes, and understandings. Place making is shaped by conflict, difference, and social negotiation among differently situated and at times antagonistically related social actors, some of whose networks are locally bound whereas others transcend national boundaries. Unlike the immigrants of an earlier generation, diasporic people now increasingly work both within their geographically specific locality, but also through networks that are not necessarily anchored in Britain but may have a transnational reach. Their sense of their locality is tied to the crisscrossing of transnational circuits of communication, and to the crosscutting of local and translocal social practices. Arjun Appadurai (1996) used the term *ethnoscape* to describe the landscape of mobile persons who now constitute the shifting world that characterizes communities like Hammertown. The cultural topography of such towns is reconstituted by tourists, immigrants, exiles, refugees and other moving groups, affecting the politics of identity, place and difference.

The community that the "lads" once inhabited was assumed to be characterized by continuity and stability. Theirs was a cohesive community in which immigrants were considered intruders and were regarded as inferior. This mode of cultural representation was based on a particular politics of difference, informed by the assumptions of power asymmetries that had emerged out of a history of colonialism. Akhil Gupta and James Ferguson (1997) identified three dimensions of contemporary cultural production that have complicated this always-idealized communitarian narrative. First, the growing economic, sociocultural, and informational interdependence across linked spaces is undermining the notions of discrete, autonomous self-contained local cultures. Second, the ubiquitous discourses and practices of postcolonialism are producing a variety of new hybrid practices that problematize the very notion of "authentic cultural traditions." And third, the boundary-penetrating processes of globalization are facilitating the social construction of "communities in the making," as imagined spaces, often occupying the same geographical locale.

These trends necessarily entail new processes of inclusion and exclusion, that is, processes that create "Otherness." In constructing the Other, a group recognizes itself through its selective memory of a common past, involving continual attempts to imagine, assert, and redefine its boundaries, in ways both routine and creative. Identity formation is characterized by its two constitutive dimensions of self-identification and affirmation of difference. Of course, under the social conditions of capitalism, this politics of difference is often an antagonistic one. With increasing mobility of people across national boundaries, the Other is both strange and increasingly in our midst. Julia Kristeva (1991, p. 20) called this "the hidden face of our identity." She has suggested that the stranger, the foreigner, is not only among us, but also *inside us.* This is an enormously significant insight. It suggests that as a result of regular cultural contact, be it physical or virtual, we acquire some of the characteristics of the Other, which has the consequence of at once creating a sense of existential unease and foreboding. In fearful anticipations, said Kristeva (1991, p. 13), the stranger looms as a powerful persecutor against whom "we" solidify to take revenge . . . must we not stick together, remain among ourselves, expel the intruder, or at least keep him in "his" place.

A number of recent theorists have discussed this politics of racial antagonism and resentment, under the global conditions of mobility. In this context, more creative discourses and practices of racism emerge, which cannot be "read off" with any predetermined logic of racial differentiation. Rather racism is best viewed as a dynamic ideological form that is continuously changing, being challenged, interrupted, and reconstructed, and that often appears in contradictory forms. Its cultural production can be expected to be complex, multifaceted, and historically specific. We need to avoid any assumption of simple historical duplication because ideologies are never only received but also constructed and reconstructed by people responding to their material and cultural circumstances in order to both understand and represent them and act in relation to them. As such, the politics of racial antagonism, like other forms of cultural politics, are created by people to find their way out of the dilemmas of everyday life they confront, produced by the conditions of rapid and continuous change.

There is nothing historically necessary about this politics. The emerging postcolonial confidence of subjugated groups need not necessarily produce resentment. Indeed, the new cultural topography of race is producing a space, at an intersection of borders, where as Avtar Brah (1996, p. 209) pointed out, "all subjectivities become juxtaposed, contested, proclaimed, or disavowed; where the permitted and the prohibited perpetually interrogate, and where the accepted and the transgressive imperceptibly mingle even while these syncretic forms may be disclaimed in the name of purity and tradition." This suggests that the outcomes of cultural intermingling are entirely contingent. Indeed, as Angela McRobbie (1996, p. 43) observed, the cultural forms produced by the new Black ethnicities in Britain have often "reached out and touched" many often socially subordinate, White young people, both male and female.

Willis provided ample evidence of the vital creativity in the production of cultural practices, but also pointed out that this creativity is ideologically laden and deeply affected by the prevailing social conditions of existence. In an era of globalization, these conditions point both to the deepening of racial antagonism, embodied in the new discourses of conservative restoration, but also to the real possibilities of antiracism, involving creative cultural practices of critical reflexivity and action.

References

Appudarai, A. (1996). *Modernity at large: Cultural dimensions of globalization.* Minneapolis: University of Minnesota.

Bowles, S., & Gintis, H. (1975). *Schooling in capitalist America.* London: Routledge.

Brah, A. (1996). *Cartographies of diaspora: Contesting identities.* London: Routledge.

Burowoy, M. et al. (1999). *Global ethnography.* Berkeley: University of California Press.

Castells, M. (1997). *The power of identity.* Oxford: Blackwell.

Gupta, A., & Ferguson, J. (1997). *Culture, power and place: Explorations in critical anthropology.* Durham, NC: Duke University Press.

Hall, S. (1996). New ethnicities. In D. Morley & K.-H. Chen (Eds.), *Stuart Hall: Critical dialogues in cultural studies* (pp. 441–449). London: Routledge.

Kristeva, J. (1991). *Strangers to ourselves.* New York: Harvester Wheatsheaf.

Massey, D. (1994). *Space, place and gender.* Minneapolis: University of Minnesota Press.

McLeod, J. (2001). *Beginning postcolonialism.* Manchester: Manchester University Press.

McRobbie A. (1996). Different youthful subjectivities. In I. Chambers & L. Curti (Eds.), *The postcolonial question* (pp. 30–46). London: Routledge.

Smith, M. P. (2001). *Transnational urbanism: Locating globalization.* Oxford: Blackwell.

Willis, P. (1977). *Learning to labour: How working class kids get working class jobs.* Aldershot, Hampshire, UK: Gower.

Willis, P. (2000). *The ethnographic imagination.* Cambridge, UK: Polity Press.

SECTION **II**

Learning to Labor in New Times

Reordering Work and Destabilizing Masculinity

JANE KENWAY AND ANNA KRAACK

Learning to Labor (Willis, 1977, first published as *Learning to Labour*) tells of a time when there were steady jobs available even for nonacademic, low-achieving, school-disaffected, White working-class boys and when there was an identifiable British working class to be reproduced through schooling and work. It tells of work in "Hammertown" in the British Midlands in the early 1970s in conditions close to full employment. The Willis study seeks to explain the reproduction of the male working class and the role of "the lads" and their education therein. Willis explains how cultural and institutional forms contribute to social reproduction. He illustrates how, in their manner of resisting school, the lads readied themselves for factory work and excluded themselves from opportunities for social mobility through education. Economic circumstances have changed dramatically since *Learning to Labor*, and this leads to somewhat different questions. What are contemporary economic conditions and what happens to working-class masculinity under such conditions? Such questions have prompted a number of studies in Britain designed, in effect, to empirically and theoretically update the issues addressed in *Learning to Labor* and indeed to address some of its absences. These studies include Mac an Ghaill, (1994), Arizpe and Arnot, (1997), O'Donnell and Sharpe (2000), and McDowell (2000, 2002).

This chapter complements such work, foregrounding "the prism of space" (Urry, 1994, p. 14). It focuses on two localities and on the reordering of work and the destabilizing of local working class masculine identities and relationships. It asks, how do nonacademic, school-disaffected, White working-class boys respond to such detraditionalization and with what effects? It draws from a wider study (Kenway & Kraack, in progress) that considers youthful masculinities and gender relations in marginalized, stigmatized, but also sometimes romanticized and exoticized places outside of Australia's capital cities.[1] This broader study points to the intersections between the changing social and cultural base of place, and identities, relationships, and inequalities as they are increasingly caught up in, and also attempt to stand apart from, globalizing flows. With its focus on the "globalizing local," this research links ideas associated with critical (Willis, 2000) and global (Burawoy et al., 2000) ethnography, and we call our approach critical local/global ethnography.[2] This chapter arises from 3 months of fieldwork in two localities. In-depth semistructured interviews were carried out with 36 young people; weekly, for 6 weeks, the 24 males were each interviewed, and the 12 females were interviewed fortnightly. Loosely structured focus and affinity group discussions were held with mothers, fathers, community members, teachers, youth workers, and welfare service providers. Informal conversations were held with a wide range of local people. The researcher also spent time at a variety of community and youth-specific locales (e.g. the school, beach, and main street) and events (e.g., sporting matches, discos, local carnivals). We use pseudonyms for all localities and participants.

The Contemporary Economic Order

The working world of Willis's lads is set against a backdrop of economic security and predictability in England. From World War II through to the late 1960s the global economy prospered and Britain's industrialized economy thrived with it (Currie, 1983). Yet in the late 1960s/early 1970s, underlying structural, industrial and economic weaknesses became evident in the global economy (Hall, 1983) and the British economy was rendered unstable. Indeed, since the days of "the lads," economies in various parts of the world have altered in remarkable ways. We begin with an overview of contemporary economic conditions.

Structural shifts in the economy in "First World" countries have involved a move away from primary and secondary to tertiary industries, particularly to the service sector. This has been variously described as a shift from Fordist to post- or neo-Fordist, or from industrial to post- or deindustrial production (Bauman, 2000; Harvey, 2000). These shifts have often included the closure, restructuring and downsizing, and indeed "off-shoring" of "heavy" manufacturing industries. Further, the center of economic gravity has altered and has become more global and less national and local. Survival needs and the drive for competitiveness have led small businesses to either close or to join bigger ones and bigger businesses to become international or global. Many public enterprises have become private and have then followed this pattern (Beresford, 2000). Local business sensibilities have been replaced either by national or by nonterritorial sensibilities. Global corporations have an increasing presence everywhere. Workplace restructuring has usually included the reduction of the workforce, intensification (longer working hours, increased productivity, and less pay), casualization, and technological enhancement. New approaches to management include an increased sensitivity to risk. Despite the neo-liberal rhetoric about leaving economic growth to market forces and despite various practices of deregulation, governments have acted as mediators among global, regional, national, and local economic trends. They have sought to sustain national and state economies by steering them in particular directions away from certain industries and business practices and toward others. This takes the form of policy advice, various deregulating and regulating practices, sundry incentives and disincentives, and strong intervention in the ideological climate.

As Massey (1995, p. 189) explained, there exists a "geography of production" and this involves a "spatial divisions of labour." Different patterns of economic activity in different locations and uneven economic growth and decline mean that the broad patterns associated with economic globalization as described earlier and the associated changes in the world of work are manifest somewhat differently in different places. Deindustrialization is not evenly spread, and there is an increasing tendency to relocate production from "First World" to "Third World" countries or to distribute it across multiple sites (Harvey, 2000). Further, as economic production in "First World" countries is increasingly dematerialized and veers toward the production of services and symbolic goods as described by Lash & Urry (1994), those places involved in primary and secondary material production are economically undermined. They are particularly subject to the flight of capital, and the associated downsizing or closure of local private and then public industries and services. The economic base of place is also altered by ecological globalization. In the interests of environmental sustainability, governments now undertake risk management in local economies. Together these factors have disrupted local economies and led local entrepreneurs to develop new industries in an attempt at local economic recovery.

Contemporary Workers

In these circumstances workers' conditions have been reconfigured and their identities challenged. The "First World" global work order consists of a small labor elite (the highly skilled, highly privileged professions) and an increasing number of people in casual, poorly paid and insecure work (May, 2002). The key features of desirable workers for the contemporary "First World" work order include mobility (they must not be rooted in place), flexibility (they must be prepared to work in any mode, at any time, for any pay), increased expertise (they must have more technical rather than manual knowledge and skill), and increased cultural (style) and social (networks) capital. Loyalty to tradition, location, and social class are understood by "industry" as impediments to growth. Indeed, as Bauman pointed out, "technological progress is measured by the replacement and elimination of labour" (Bauman, 1998b, p. 65).

The literature on the implications of deindustrialization for subgroups of working class school boys shows how these groups reinscribe themselves around academic achievement, high- and low-status vocational courses, and indeed around "new work areas such as business, design, media, and information technology" (O'Donnell & Sharpe, 2000, p. 134). This literature points to the ways that some young working class males are inventing themselves as "new workers" and to the fact that some others, particularly those who subscribe to working-class "macho masculinities," are not. However, such research offers little sense of the gendered ways in which pertinent young males get around the identity problems that arise in the so-called feminized work and labor markets. The casual work now available to them is not only insecure and poorly paid and difficult to class, but often invokes the "feminine" other to the working-class masculine described by Willis in his discussion of "labour power and patriarchy" (1977, p. 149). The term *feminization of work* commonly refers to the trend for an increasing number of workplaces to emulate the work and working conditions that have historically pertained to the "female" retail and service sectors. This involves the gendered convergence of labor market and work experiences and is part of what Bakker (1996, p. 7) called the "gender paradox of restructuring," involving the "contradictory effects of the dual process of gender erosion and intensification." We next show how working class masculinity is imbricated within this dynamic.

Detraditionalizing Masculinity in the "Globalizing Local"

For many years the main economic base of the two Australian localities discussed here has been power generation in the country city of Putland and fishing and timber in the coastal town of Paradise. The history of work in each location is closely tied up with what is conventionally thought of as men's work and with particular manifestations of masculinity. Males earn respect and reputation by performing a job well and diligently and by working hard to earn a decent wage—by, as Willis put it, "Doing a hard job well and being known for it" (1977, p. 52). Logging, fishing and industrial work all require "heroic" (Willis, 1977, p. 150), hard, sometimes grueling physical labor and involve various kinds and degrees of manual skill and physical toughness. In addition, logging and fishing occur out in the elements and involve battling with nature and extracting its bounty. They entail physical danger and call into play the camaraderie that arises from shared risk. In contrast, the industrial work associated with the power industry in Putland involves the mastery of machinery, and males develop close affinities on the shop floor. The masculinities invoked here equate with what Vashti Kenway (2001, pp. 7–8), drawing on Connell (1995), called "hegemonic industrial working class masculinity." As she points out, this includes "a 'hard bodies,' 'hard emotions' response to the world. [And] a mode of embodiment that signifies strength, mobility, autonomy, solidarity and a capacity to dominate space." Putland and Paradise have historically developed their self-concept around a particular place-based version of "hegemonic industrial working-class masculinity," which is central to the manner in which identities, work, and all relationships are valued. Others' work plays no part in the identities of each place and is either ignored or belittled for its softness and lack of physicality. The broad economic changes just outlined have, however, challenged each locality's character and the identities and relationships of local people, who have, in the words of Bauman (1998a, p. 18) "watched helplessly, the sole locality they inhabit moving away from under their feet." As we will now explain, the various reactions of White working class males are similar to those discussed in O'Donnell and Sharpe, (2000, p. 127); generally they are defensive, reactionary, progressive, uncertain, and confused. Yet there are also different patterns of effects in both places.

"Men Were Put on the Scrap Heap"

Located near rich deposits of brown coal that are excavated for the production of electricity, Putland was once a thriving "power town," providing over 85% of the State of Victoria's electricity (Local Government Board, 1994). But the neo-liberal privatization and deregulation reform policies pursued by successive Victorian state governments since the late 1980s have undermined Putland's economic base. The privatization and restructuring of the State Electricity Commission have involved major job losses (Kazakevitch, Foster, & Stone, 1997). This has had a significant social and psychological impact on the locale.

Before this restructuring, male jobs were plentiful, secure, and well paid, and there was intergenerational employment for males. Sally, a youth service worker, explained, "You could always get work at the SEC. It was slow, easy and comfortable. You didn't need an education, you started at the bottom and just worked your way up." Boys whose fathers worked at a power station were almost guaranteed an apprenticeship. Our conversations with local people are suffused by a melancholy discourse of loss and defeat, and this flows into pessimistic views about the present and future of Putland. Sometimes this discourse is also taken up by the young, who portray Putland as a "ghost town," a "lonely city."

"The mark of the socially excluded in an era of time/ space compression is immobility," argued Bauman (1998a, p. 113). According to Bauman, the excluded are those who have been "left behind," constrained by space, and also those who have no choice but to move. Putland is caught up in the class and gender politics of such mobility and immobility. With the downsizing of the power industry came worker redundancy and the search for new employment. The local working class has been disrupted and the industrial foundations of workers' identities have been lost. Some men have used their redundancy payouts to start small local businesses. Some survived; many failed. Others have searched for work locally, but, unable to find it, have reluctantly "gone on the dole." Others feel they have no tolerable choice but to leave their families and to join the many "mobile" and "flexible" new workers displaced and on the move due to economic globalization. Some have found work elsewhere and fled with their families. Other families have stayed behind "because the kids are settled here and they have a house here," Sally made clear. "This is having a big impact on families," Georgina (a service worker) explained. Fathers are away for various stretches of time. Moreover, as some of the boys and girls told us, even those fathers who are still working in Putland are not necessarily a strong presence at home. Those with small businesses work very long hours and are commonly, as Ted (age 14), noted, "too busy to be worried about us kids."

The families who have stayed in Putland are the "locally bound"—left behind as capital and influence have flown. They have to do what Bauman (1998a, p. 8) called the "wound licking, damage repair and waste disposal." The gendered dynamic to being "locally bound" in Putland is a clear example of "gender intensification" (Bakker, 1996) for females. The absence of fathers means that more family work falls on mothers, whether they are in paid employment or not. This work includes dealing with the psychological fallout of neo-liberal economic globalization, the emotional upheaval that often accompanies the forced loss of men's jobs, status, and identity, and the subsequent stresses of change. Predictably, though, despite the implications for women, children, and families and indeed for the town itself, this changing economic context is largely framed as a "crisis" for men and boys by many of local adults. Elizabeth, a long-time local, observed, "Men were put on the scrap heap. There was a feeling that they were useless."

There is a general view that when fathers lose their jobs and cannot get work, this impacts particularly on sons. The fact that significant numbers of hard-working, able-bodied men were not wanted by their employer and even by many subsequent potential employers cast serious doubt on their worth and on their particular ways of being male. Both were socially surplus and disposable. However, such deeply entrenched ways of being male are not so easily disposed of by the males themselves, and notions of worthwhile work and the admirable worker remain from the past and indeed across the generations. Local ideologies of masculinity have not been weakened even though there is no economic base to support them. This is evident in the hopes of quite a sizable proportion of young adolescent males and in their views of education (see Kenway & Kraack, in progress, chap. 5, for other standpoints).

Local middle-class entrepreneurs consider education an important part of an economic renewal strategy for Putland. There are moves afoot to establish an Education Precinct on the regional campus of Monash University. This proposal builds on ideas about the vocationalization and technologization of the secondary school, which, incidentally, also set the scene for Mac an Ghaill's 1994 study of "macho lads" and "academic achievers" in England. The Precinct is also based on the notion of borderless and "lifelong education," a notion informing the Australian government's attempts to build a globally competitive "knowledge economy." The idea is that upper secondary schooling, vocational education and training, and university courses are provided on one campus, thus allowing students to move relatively easily across the three types of provision. Such options for educational mobility were not available to the lads and their peers in *Learning to Labor*. But had they been, the lads probably would have scorned them. Certainly, similar boys in Putland don't accept such ideas. They expect to leave school as soon as possible and to get an apprenticeship. "Having a trade is like having a job for life," said Ted (age, 14), who doesn't care what sort of work he gets after he leaves school as long as it is a trade. For these boys, school is either a place where they wait, impatiently and often disruptively in a manner similar to Willis's lads, until they can legally leave and take up an apprenticeship. Or it is where they get the "hands-on" or practical knowledge necessary to prepare them for an apprenticeship. Such boys love the "tech shed" at school, but not what is described as paper-work—"too much" writing or "too much" theory. Terry, age 15, is typical.

> I am not really interested in any of the stuff like being a lawyer or accountant . . . I want something that is hands on. I hate sitting there and doing nothing. . . . If there is paperwork and stuff involved I will do it, but I would rather be out in the machine shop doing something than inside the shop writing on paper. . . . It just seems more challenging to be out in the workshop.

As Collinson and Hearn (1997) observed, from the point of view of male manual workers, paperwork is not real work, and indeed, although Terry did not say so, it is also seen as effeminate. Further, like the working-class males in Willis's study, for these boys "practice is more important than theory" (Willis, 1977, p. 56).

There is a popular view among boys like Terry (and their parents) that doing "hands-on" at school and then going into a trade are what ordinary boys do—especially boys who are "good with their hands but not their heads." Yet, as teachers and youth workers tell us, many contractors cannot afford to take on apprentices and the restructuring of the power industry has dramatically reduced the apprenticeships offered in the district. Further, those few that are available locally through the Commonwealth Government's New/Modern Apprenticeship Scheme are highly competitive and this involves "lots of aptitude, medical and psyche tests." "Nonacademic" students compete against the high academic achievers and usually miss out. Missing can cause family conflict, especially between fathers and sons. Some fathers cannot admit that a trade is no longer "a job for life," even though this notion has been so patently undermined by the Putland experience. The continuities between school, work, and home experienced by the lads in *Learning to Labor* do not exist for such boys in Putland either socially or culturally. Although men's work has been detraditionalized in Putland and the material base for it has all but vanished, the values associated with traditional hegemonic working-class masculinity have proved very difficult to dislodge. Indeed, they provide intergenerational camaraderie between fathers and sons. But the boys who subscribe to such values are undergoing what Mac an Ghaill (1994) called a crisis of "working class masculinity" and what O'Donnell and Sharpe (2000, p. 134) more accurately described as "a crisis of macho working-class masculinity."

Despite the restructuring of Putland's economy and the changed nature of local employment, many fathers cannot *unlearn* the attitudes associated with regular skilled manual employment and local hegemonic working-class masculinity. Indeed, they have become melancholic figures living in the past and sidelined in the present.[3] Having a job is tightly connected to self-respect, while lacking one is shameful and attracts disdain. Many fathers and sons hold these views. Take the case of Brett (age 13), whose father works at Power Bricks, where the number of workers has dropped dramatically over recent years. Unlike many of his friends' fathers, Brett's has not been made redundant. He describes those who lost their jobs as "slack," "lazy," and "soft." His father's continued employment affirms his view that his father is superior. He boasts that his dad can "work rings around the other guys." He works hard and doesn't "bludge" off the social welfare system.

In Putland, earning an income and financially supporting the family are masculine imperatives. Unemployment is associated with laziness, weakness, and passivity—in fact, with a lack of masculinity. This view of masculinity is a key element in local social constructions of the unemployed and of the associated politics of resentment directed at those who have been 'left behind' in place, but out of work and who suffer "enforced immobility" (Bauman, 1998a, p. 121). Indeed, as we have shown elsewhere (Kenway & Kraack, 2003) the economic and existential uncertainties associated with economic globalization have contributed to deep divisions among those on the lower rungs of the global economy in Putland and elsewhere. The sense of working-class collectivity, solidarity, and its predictable reproduction across generations so evident in *Learning to Labor* is now seldom evident in Putland. Meanwhile, the boys who constitute this fraction of Putland's working class face the prospect of either joining the "bludgers" they despise, of undertaking a form of education and work that they also despise, or of joining the growing ranks of those who have little choice but to move.

"What Future Is There for Boys with Aprons?"

The story of globalization in Paradise has some things in common with the Putland story but also involves some significant differences associated with what Beck (1992) called "risk society" and Giddens (1994, p. 20) called "high consequence risk." The key themes in Paradise are associated with the government's regulation and "risk management" of the timber and fishing industries in the interest of environmental conservation. Although "the state" has deliberately loosened its grip in Victorian Putland, it has tightened its grip over Paradise in New South Wales (NSW) (Bochner & Parkes, 1998). In addition, the flight of global capital has meant the closure of the Heinz cannery processing plant. Overall, there have been significant job losses (Eden Business Challenge, 2000).

Paradise has suffered social dislocation similar to Putland. Again, a town has been severely shaken; there is talk of a town dying. A middle-aged male timber worker puts it bluntly: "Paradise is a working man's town but it has no jobs." A study of the social impact of the changes to the Paradise timber industry identified higher levels of stress and insomnia, increased use of prescription drugs, feelings of powerlessness, heightened fear of family breakup and of not being able to meet financial commitments, and higher levels of physical and verbal violence (Bochner & Parkes, 1998, pp. 18–20). Again, the despondency is not restricted to adults. Many young people feel that they have no future due to the lack of jobs, and their subsequent feelings of worthlessness are exacerbated by the strong local work ethic. Prior to the closure of the cannery there was a sense of hope and, indeed, quite strong resistance to the globalizing forces associated with environmental regulation. This was evident in a truck blockade of parliament house in Canberra in the early 1990s and in similar protests in Sydney against the NSW government. The government and "the greenies," "ignorant" city dwellers, "outsiders with no understanding of local issues," were seen as the root of the problem.

The town is now split. According to Grant (age 15), "The loggers don't like the greenies, the fishos don't like anyone, the greenies don't like the fishos or the loggers." And then there are the "druggos," the "alternative lifestylers," and the "hippies," all of whom want to "close down the chip mill" and "get rid of jobs," many boys tell us. Generally, environmental regulation and the Save the Forest Campaign conducted by environmental activists were seen as an attack on the values associated with local lifestyle and on the timber cutters themselves. As Bochner and Parkes (1998) showed, the timber workers felt confused about their negative public image and suffered an overall loss of self-dignity that left them feeling resentful of outside interference. This spilled over into serious conflict with environmental activists, and many stories were shared with us about the provocative behavior of greenies and equally the hostile and sometimes violent behavior of those who opposed them.

There are several implications of this economic and social upheaval for intergenerational relations among males. The first has strong parallels with Putland. Before the restructuring of the timber and fishing industries, boys found it easy to follow their fathers into work. However, now there are not even enough jobs for the current work force. Even so, some fathers have difficulty understanding why their sons are finding it so hard to get a job, when they just "walked" into their jobs once they were working age. There is a form of denial here, and this is manifest in the quite commonly held view that "If you're prepared to put in the hard yards [the hard work], you'll always get a job." Thus, some fathers are inclined to blame young men for their lack of work.

To achieve respect in Paradise, young men must gain employment. Those without work are often constructed as "just plain lazy" and are an embarrassment and annoyance to their fathers. Witness this father's comments about his son: "I get out of bed about seven or eight a.m., but he doesn't get out of bed until ten a.m., and he will just sit around the house all day in his boxers and watch TV." He proudly described the change in attitude of his older son once he got a job:

> My eldest bloke, when he was going to work with forestry, he was up at half past six, and that was unheard of. He just used to get up himself, yeah. That really surprised me. Used to be a fight every morning to get him out of bed. (Fathers' focus group)

The context of globalized restructuring of traditional industries and rising unemployment is unaccounted for in such fathers' constructions of young males.

However, whatever their opinion of greenies and governments, some fathers are heeding their lessons about the future.

> I come from a long line of timber cutters. I followed my father into the industry. But I am not going to let my sons follow me. . . . It's just not acceptable these days—because of the greenies and because it is a dying industry. (Fathers' focus group)

Environmentalism is also putting some young men off these primary industries. James, age 16, typifies this view.

> The chip mill, all the major industries like the fishing, . . . they can't go on forever the way they are doing it, . . . and that is why I don't want to be a fisherman. The industries are going to be gone eventually, and the same with logging. . . . So it is just a waste of time getting a job in logging.

Clearly, the young males of Paradise are negotiating some powerful and conflicting local, state, and global forces associated with the world of work. To be valued as males in the local culture, they are expected to have work, but there is not enough work for all of them, and the available local work is insecure casual work either in the traditional local industries or in the fledgling tourist industry. Further, they have grown up in an atmosphere hostile to outsiders and the outside world and this implicitly discourages them from migrating elsewhere for work. Yet to stay locally is to be subject to a depressed economy and culture. If they seek to reinvent themselves in tune with the tourist industry, this is seen to subscribe to "ritzy" values that are alien to this "working man's town" and worse still to the feminine values associated with women's work. Boys who do so put others' perceptions of their masculinity at risk. Note the remarks of a long-time male resident (aged 65):

> This town is made up of the Ockers, you know like the timber industry, the bush fellas and the fishermen. They are hard working types. . . . They work with their hands and they can't be turned into office boys. They'd be out of place if this became a big tourist industry. There is an outdoor working culture. Their jobs have diminished. There are tourism jobs for girls, but that doesn't help a hard working person.

So what do boys do when they leave school? They do what they can and they do things to affirm themselves. Some, but not many, leave town for further study or work, some get casual work when it is available, some go on the dole, and some get into trouble. And, of course, those who stay in town but remain outside the full-time workforce have time on their hands and many go surfing. Despite all its masculine virtues, fathers do not regard surfing as a valuable way for their under- or unemployed sons to spend their abundant time. Furthermore, some senior teachers associate surfing with what they scornfully call "beach culture," which is seen to distract local boys from the serious work of schooling.

Ironically, beach culture, differently defined of course, is the basis for the multipurpose wharf that local entrepreneurs hope will soon be built and rescue the Paradise economy. Certain local residents also see tourism as the answer to their town's plight, although others vigorously oppose it unless it is the sort of tourism that involves "those who'd want to come here and get their hands dirty" (elderly local male). Further, some local educational entrepreneurs have developed a marine studies program at the high school. This program includes units of study such as diving, safe boating, and Coxin's certificates, and provides students with a qualification to undertake work in any marine area, from deck handing on a fishing boat to running tourist charter boats. This is stroke of brilliance. It builds young males into the expanding tourist industry in ways that draw on the masculinities most valued in Paradise. But masculine values are also being detraditionalized.

Many young people, like James mentioned earlier, see the old industries as dying and obsolete and are turning to the hospitality industries. Garth (age 14) exemplifies this trend:

> These days you have to get into hospitality, the retail trade. . . . I know one [friend] who wants to drive boats up in the islands. . . . He said his brother drives boats for some fishermen, and it is a charter type thing. . . . Another friend wouldn't mind being a chef.

Garth is also adjusting his views of the gendered division of labor and is redefining as masculine, work that has traditionally been defined as feminine. Adkins (1997) called this process *retraditionalization*. Garth thinks that retail work is for women but that "In the hospitality trade, its better to be a man, like in the kitchen or something like that." Despite their fathers' views about the threats to their masculine identity, some Paradise schoolboys have embraced tourism and are taking up courses and work experience that will lead them to a career in hospitality. "The two most popular choices at school are now marine studies and hospitality courses," a teacher reports. But, again, this is not how the fathers necessarily see it. Fathers who have invested in the forms of masculinity associated with hard physical outdoor labor find it difficult to respect sons who undertake such "feminized" work:

> They are pointing kids to hospitality and stuff like that at the high school. I guess that's directly related to losing the industries we're losing and trying to put something else in there. But they're getting boys in there when they should be trying to learn how to do something with their hands. What future is there for boys with aprons? (Fathers' focus group)

Conclusion

Learning to Labor is a book of its time and place. We have written of more recent times and other places that nonetheless carry strong traces of the working-class masculinity discussed by Willis. Indeed, we have shown how each locality's traditional culture and identity has arisen from men's classed work and how the masculinity associated with such work still holds sway, particularly in Putland. However, contemporary economic trends have clearly destabilized local working-class work and demoralized local working-class men. As a consequence, the reproduction of working-class masculinity has been ruptured. By and large, working-class boys no longer get working-class jobs and cannot reproduce their fathers' class cultures. However, despite this, some try to do so and others try to make them. Memory and custom have collided with the present, and such collisions are personally and poignantly manifest in tense intergenerational relationships between some fathers and sons and also in the intensification of women's emotional labor.

Young males are caught on the cusp of the old and the new and react differently to the competing imperatives involved. Even though they cannot walk into work as did Willis's lads, nonacademic, White working-class boys in Putland still subscribe to traditional views about masculinity and work and refuse to reinvent themselves for the new educational and economic order. These boys neither seek nor find viable alternative versions of manhood. Indeed, in monocultural Putland there are few alternatives, and anyway to subscribe to alternative masculinities would be to psychologically wound their already wounded fathers and to go against local common sense about meaningful work. Even the prospect of joining the working-class-without-work, be they locally bound or mobile, does not encourage these boys to develop alternative forms of expertise or to be flexible about their gender identities in ways that might equip them for alternative labor markets. However, there is also evidence of an emerging detraditionalized masculinity in the more diverse and dynamic culture of Paradise. This involves some young males turning to the tourism and hospitality industries and ideologically leaving behind notions of the working class. Yet, even in relation to such nontraditional work these young men sometimes retraditionalize it in gender terms. They do this by either picking up more "masculine" aspects of such work or by reinscribing the traditionally feminine work they do as masculine. Overall, across both locations, we see that hegemonic working-class masculinity and its cross-generational reproduction have been profoundly destabilized, and the traditional gender order of each place is both eroded and, paradoxically, intensified.

Acknowledgment

We thank Vashti Kenway for her contributions to this chapter.

Notes

1. This 3-year study was funded for 1999–2001 by the Australian Research Council's Large Grant scheme and was called *Country Boys in Uncertain Times and Places*.
2. For an extended discussion of this approach to ethnography and the debates within which it is immersed see Kenway and Kraack (in progress).
3. We acknowledge here Vashti Kenway's (2001) work on masculinity and melancholia in "Brit Grit" films.

References

Adkins, L. (1997, July). *Community and economy: The retraditionalisation of gender.* Paper presented at "Transformations: Thinking through feminism," Institute for Women's Studies, University of Lancaster.

Arizpe, E., & Arnot, M. (1997, April). *The new boys of the 1990s: A study of the reconstruction of masculinity in relation to economic restructuring.* Paper presented at the American Education Research Association Conference, Chicago.

Bakker, I. (Ed.). (1996). *Rethinking restructuring: Gender & change in Canada.* Toronto: University of Toronto Press Inc.

Bauman, Z. (1998a). *Globalisation: The human consequences.* Cambridge, UK: Polity Press.

Bauman, Z. (1998b). *Work, consumerism and the new poor.* Buckingham: Open University Press.

Bauman, Z. (2000). *Liquid modernity.* Cambridge, UK: Polity Press.

Beck, U. (1992). *Risk society—Towards a new modernity.* London: Sage.

Beresford, Q. (2000). *Governments, markets and globalisation: Australian public policy in context.* St. Leonards: Allen and Unwin.

Burawoy, M., Blum, J. A., Sheba, G., Gille, Z., Gowan, T., Haney, L., Klawiter, M., Lopez, S. H., Riain, S., & Thayer, M. (2000). *Global ethnography: Forces, connections, and imaginations in a postmodern world.* Berkeley: University of California Press.

Bochner, S., & Parkes, L. (1998). *The psychological effects of the timber industry in the Eden region of New South Wales: A critical review of social impact studies conducted between 1991–1995.* Report prepared for the NSW Forest Products Association, Sydney, NSW.

Collinson, D., & Hearn, J. (1997). "Men" at "work": Multiple masculinities/multiple workplaces. In M. Mac an Ghaill (Ed.), *Understanding masculinities* (pp. 61–77). Buckingham: Open University Press.

Connell, R. W. (1995). *Masculinities.* St Leonards: Allen and Unwin.

Currie, D. (1983). World capitalism in recession. In S. Hall & J. Martin (Eds.), *The politics of Thatcherism* (pp. 79–105). London: Lawrence and Wishart.

Eden Business Challenge. (2000). *Business plan—February 2000.* Eden, NSW: Barclay & Donaldson Services.

Giddens, A. (1994). *Beyond left and right: The future of radical politics.* Stanford, CA: Stanford University Press.

Hall, S. (1983). The great moving right show. In S. Hall & J. Martin (Eds.), *The politics of Thatcherism* (pp. 19–39). London: Lawrence and Wishart.

Harvey, D. (2000). *Spaces of hope.* Edinborough: Edinborough University Press.

Kazakevitch, G., Foster, B., & Stone, S. (1997). *The effects of economic restructuring on population movements in the Latrobe Valley.* Canberra: Department of Immigration and Multicultural Affairs.

Kenway, J., & Kraack, A. (2003, March). *The politics of resentment and mobility: Local/global power geometries.* Keynote address given at the Gender and Education conference, Sheffield, UK.

Kenway, J., & Kraack, A. (in progress). *Masculinity beyond the metropolis.* Hampshire and New York: Palgrave.

Kenway, V. (2001). *Dodos, dinosaurs and men: Representations of melancholy masculinities in* Brassed Off, Billy Elliot *and* The Full Monty. Honors Dissertation, Melbourne University, Melbourne, Australia, 2001.

Lash, S., & Urry, J. (1994). *Economies of signs and space.* London: Sage.

Local Government Board. (1994). *A vision for Gippsland: Gippsland area review, Interim Report.* Victoria: Local Government Board.

Mac an Ghaill, M. (1996). "What about the boys?": Schooling, class and crisis masculinity. *Sociological Review, 44*(3), 381–397.

Massey, D. (1995). *Spatial divisions of labour: Social structures and the geography of production.* London: Macmillan.

May, C. (2002). *The information society: A skeptical view.* Cambridge: Polity.

McDowell, L. (2000). Learning to serve? Employment aspirations and attitudes of young working class men in an era of labour market restructuring. *Gender, Place and Culture, 7*(7), 389–416.

McDowell, L. (2002). Masculine discourses and dissonances: Strutting "lads," protest masculinity, and domestic respectability. *Environment and Planning: Society and Space, 20,* 97–119.

O'Donnell, M., & Sharpe, S. (2000). *Uncertain masculinities: Youth, ethnicity and class in contemporary Britain.* London & New York: Routledge.

Urry, J. (1995). *Consuming Places.* London: Routledge.

Willis, P. (1977). *Learning to labour: How working class kids get working class jobs.* Hampshire: Gower.

Willis, P. (2000). *The ethnographic imagination.* Cambridge: Polity Press.

CHAPTER 7

Revisiting a 1980s "Moment of Critique"
Class, Gender, and the New Economy

LOIS WEIS

December 1985

I want to go to college for four years, get my job, work for a few years, and then get married. I like supporting myself. I don't want my husband supporting me. I like to be independent. (Judy Rankin, Class of 1987 Homecoming Queen)

January 2001

My mom hit a point where she came to me and said, "Please Judy, I don't know what to do to stop it, but I just don't wanna be seeing you in your grave." (Judy Rankin Smithers, Class of 1987 Homecoming Queen)

Beginning with my ethnographic investigation of Freeway High (*Working Class Without Work*, Routledge, 1990), and culminating with intensive follow-up interviews with these same students in 2000–2001, I track a group of the sons and daughters of the workers of "Freeway Steel" and similar such industries over a 15-year time period. Exploring identity formation among American White working-class male and female students in relation to the school, economy, and family of origin, *Working Class Without Work* captures

111

the complex relations among secondary schooling, human agency, and the formation of collective consciousness within a radically changing economic and social context (Bluestone & Harrison, 1982). Most widely known, I suggest in the volume that young women exhibit what I call a "glimmer of critique" regarding traditional gender roles in the White working-class family and that young men are ripe for New Right consciousness given their strident racism and male dominant stance in an economy that, like that immortalized in the justly celebrated *The Full Monty* and the BBC serial *The Missing Postman* (Walkerdine, Lucey, & Melody, 2001), offers them little.

Now, 15 years later I return to these same students (35 of the original 51 were reinterviewed in 2000–2001), as they (and we) meet in *Class Reunion* (Weis, 2004), a study firmly embedded in what Michelle Fine and I call "compositional studies" (Weis & Fine, 2004)—a broadly based theory of method in which analyses of public and private institutions, groups, and lives are lodged in relation to key economic and social structures. Through a careful look at the high school (ages 14–18) and young adult years (ages 18–31) of the sons and daughters of the industrial proletariat in the northeast "rust belt" of the United States, I track the remaking of this class fraction through careful and explicit attention to issues that swirl around Whiteness, masculinity, femininity, representations, and the new economy. Reflective of the triplet of theoretical and analytic moves that Michelle and I put forward as signature of our work (Weis & Fine, 2004)—deep work within one group (over a 15-year time period in this case), serious relational analyses between and among relevant bordering groups, and broad structural connections to social, economic and political arrangements—I argue in the broader study that the remaking of the American White working class can only be understood in relation to gendered constructions within itself, the construction of relevant "others" as uncovered ethnographically—in this case African Americans and Yemenites ("Arabians")—as well as deep shifts in large social formations, most particularly the global economy.

Here I focus on a slice of the larger study, interrogating data collected at two points in time in light of Paul Willis's contributions regarding what he called "penetrations." "Penetrations," which Willis coined in *Learning to Labour* (1977) and later affirmed in *The Ethnographic Imagination* (2000), refer to "impulses within a cultural form towards the penetration of the conditions of existence of its members and their position within the social whole but in a way which is not centrist, essentialist or individualist" (1977, p. 119). Willis moved beyond "penetrations" to what he called "limitations": those "blocks, diversions and ideological effects which confuse and impede the full development and expression of these impulses" (p. 119). "The rather clumsy but strictly accurate term 'partial penetration,'" continued Willis, "is meant to designate the interaction of these two terms in a concrete culture.

Ethnography describes the field of play in which the impulses and limitations combine but cannot isolate them theoretically or show them separately" (p. 119).

In this chapter I turn my attention to the possibilities opened up by one such cultural "penetration" over time, using, by way of example, the young Freeway women's "glimmer of critique" that I flagged in the mid 1980s. To be clear, by critique I mean narrative data that represent a critical awareness or knowledge of class structures, racism, sexism and/or the globalizing economic in interpersonal and/or structural relations. This, I would argue, parallels Willis's concept of "penetration," thereby enabling me to probe carefully, using data collected at two points in time from the same individuals, where such cultural "penetrations" sit as the young women move toward adulthood in a radically changing economic and social context.

Here I move through working-class White women's lives not on a wholly theoretical level but on a more practical lived level, as they have families and assume positions as wage laborers. Given their "moment of critique" during adolescence, the question is, what elements of critique, or "penetration" in Willis's parlance, were young White working-class women able to live out and sustain as they plunge toward adulthood?

Freeway, 1985 and Beyond

> Best are the freedom dreams. Steering wheels so real in the hand, the spring of the accelerator, gas tanks marked FULL. . . . We take the freeways, using the fast lanes, watch for signs saying San Francisco, New Orleans. We pass trucks on great interstates, truck drivers blowing their airhorns. We drink sodas at gas stations, listen to country music stations, we pick up Tijuana, Chicago, Atlanta, GA, and sleep in motels where the clerk never even looks up, just takes the money. (Fitch, 1999, *White Oleander*, p. 348)

Young women, unlike their male counterparts in working class Freeway, take a stab at reworking gender while still in high school (Weis, 1990). Unwilling to accept the lives of their mothers and grandmothers as their own, Freeway High White girls strut forward, exhibiting an inchoate sense of "girl power" while attempting to remake the class/gender intersection more to their liking, engaging, it can be argued, in a process of the "re-making of girls and women as the neoliberal subject: a subject of self-invention and transformation who is capable of surviving within the new social, economic and political system" (Walkerdine et al., 2001, p. 3). For the Freeway youth, this means a female based income, one earned in the public wage labor sector; a perhaps ill-defined sense of independence ("the freedom dream"); and a life that can conceivably move forward comfortably even if they experience the divorce now so commonplace in their community—a phenomenon that virtually every young woman comments on in the 1980s.

Energized by the possibility of a life markedly different from that of their mothers, young women generate a female version of life in a working-class community under the new economy. Given kaleidoscopic changes in the global economy (Reich, 1991, 2002) and the virtual excisement of the former industrial proletariat, their men would no longer be able to "support" the family through earning the working-class family wage packet, at one and the same time as corporate America seeks female labor in a wide variety of service positions. These young women are, in addition, desirous of continuing their schooling, not ensnared by its hegemonic working-class masculine coding as negative (Arnot, chap. 2, this volume; Arnot, 2002; Connell, 1995; Reay, 2002; Weis, 2004; Willis, 1977), and look forward, for the most part, to some form of postsecondary education in spite of the fact that they, like the young men, bounce through the contradictory code of respect in relation to school knowledge and culture (Sennett & Cobb, 1972) while in high school (Weis, 1990, 2004). Finding it psychologically easier than their men to land on the substance side of this class-embedded contradiction with respect to schooling, young Freeway women exploit a myriad of educational opportunities. As the men in their lives experience increased unemployment and what they see as underemployment—the economic sector with which they are historically linked being virtually excised—White working-class women are reveling in the moment of possibility in economic and cultural terms (that "freedom dream") that they desire.

Data suggest that 1985 young White Freeway women envision their lives very differently from girls in previous studies and very differently than investigators such as Lillian Breslow Rubin (1976) and Glen Elder (1974) suggested that their mothers and grandmothers do. Articulating a challenge to the Domestic Code, they suggest strongly that the domestic is not primary; wage labor is. If patriarchy rests on a fundamental distinction between men's and women's labor and the domination of women in both the home/family sphere and the workplace, these girls exhibit the glimmerings of a critique of that. They understand to the point of being able to articulate that too many negative consequences result if one depends on men to the exclusion of depending on oneself, and this suggests the necessity of engaging in long-term wage labor. Significantly, they do not offer the part-time wage labor solution (Valli, 1986) and/or flights into fantasy future (McRobbie, 1978) so characteristic of girls in previous studies. In this sense, then, their emerging collective identity embodies a critical moment of critique of an underlying premise of patriarchy, that being that women's primary place is in the home/family sphere and that men will, in turn, take care of them. In so doing, they question the basis of the "family wage," which the young men in 1985 Freeway voraciously affirm (Weis, 1990). Indeed, as numerous investigators point out, the "family wage" ideology lies at the very heart of industrially based White working-class male identity (Arnot, chap 2., this volume; Connell, 1995; Nayak, 2001; Reay, 2002; Walkerdine et al., 2001; Willis, 1977, 2000).

As men struggle to cope with the changes that confront them, clinging, through high school, to a fantasy future linked to the patriarchal family/work site of past years (Weis, 1990), women, in contrast, "positively face the prospect of self transformation" (Walkerdine, et al., 2001, p. 20). Like the postman's wife in the BBC serial who "comes to life after her husband's disappearance" (after being laid off, her husband traverses the country delivering "one last letter"; she, on the other hand, becomes an interior decorator of some note), the young Freeway women face the prospect of transforming themselves with gusto, moving quickly to remake themselves in the face of educational and workforce opportunities.

By way of example, of those interviewed in 1985, 48% of the women completed their BA as of 2001, as compared with 29% of the men. Every single woman interviewed in 1985 and reinterviewed in 2001 pursued some form of higher education, whether 4-year university, comprehensive college, community college, or nursing school. Men, on the other hand, have a far less noteworthy record in the education arena, with 50% attending some form of postsecondary education and less than half completing their intended program. Both the men and women are from similar family circumstances: 79% of men come from families that owned their own homes in Freeway while they were growing up (the great symbol of working class stability), whereas a comparable 76% of the women come from such homes. All the women but one currently work in the wage labor sector, with jobs like respiratory therapist, teacher, registered nurse, licensed practical nurse, chemical engineer, catering manager, paralegal, vascular technician, waitress (simultaneously a full-time student in a teacher education program), social worker, and health plan representative. Compared with the Freeway men whom I interviewed (Weis, 2004), the women have moved into postsecondary education and accompanying skilled positions with some dexterity. The question must be asked, though, to what extent does this represent a lived-out challenge to the gender regime deeply embedded in the White working-class community? What is challenged by this "moment of critique"/cultural penetration, and what remains the same?

Here I offer brief portraits of two young women in 1985, all grown up by 2000. Judy, who we met in the chapter header, a former homecoming queen whose working-class life seemed so perfect when I met her in 1985, reveals how the brutality of her patriarchally bound existence as a teenager rendered her life pure hell. All smiles, kindness, and exuberant beauty, a fine student in the context of Freeway High, which prepared students only minimally for college entrance, Judy lets us in on her secret—only too happy to do so in order to help the next generation of young women, her niece included, who she fears is entrapped in the same vicious dynamic as she was.

Suzanne, still angry at her drunken father who off-loaded his pain on a human triangle encircling herself, her mother, and all Black Americans, lived, as it turns out, in a home totally out of control in the 1980s. Suzanne had few friends and a sarcastic mouth, set in sharp contrast to Judy's, yet Suzanne also had her secrets. She had a boyfriend who was 13 years older than she was and a father who flew into drunken rages at all hours of the day and night. Both from working-class families filled with sharp secrets, Judy and Suzanne, as emblematic of White working-class Freeway women, lived "worlds of pain" (Rubin, 1976), although Judy projected a "good girl" image whereas Suzanne exuded venomous "bad girl" anger. Both, however, wanted out of life as they knew it. Striving for a job, space, and time, neither saw the ostensibly soft hand of male support as desired, or as a solution to their problems. What I did not know when they were teenagers (although I knew them fairly well) was the deeply rooted male brutality—both physical and emotional—that laced their existence. In retrospect for each, it is the pain linked to physical and emotional violence that they desperately wished to escape: An envisioned job, a metaphoric ride on the "freedom train," was seen as a way out.

The stories that follow illustrate the pain and brutality that fester barely beneath the surface of this class fraction, spearheading, at least in part, a critical moment of critique regarding gender roles and relations among White working-class women in the mid 1980s. To be sure, the opening up of the economy to women and the larger middle-class and virtually unacknowledged (by this group) women's movement offer important contexts for the young White working-class women's expressed desires and subsequent actions. But, as I argue here, it is the seen and felt brutality that in large part triggers the critique; the changing context enables the critique to land, rather than being wholly stalled, or turned inward on self.

Although they were teenagers in the mid 1980s, and unable to articulate the linkages, it is clear from an adult perspective, mine as well as theirs, that the brutality underlying patriarchal domesticity in White working-class communities is much of what these women wish to escape. As such, their stories must be read as emblematic of what such a moment of critique can become—what a movement of women at the end of the century, whether understood this way or not, is able to build toward as the American White working class remakes itself against the kaleidoscopic backdrop of changes in the U.S./world economy.

Judy

JUDY: We had a lot of ups and downs—the steel plant was closing. A lot of ups and downs, just with the steel plant and my Dad being out of work and that type of thing. And my mom went to work when I was eight, just for that reason. And she felt guilty about it forever, and still probably does. But otherwise I think we were pretty normal. I mean, my mom tried her best to do everything she could for us. Took us on trips and did that type of thing. We lived in a very small apartment though.

LOIS: So this must be like a palace to you [her current house which is not in Freeway but sits on a large plot of land in a fairly rural area].

JUDY: This is my dream home [laughs] . . . yeah, this is truly, yes, this is. Actually my husband grew up in a nicer house than I did [in a first-ring suburb], but we grew up in a little apartment that was three bedrooms and one bathroom and it was very small [for five of them].

LOIS: When you were in high school you did talk to me about your dad being laid off. Do you reflect back on that at all?

JUDY: At times, yeah. Especially now with having kids [one 3-year-old and one 2-months old]. I think back . . . like I said, I remember the first time my mom really talked about going back to work and how guilty she felt leaving me when I was eight. And like now . . . when I think back about how my Grandmother used to come, or my Grandfather would come down [they lived upstairs] if I was sick because my Mom had to go to work, and take care of me, and my Mom wouldn't have done it if my Dad wasn't laid off at the time. Because actually it was more when I was in junior high school when a lot of it was going on.

LOIS: What did your mom do when she went to work?

JUDY: She's actually still doing it. She works . . . it's almost like an accountant, but she doesn't have an accounting degree. And it's called Jacobbi's now. It used to be called Augustine Electric. So she worked there. Still does. Now I'm happy for her 'cause she does it. It's definitely her pride and joy. She does very well at it and she loves it. Loves the freedom of money finally. . . .

When my dad was laid off, and then go back, and he would get unemployment, I think it bothered him a lot. But my dad's not the type that would go out and get another job. Not that he *couldn't* do it. I don't know. He just, he didn't. Because there was like, the steel plant was all he did and all he knew. And that's, I mean, I can never see him even like going to Home Depot to work because I don't think he has enough self-confidence. I don't know if that's what it is, but even now, with being retired. The steel plant opened back up but under a different name for a little while. And they called him, and he went back for a few months and then stopped. He was getting paid garbage money and he was standing in oil and it just wasn't his thing. He didn't go back after that. So, but he was in his late fifties when the steel plant closed finally [completely], and he retired. He was, pretty much collected unemployment, and I mean, I think he just had hoped that it would always be there and it would be fine. . . . My dad used to do like little projects around the house . . . the house we lived in was four apartments. It was actually my dad's dad's house. And when he passed away, my dad and his brother got the house, so they split it . . . and my dad would do little things around the house. Type of fixer up things. Not decorative or major projects, but just putter around. As far as like laundry, cooking . . . [laughs] . . . he didn't do any of that, really. Yeah, he was just home a lot. That was it. I mean, there was definitely some tough problems there. I mean with my dad and my mom. And so for a while it was very rough. And I think it all stems back from that. Plus my dad was injured in the steel plant. He had his fingers cut off. So that had a big psychological effect on my father. I mean, I didn't like to go back to think about when I was growing up and like, now, like I said, I've been thinking about it. And I think that [his injury] played a big part of it, and he probably should have done something to even get out of there [the steel plant], but he didn't. It's just, like I said, that's all he knew. And if it was up to him I think he'd still live there [in Freeway—in the same house]. . . . Yeah, he just wanted to stay in his little world.

Lois: Can you describe for me where you live now?

Judy: Oh, it's tremendously different [laughs]. This is like my own little piece of heaven here, actually. I just wanted property, 'cause, well, in Freeway the house next to us, you could stick your arm out the window and it was right there. You heard everything. Everybody heard everything. And I just wanted space. So now we own thirteen acres . . . and the house is, to me, it was huge compared to where I grew up.

Almost from rags to riches would be the way in which Judy describes her life—a life that began in a run-down section of Freeway and meandered to a beautiful home on Salk Island. She, a 2-year college graduate and radiologic technician in a local hospital, and her husband, a construction worker, have pieced together a materially comfortable life 20 miles from Freeway, one that rests largely for him, and partially for her, on the skills and contacts embedded within the White working-class community. Her husband's job as a construction worker represents the culmination of a set of skills obtained as a youth, and he now works for a family friend. Judy works at General Hospital, a job known to her courtesy of her sister-in-law who also works there. It is these skills and contacts that not only helped Judy and Ron obtain jobs, but also enabled them to build their home (the contractor, for example, is a family friend and her husband and his friends did much of the work themselves), a scenario duplicated by many of the "settled livers" interviewed in 2000[1] (Weis, 2004).

Judy and Ron's present "settled" lifestyle is as dependent on Judy's job as her husband's, for it is the two-income family and the collective production of domesticity that enables the necessary cobbling together of resources, both human and material. The young Freeway women's teenage desire to "be independent," "get a job," "not live off a man," and "live my own life" has encouraged these women to seek postsecondary education with a vengeance (Fine & Weis, 1998), as well as work in a wage labor capacity. Ironically, of course, it is the very desire to escape brutality and dependence on a male breadwinner that has enabled/encouraged familial dependence on the two-income family. Thus, young women's push for "independence" *has* served to alter gender relations in the family, at least to some extent. In this sense, then, these women have lived out the "moment of critique" around patriarchy and wage labor articulated in high school. They are not wholly economically dependent on a man. Rather, men and women are now economically dependent on one another if a comfortable family lifestyle is to be attained.

On another level, however, the youthful moment of critique has not necessarily interrupted male brutality in women's lives, even though, as I suggested earlier, it is the brutality that in large part catapulted this set of changes to begin with—a brutality that sweeps through the White working class with a vengeance (Fine & Weis, 1998). Although the new economic and social context enabled White working-class women to at least imagine exiting lives laced with home-based violence, Judy, like many others, harbored a dark secret, one that she took great pains to conceal.

Judy: My [other] brother is an electrical engineer. He actually did go away to school, just for a couple of years. Ended up coming back and finished up at State College. And he got a job and was doing really well, and my sister, the same thing. *And I wanted that.* And then I think going around to . . . like in our senior year when you had the chances to see colleges, or like college representatives would come, and sometimes these girls would come in and they're all dressed up and I'm like, "That's what I want. I wanna be like that. I wanna have a career and be independent and just be like that." *Do* something instead of being a stay-at-home mom. Or . . . I'm not saying there's anything wrong with that either [being a stay-at-home mom], but I just wanted, I wanted that . . . I guess, the self-esteem and self-confidence in myself. I didn't wanna depend on anybody. And the not depending on anybody thing I think comes from [everything] with my dad and how my mom and dad were, and I just didn't wanna be like that. I didn't wanna live a life like that.

Lois: How were they? You've talked about that twice now. . . .

Judy: They had their rough times. My dad at times was abusive to my mom. More physically than mentally. Mentally he was fine. I think it was . . . now thinking back on it . . . I think it was just problems he had from the steel plant and all that. But . . . sorry [she is crying]. Yeah, and it was bad [crying] . . . that's why I said, I just wanted bigger and better. My family and my kids . . . and I have a wonderful husband.

Lois: You're so lucky.

Judy: I am. He's wonderful. He knows all about it, so . . . I wouldn't even think that [the abuse] would ever even happen here. I know it wouldn't, and I love that comfort, knowing that it wouldn't.

Lois: Do you think that's one of the reasons why you wanted to get out of there?

Judy: Yeah, I think like . . . get me outta here [Freeway] and I'll forget all about those horrible times. That's how my mom deals with it, because when we talk or, my dad was getting a little funny actually a month ago. That's why this is . . . [laughs] . . . a little upsetting. It was getting a little on edge again, and I was, I was getting nervous again about it, and I brought it up to my Mom. And she'll almost act like it didn't happen. Or she'll say like, "It wasn't that bad." And then like I have these vivid memories and I'm like, "What do you mean it wasn't that bad? How can you say it wasn't that bad when we spent nights locked in the bathroom 'cause it was the only door in the house that locked" type of thing, you know? And I was more like, "Oh, how could this be happening."

Lois: Was he drinking?

Judy: No. You almost wish it did [explain it] 'cause you had a reason, you know? Or it's easier to get help that way. His was definitely . . . I mean, I don't know if he ever had a nervous breakdown. Now I think that's probably what happened at some point in time. And I think he probably needed help but never did anything about it. And my mom hid it from everybody. I don't think anybody knew. I mean, she would just call in sick to work . . . she had black eyes. I remember her laying on the couch with the black eyes and stuff, and she would just call in sick to work, and nobody would know. . . .

   That was like a big part of my childhood, 'cause I remember it always being there. I don't remember a point when it wasn't. Yeah . . . I wanted out of there [Freeway] for that reason, I'm sure.

Lois: Did anybody try to tell him to get help?

Judy: He's not open to that . . . I mean . . . and it happened when we were older. I called the cops twice. And there was a whole embarrassing thing, 'cause of course, the front pages of the local newspaper, and they would put the Sheriff's Reports in there. And it said, "Domestic, 25 Seneca" in there. And I remember somebody came in school the next day and said, "What happened at your house?" And I made up this whole story about these people living upstairs had this fight. And I was like, "This is terrible." I was embarrassed. I acted like it didn't happen. Maybe it was in my thinking [that] I didn't *want* it to happen. And now when I think, thinking about it, me and my sister and brother have turned out pretty good [laughs], considering how bad it was. . . .

So, I'm sure that was why I wanted out of Freeway. 'Cause going through there, I mean there are memories that come back, you know. I mean, yes, I have great memories through high school and stuff, and that's what you focused on. And I guess that's part of why you try to stay positive and try to view things positively because you wanted to leave all that behind and make a better life for yourself.

Judy and her family fell victim to the abusive elements festering within White working-class male culture. Although she sees her current marriage as more than she could ever have hoped for, her escape from Freeway, and simultaneously Carl, her low-key Freeway high school boyfriend, led her down a treacherous path, one laced with abuse. Meeting Mike in college, she envisioned him as a way of "getting out of the Carl situation" and moving along the road to new experiences, although her first step in this direction was to hook up with another man from Freeway, who, as it turns out, was exceedingly brutal. Having met at a local softball game, she and Mike dated for 3 years, she still smarting from the pain.

JUDY: I guess when it first started happening, yeah, it's just like that little push, little shove, and I didn't . . . I guess I just didn't think of it, and I didn't think that it was gonna go anywhere. And then as it got worse I think I was more like, "I can't believe this is happening." You know, it's not real, or it's gonna stop. And I was ignoring it, probably how my mom just like ignored things [the abuse] and didn't do anything. I just let it go. And I could say that I was in love with him. Definitely. I mean, if he wasn't like that, we'd probably still be together. . . .

He was unbelievably jealous. Unbelievably. I mean I couldn't even look at somebody the wrong way sometimes and he would start. He was just very obsessive type of thing. And then I got to the point where people started finding out. My mother started questioning and, you know, I'd have bruises. He did stuff in front of all my friends. We went to Chowder Point and it was really bad there. And that actually distanced most of my friends because most of them were just like, "Judy, you need to get out of it," and "Judy, why are you still going out with him? If you go out with him, we're not gonna bother with you guys anymore 'cause we don't wanna deal with it." And that's kinda what happened. And I did. I stayed with him and there was definitely a few years there that I was not as close with everybody because of it. . . .

My parents were upset . . . my brother saw something . . . when he [Mike] hit me . . . and he [brother] got really upset and called Mike's parents. And I knew it was, it was just out of control. He [Mike] was out of control. But at one point he was going for counseling. I actually had him talked into that, and he was doing it, so I'm thinking to myself . . . I can do this, I can change him, it'll get better. And I think that was stemming from my father, thinking, you know, "I can help this, I know. It can get better." And I wound up getting to the point where I had to get restraining orders and stuff. Actually I had to get two restraining orders. Yeah, I got one and then, of course, I wound up going back to him. But then, when I started going to County Community College we separated for like nine months. I ran into him at a bar and he's like, "Judy, I wanna talk to you." We started talking. He seemed genuine and sincere and then we started dating. But something wasn't right there, and then he started again. And then he actually attacked me . . . right in front of all these people, and scratched my car and all this stuff. And that was when I was like, "I've had it." I already had enough self-confidence and I think my self-esteem was back so that I was like, "No, I don't need this. I'm not gonna put up with this." And I got another restraining order at that point and that was when we severed our ties. And I did, I mean, he lived four houses away from me growing up, and then I wound up moving to that apartment [her parents' apartment in Freeway], and I was in college and I ran into him a few times there. . . . I mean we talked a couple of times and then a couple of times in the middle of the night he'd come to my apartment. And then I just wanted nothing to do with him. And I was happy to say that at that point, because at one point I would have probably have done anything for him.

Lois: And if you had a niece who was in this situation, what would you tell her to do?

Judy: I have two. We're approaching this point. I guess [I'd tell them] always be self-confident. To really look for help and hopefully they'd have a friend or someone that they could talk to that would always be there and stand by them. And not leave them to be . . . like [thinking] this is all you have, you know? To let them know that there is more out there. To be so much more self-confident themselves that they don't need that; they don't need anybody. Honestly, I would love to talk to girls in these situations because I've been there, and I know how hard it is, and I know how hard it is to get out. *And just do it!* I mean, it was really bad there for a while. My mom hit a point where she came to me and said, "Please Judy, I don't know what to do to stop it, but I just don't wanna be seeing you in your grave."

Two restraining orders later (one was useful; the other was not), Judy exited this situation. Terrified to go to a battered women's shelter because her one phone call to Safe Haven led to a connection with someone she knew on the other end of the line, Judy took years to extricate herself from abusive relationships. Spending her entire childhood hiding the abuse in her family, and later as a young adult fleeing those who might know her and label the abuse for what it was, this mid 1980s homecoming queen harbored her secrets well. Crying as she took the blood-red roses at her high school prom, Judy, a young woman determined to "support herself" and "be on her own," like virtually all of the young women I interviewed in 1985, lurched from the violence of her home to violence embedded within young love. Now a radiologic technician whose income enabled the construction of her dream house, Judy walked a path strewn with sharp rocks. Part of a collective expression of "a moment of critique" among White female working-class youth in the mid 1980s, she continued forward toward her dream, but she, like most of the working-class White women I worked with when they were teenagers, was unable to escape fully the physical brutality associated with men in her life. Looking around her kitchen filled with wonderfully happy cut-and-paste glittery pumpkins produced by her family, she reflects on her struggles and triumph.

Suzanne

Suzanne, in contrast to Judy, has no children and is not married. Informing me in 1985 that "Marriage was invented by somebody who was lucky if they lived to be twenty without being bit by a dinosaur," she retains her feisty sarcasm 15 years later. But Suzanne also has a story to tell. Currently a seventh-grade math teacher in a city middle school, she, like Judy, lived her dream of "not being trapped." As she said in high school, "Back when they [parents] were kids, like . . . girls grew up, got married, worked for a couple of years after graduation, had two or three kids, had a white picket fence, two cars. Things are different now. . . . You've got to do it [make a good life] for yourself. I don't want to be Mrs. John Smith. I want to be able to do something." Besides, she tells me in 1985, "You can't rely on them [men]—it's like, I know a lot of older guys, they drink all the time."

SUZANNE: Dad spent most of my growing up years either at work—he's a city firefighter and also worked at Macey Boiler Works—or at a bar for seventy to eighty percent of my growing up time. Mom went back to work when I was about eleven or twelve years old. When she went back to work it was very part-time [she is a waitress]. There's a lot of family conflict because of dad being so unavailable. Mom found comfort elsewhere. I ended up getting involved with somebody much older than me in high school . . . I met Joe [long pause] probably eighth grade summer, going into freshman year. I met him when I was thirteen. We became involved, sexually involved, at sixteen, but he was much older than I was. He was about seven years older than I was at the time. He was 21 when we met. We ended up being together pretty much on, most of the time, for about eight years. Yeah, it was very long-term. Did not end well. It was very ugly. . . .

As I look back on it, quite honestly, parts of the relationship were extremely destructive. Parts of it were very instructive in that I learned a lot, especially sex. He was the first one that I was ever with. He was very active, and had no problems teaching me everything he knew, for better or worse. And, of course, you know, of course you're learning something and you take a certain pride in learning how to do something well. And I look back, though, it was destructive, in that in a way he developed into a father figure for me. I would look to him for guidance when I really should have had a father to look to for guidance. We would get into extremely heated arguments. I mean, oh! It was a very passionate relationship on all levels, not sexually passionate . . . if we fought, we fought all out! I mean, we threw everything that we could at each other. He was good at throwing things back at me, and I was never as good at throwing things back at him as he was to me. He would remember something I had done six months, a year, two years earlier, and throw it back in my face. . . . You know, now I have the wisdom of knowing better and I can say that it [the entire relationship] was blamed on my father and his drinking because I couldn't run to him [for support]. First of all, I didn't have a male adult in my life to learn how adult men treated adult women. My father's the kind that would come home and yell and scream. You know, he's gonna "sell the house, kill the dog" . . . you know . . . usually it was only after he had been drinking. Mom has typical dependencies for spouses of alcohol abusers. You know, the whole co-addictions. She's addicted to nerve pills to retain her sanity. And, of course, if he took something out on her, she would take it out on me. If he took something out on me, I took it out on her. If they took something out on me, I took it out on Joe. So there was the whole interaction of things going on. And the further away from high school that Joe and I got, the more brutal our arguments about things would become. It eventually got to the point where he would scream at me, "You have nothing to say! Don't even say anything; you have nothing to say about this!" And eventually it became true. I had nothing to say.

Like Judy, Suzanne centers on her father as the source of current and past problems, a centering that rests squarely on abuse associated, in Suzanne's case, with alcohol. Her relationship with her father, or more accurately the lack thereof, colors her relationship with all men, and she attributes her destructive involvement with Joe to this source.

It is certainly true that individuals from a variety of social classes, both men and women, abuse alcohol. It is also true that such abuse saturates a family, causing untold damage to all family members—partners as well as children. What is striking about the Freeway data in this regard, however, is its very *layered typicality*; whether with respect to physical violence or obvious alcoholism, a very high proportion of the White women I knew in 1985 narrate, as adults, a set of family encounters with alcohol and/or domestic violence that spans generations. This mirrors what Demi Kurz (1995) uncovered as well as what Michelle Fine and I discussed in *The Unknown City* (1998), where an overwhelming majority (92%) of the White working-class women we interviewed across two cities reported childhood abuse (physical or sexual) and/or adult domestic abuse (aimed at themselves or a sister) at the hands of a father, a mother's boyfriend, or the woman's husband or her boyfriend. Contrary to the Norman Rockwell images of a family sitting down to eat dinner, these women's lives drown in various forms of abuse, leaving them too emotionally bereft, in many instances, to deal with the festering anger among the men who continue to surround them.

For Suzanne, the "not talking" with her father, for example, continues well into her adult years:

SUZANNE: Dad and I are better off not talking about anything controversial whatsoever. Dad's not capable of having an intelligent conversation; he just doesn't have the resources.
LOIS: You told me that when you were in high school. Has anything changed?
SUZANNE: No, nothing! It's funny that I was that articulate in high school! Yeah, he's just not capable of having an intelligent conversation with someone.
LOIS: Did anyone ever try to get him into a program? Or rehab?
SUZANNE: Oh, God, no! You're just asking for trouble. I can remember having an argument with my father, this was the first time I ever moved out of this house. It was in the springtime of '94, because it was right around

Valentine's Day and it had gotten to the point . . . I had gone into a rather severe depression that semester [in college]. This was after the first time I dropped out of college. Because this was '94, just before I graduated . . . the second time I went back. And in the spring of '94 around Valentine's Day, things in this house were horrendous. I was not functioning at all. And I had to function somewhat because I just had to get out of the house. This is not a house that you can just stop functioning in, because as soon as you stop functioning, it gets very ugly. I moved out of this house. I moved in with a girlfriend out in Centreville, and I'm pounding out of my room with my things and screaming at my father . . . because my father was home, drunk as usual, Mom was at work, and I looked at him and I said, "What do you care about? All you do is sit on a barstool and watch the world go by. You don't care what happens in here!" And he turned to me and looked at me and he said, "I've earned my right to drink." I thought, you know, fine. You've earned your right to drink. You've earned the right to not have a family, because you don't have one. And, you know, from that day on, I realized there's no point in ever trying to get him to stop. I don't want him to stop. I wish to God he'd drink himself into his grave, quite frankly. Or at least move away from here and not come back, because he's more damaging than he is anything else. I can't say that I wish him dead. My mother can. I can't. . . .

Lois: Your mom ever say anything to you about not getting married because of her own situation?

Suzanne: Never. Well, she didn't have to say, "Don't marry a man that drinks." No, she would prefer that I was married, because she is under the impression that I cannot take care of myself, you know, with the debt that I have and the disasters that seem to happen [she is a teacher but has lost two jobs], she just doesn't think I can take care of myself. And she thinks I need someone to do that for me, which I don't agree with.

Whether Suzanne "needs someone to take care of her" or not is not at issue here. What is important is that Suzanne has lived out her teenage dream—she is "independent," earns her own money, is not married, and has no children. In her 1985 words, she is not "Mrs. John Smith" crawling behind a "white picket fence." For Suzanne and the other 1985 Freeway girls, "Best are the freedom dreams," and Suzanne has lived this "freedom."

On the down side, Suzanne was in a highly abusive relationship with a man 7 years her senior from the time she was 16: a relationship that began, although nonsexually, when she was 13. She hates her father, who continues to drink, verbally abusing her, her mother, and all Black Americans when drunk. She attributes her own destructive relationship with Joe to the fact that she has no father. Within the last 2 years Suzanne has suffered two nervous breakdowns, having lost one teaching job and enduring seemingly endless bad encounters with men. At one point last summer, she could not get up from the couch for a full week—she just lay there, crying.

Suzanne did not emerge unscathed from the "freedom" train—she and a high proportion of the young Freeway women continue to suffer under the men of their class, as it is the men of their class whom they meet and interact with. I asked her at one point where she meets men. She responded that she goes to bars. "Which bars?" I said. "Oh, you know," she responded, "the ones that people like me go to—the guys are rough, not very educated, and like to have fun. I don't go to bars that educated guys go to." "Why?" I asked. "I don't feel comfortable there," she responded. "I need to be with people who are from places like Freeway." Suzanne is a seventh grade math teacher in a city school. Her social class of origin—her class-embedded *habitus* (Bourdieu, 1993) and accompanying assertions of physical male dominance—travels with her.

The hand of the male is not soft for Judy, Suzanne, or the majority of the Freeway girls, now women. The bruises, Black eyes, thrown plates of spaghetti, angry phone calls at three o'clock in the morning—all encircle life with men they have come into contact with over the years, beginning, in many instances, with their fathers. In the case of Carla, a third woman in the cohort sample, her mother "just knew"—there was something mean about Tom (Carla's former boyfriend who beat her mercilessly). She was right. One drunken night he called her up after slamming her daughter's head against the wall, threatening, "You better say goodbye to your daughter because this is the last time you're ever gonna hear from her."

Concludsion

Juxtaposing the deeply etched youthful desire for "independence" against the women's now held full-time and relatively stable positions in the labor force, the question arises, what came of, and was able to come of, the moment of critique packed within modal working-class female culture as it emerged during the high school years? In other words, where can such a "cultural penetration" deposit, and why?

Significantly, all live to an appreciable extent their fantasy of not being wholly dependent on a man, yet a very high proportion of the women, like Suzanne and Judy, experience horrific episodes of abuse at the hands of men. Certainly not all of the Freeway women have experienced such violence either during their youth or since high school, but most have, to the point where those who have not lived through violent episodes are the exception rather than the rule, signifying the very *layered typicality* of the experience. Although Freeway men may live distanced from their expressed high school desire to set up patriarchal families in which they labor outside the home/family sphere and women reside within it and tend to it (Weis, 1990), the physical brutality that is all too common speaks to an underlying male desire to control and dominate their women.

For women, then, the lived-out "moment of critique" has not wholly been able to challenge all that goes on in the private sphere, although this certainly was their teenage desire. The new collective unit (the family of varying forms; Weis, 2004) on which working-class men and women are now totally dependent if a "stable" life is to be accomplished is punctuated by raw physical male power, much as the working- class collective of old was punctuated by raw bursts of violent capitalist power, as supported by the state. Both the fundamental site of collectivity *and* essential punctuating moves of physical power, as a disruption to this site, have altered under the new economy.

In 1985 the Freeway girls offered the glimmerings of critique of women's place in both the home/family sphere and that of wage labor, challenging the notion that their primary role is to take care of their husbands' children in return for which their husbands' family wages will support them, thus challenging the secret guarantee of the family wage: sacrifice, reward, dignity (Willis, 2000). Additionally, they pierced the notion that they must account to men—that they must listen as men tell them what to do, where to go, when to have children, and what to buy, thus chipping away at the ideology of thoroughly separate spheres for women and men and the accompanying notion that they must occupy a subordinate role.

It is arguably the case, then, that the Freeway girls' identity must be understood in terms of a radically changed economy as well as in relation to altered understandings of women as a sexual class in general, even though the resurgence of the women's movement has been spearheaded and certainly colonized by the middle class. Some of the middle-class struggles have clearly filtered down to these girls, and their beginning critique of women's place must be seen as linked to these broader struggles in key ways. The language of "independence," for example, is tied discursively to a middle-class women's movement and picked up by working-class girls, whether they consciously identify with this movement or not.

What working-class Freeway women have not been able to do, however, is escape the violence associated with the ways in which patriarchy plays out historically and continues to play out in this particular class fraction. It is this element of class association and embeddedeness, this *habitus* if you will (Bourdieu, 1993), that the daughters of the industrial proletariat have not, as a collective, been able to escape. Indeed, it is arguably the case that such abuse is on the rise as working-class men move away from older patriarchal notions in some part of their lives yet retain violent elements meted out in the domestic realm. Given that longitudinal physical abuse data are difficult to read because any rise in such abuse may signal greater frequency of abuse or simply more extensive reporting of such abuse, it is difficult to establish with any certainty whether or not abuse in working-class communities is on the upswing as a result of changes in the economy and family structure. In a frightening turn of events, though, it is conceivable that the physical cruelty of White working-class men (whether more extensive than in the past or not) becomes their last defensive resort—their last solidly and visible patriarchal stand in a world that has stripped them of alternative forms of power. Under this scenario, the power left to them, as a group, is their physicality, and they employ it, whether consciously or not, to stake out a form of continued dominance vis-à-vis women and children in the home.

This underscores points made by Angela McRobbie (1980) and more recently Madeline Arnot (chap. 2, this volume). As Arnot notes, what McRobbie found most striking was how "unambiguously degrading to women is the language of aggressive masculinity through which (Willis's) lads kick against the oppressive structures they inhabit" (p. 38, as cited in Arnot). *Learning to Labor*, which can be read as a classic piece on White working-class masculinity (Arnot, chap 2., this volume), is peppered with references of utmost brutality against women, suggesting that "the violence of the imagery, the cruelty of the lads' sexual double standard, the images of sexual power and domination become the lads' last defensive resort" (Arnot, chap 2., this volume). Given changes in the world economy that render substantial *economically* based male power in the White working class less and less likely, it is arguably the case that raw physical power becomes the last line of defense, building on already existing sensibilities regarding women in this class fraction (Nayak, 2001; Reay, 2002). Certainly, many White working-class husbands and fathers (some of whom are currently married to the Freeway women) do not fall victim to this brute physicality as an expression of desired and yet stripped down dominance and superiority. Yet data suggest that enough of these women have experienced such raw physical abuse so as to render violence against women typical.[2]

Critique, then, such as that expressed by the young Freeway women, although not necessarily "fizzing out" as some of our earlier short-term studies suggested (Weis & Fine, 1996), takes different shape and form by gender, and, I am quite certain, moves forward in the real world in markedly different ways. Paul Willis's extraordinarily insightful set of understandings around the theoretical constructions associated with penetration, partial penetration, and limitation, useful as they are, *play over time*. What I am suggesting here is, not only do they play differently over time for men and women, but that a "moment of critique" such as I stumbled on in the mid 1980s is multifaceted, with long-term follow-up studies allowing us to unravel the "sticking power" of varying elements of such critique in concrete political, economic, cultural and discursive settings.

The Freeway girls "all grown up" in 2000–2001 reveal that although their mid 1980s moment of critique enables some semblance of control over work and family life, it does not enable them to escape the male-based physical abuse of this class. Ironically, although it is the skills and contacts embedded within White working-class *habitus* that enable the "accomplishment" of "settled" life within this specific class fraction under the new economy, a topic that I take up at much greater length elsewhere (Weis, 2004), it is, at one and the same time, the physical domination as embedded within this same *habitus* that "causes" the violence noted here. Thus, both "good" and "bad" elements of White working-class *habitus* are carried on the backs of women (and men, of course) as they move into the 21st century, carving, with men, a new class fraction under the restructured economy.

Notwithstanding occupational segregation and the continued "double burden" (wage labor/family) of women across social class context, the White working class has moved into the 21st century with women figuratively working side by side men in both the home/family sphere and the public sphere so as to bring in income and raise the next generation. Just below the surface of this newly minted collective, however, rests the potential physical dominance of the White working-class man, a dominance intensified perhaps by a deep and targeted sense among White working-class men that their masculinities are under siege in the new global economy. The apparent seamlessness with which this new White working class fraction is accomplished, then, is, on closer scrutiny, perhaps being shredded from the inside.

Notes

1. Here I am employing an updated version of the "hard" versus "settled" living binary embedded within the literature on the white working class (Howell, 1973). I explore this at length in *Class Reunion* (Weis, 2004).

2. I want to make it clear here that White working-class identity as expressed within my original ethnography addresses what can be seen as *modal* cultural forms. Diane Reay (2002) recently took me to task for my apparent "homogenization" of White working-class male forms, suggesting that such homogenized accounts of White working-class masculinities not only ignore difference within masculinities but leave this class to "bear the weight of White racism and male sexism" (Reay, 2002, p. 222). I agree with her latter point wholeheartedly. When we point fingers at this group and locate racism and sexism within it, we ignore the differently coded but nonetheless real racism and sexism within the middle and upper middle classes, for example, as well as racism and sexism embedded within economic and state policies, which are most definitely not crafted by the White working class (but may, nonetheless, benefit them as "Whites"). This is obviously not my intent, but I recognize that

a focus on one group inadvertently tends to "black out" the ways in which these same characteristics may be embedded within another group or broad-based policies. Michelle Fine and I have taken up this point elsewhere (Fine & Weis, 1998), arguing strongly that White working-class men and women, and particularly men, often bear the brunt of broad class-based racism and sexism simply because they speak out whereas others offer more coded versions of similar sentiments.

With respect to Reay's point about homogenization, I do not mean to imply that all men and women from the White working class live out the stories presented in any of my writing or *necessarily* exhibit the range of characteristics embedded within the stories. However, I do suggest that these are *modal* stories—that a *significant* proportion of the specified group could tell a similar story, as evidenced by Reay's own admission that "my own childhood and adolescent experience of white working class masculinities was one scarred by violence, both physical and verbal abuse plus the more symbolic but equally damaging violence of deeply entrenched sexism and racism within the male dominated coal mining community I used to be part of" (p. 222). Again, then, I do not mean to imply that there are not varying masculinities or femininities within this class cultural group. Obviously there are. What I do suggest though, in line with a range of scholars such as R. W. Connell (1995), Kenway and Fitzclarence (1997), and others, is that particular masculinist constructions are highly valued—or hegemonic—thereby providing the center with which and against which all other competing masculinities (or femininities) must emerge. My point in this chapter, then, is not that every White working-class woman has the experience outlined here, but rather that my data suggest its very typicality, a typicality that should not be ignored as we focus on the adult "living out" of culturally rooted "penetrations" observed during teenage years (metaphorically ours and actually theirs).

References

Arnot, M. (2002). *Reproducing gender: Essays on educational theory and feminist politics.* New York: Routledge Falmer.

Bluestone, B., & Harrison, B. (1982). *The de-industrialization of America.* New York: Basic Books.

Bourdieu, P. (1993). *Sociology in question.* London: Sage.

Connell, R. W. (1995). *Masculinities.* Cambridge, UK: Polity Press.

Elder, G. (1974). *Children of the Great Depression.* Chicago: University of Chicago Press.

Fine, M., & Weis, L. (1998). *The unknown city: The lives of poor and working class young adults.* Boston: Beacon Press.

Fitch, J. (1999). *White oleander.* London: Virago Press.

Howell, J. (1973). *Hard living on Clay Street.* Garden City, NY: Anchor Press.

Kenway, J., & Fitzclarence, L. (1997). Masculinity, violence and schooling—Challenging poisonous pedagogies. *Gender and Education, 9,* 117–33.

Kurz, D. (1995) *For richer, for poorer: Mothers confront divorce.* New York: Routledge.

McRobbie, A. (1978). Working class girls and the culture of femininity. In Women's Studies Group (Ed.), *Women take issue* (pp. 96–108). London: Hutchinson.

McRobbie, A. (1980). Settling accounts with sub-culture. *Screen Education, 34,* 37–50.

Nayak, A. (2001, May). *Ivory lives, race, ethnicity and the practice of Whiteness in a northeast youth community.* Paper presented at the Economic and Social Research Seminar Series: "Interdisciplinary Youth Research: New Approaches," Birmingham University, U.K.

Reay, D. (2002). Shaun's story: Troubling discourses of white working-class masculinities. *Gender and Education. 14*(3), 221–234.

Reich, R. (1991). Why the rich are getting richer and the poor poorer. In *The work of nations* (pp. 208–224). London: Simon and Schuster.

Reich, R. (2001). *The future of success.* New York: Alfred Knopf.

Rubin, L. (1976). *Worlds of pain.* New York: Basic Books.

Sennett, R., and Cobb, J. (1972). *The hidden injuries of class.* New York: Vintage.

Valli, L. (1986). *Becoming clerical workers.* Boston: Routledge and Kegan Paul.

Walkerdine, V., Lucey, H., & Melody, J. (2001). *Growing up girl: Psychological explorations of gender and class.* New York: New York University Press.

Weis, L. (1990). *Working class without work: High school students in a de-industrializing economy.* New York: Routledge.

Weis, L. (2004). *Class reunion: The new working class.* New York: Routledge.

Weis, L., & Fine, M. (1996). Narrating the 1980s and 1990s: Voices of poor and working class White and African American men. *Anthropology and Education Quarterly, 27*(4), 1–24.

Weis, L., & Fine, M. (2004). *Working method.* New York: Routledge.

Willis, P. (1977). *Learning to labour: How working class kids get working class jobs.* Westmead, England: Saxon House Press.

Willis, P. (2000). *The ethnographic imagination.* Cambridge, UK: Polity Press.

CHAPTER 8

Learning to Do Time
Willis's Model of Cultural Reproduction in an Era of Postindustrialism, Globalization, and Mass Incarceration

KATHLEEN NOLAN AND JEAN ANYON

This chapter examines Paul Willis's cultural reproduction model, explicated in *Learning to Labor* (first published as *Learning to Labour*, 1977), and offers an analysis of the importance it holds as a critique of urban public schools in the current context of postindustrialism, globalization, and the mass incarceration of people of color—particularly Black men—in the United States. Willis's contention that working-class youth, by opposing the dominant school culture, act as agents not only in the reproduction of working-class culture, but in the reproduction of their own class position, is as relevant today as it was over 25 years ago. However, oppositional behavior in school—when enacted by Black urban youth in poverty neighborhoods in the United States—does not lead to the shop floor. Rather, in this postindustrial era of mass incarceration, oppositional behavior by working-class youth of color in educational institutions often leads them directly into the criminal justice system.

The chapter first describes how the phenomenon of mass incarceration in the United States was created. Although it is difficult to identify the myriad causes of mass incarceration, we hold that there is a relationship between such trends as deindustrialization and globalization, and the need for the management and control of a population that has become economically superfluous—particularly in urban, deindustrialized zones. In our analysis, race and class are central. The chapter next explores the changing role of urban public schools in the new social and economic circumstances. Urban public schools, we argue, have become increasingly connected to the criminal justice system and to the production of mass incarceration of youth of color therein. This "school/prison continuum" has developed through the use of academic policies such as high-stakes testing, disciplinary policies such as "zero tolerance," the use of high-tech security apparatus and police officers in schools, and the establishment of a multitude of intermediary institutions that house youth as they move between educational and custodial facilities. A most important step in this "prison track" is that truancy and the kind of oppositional behavior displayed by Willis's lads, when committed by U.S. youth of color in schools, is criminalized.

However, it is not only oppositional youth who get criminalized. Dominant media representations that depict urban youth of color as dangerous criminals and the source of urban chaos and the media's sensationalist coverage of school violence serve to demonize inner-city youth of color as a group. These media representations generate fear of young Black men and other youth of color and support school discipline policies, such as zero tolerance, that place even youth of color who accommodate to school protocols in jeopardy of being constructed as troublemakers—or worse, criminals.

We posit finally that Willis's model of cultural reproduction, as a dialectic between opposition and reproduction, offers today a much needed sense of possibility for political action. Although laden with contradictions, the cultural productions of youth of color, at times, can lead to youths' reclaiming their individual and collective identities, social critique, and the possibility of organized resistance.

The Social Context

In 2000, the prison population of the United States exceeded 2 million for the first time. Currently, about 6.6 million Americans are incarcerated, on probation, or parole—an increase of 258% since 1980. The ratio of incarcerated people is now 702 per 100,000 people (in contrast to 97 per 100,000 in 1972), the highest reported rate of incarceration in the world. The explosion in the number of people involved in the criminal justice system has had its most dramatic effects on communities of color, especially African American men. In fact, about two-thirds of the people in prison are racial and ethnic minorities, and about half of the prison population is African American, although they represent only about 13% of the total population (Mauer, 1999). Among African American men, the most adversely affected population is men between the ages of 16 and 25. An astounding one out of every three young Black men are either incarcerated or otherwise involved in the criminal justice system, and for the first time in decades, there are more Black men headed to prison than to college (Justice Policy Institute, 2000).

The number of children (those under the age of 16) involved in the juvenile justice system has also increased (Zimring, 2001). Moreover, national statistics reveal alarming patterns of bias against African American and Latino youth. They are overrepresented in the juvenile and criminal justice system, and are subject to harsher treatment than whites. For example, African American youth are more likely than Whites to be "waived" into adult court. They are more likely to be detained, and six times more likely to be incarcerated than White youth for the same offense (Jones & Yamagata, 2000).

The rise in the prison population began in the 1960s, but the dramatic shift in adult incarceration occurred over a decade later, in the early 1980s. This increase marked a new era in the American criminal justice system. An increase in the juvenile population involved in the criminal justice system followed a decade later and continued throughout the 1990s (Zimring, 2001). Although there is some debate about the causes of this phenomenon, we argue that it is the result of complex interactions of economic, political, historical, and discursive forces.

Loic Wacquant (2002) posited that since the inception of the United States, there have been four racialized economic institutions: slavery, Jim Crow, the ghetto, and—beginning in the late 1960s—what he calls the hyper-ghetto/prison. Within this framework, Wacquant offers an historical analysis of the capitalist classes' interest and investment in institutions created for the management of forced and low-wage labor and racial containment (see also Wacquant, 2001).

As early as the 1920s, African Americans living in the South were drawn to Northern industrial cities seeking employment and escaping the Jim Crow South. By the 1950s, Southern Blacks were migrating to Northern industrial cities at unprecedented rates. Although employers actually encouraged migration and sought to hire Black workers at times, such as during World War I when there was a dearth of European immigrant labor, Black workers were more often excluded from skilled jobs by employers and trade unions (Anyon, 1997). Nevertheless, for the most part, the 1940s and 1950s marked a period of economic expansion, and African Americans in urban neighborhoods enjoyed more employment opportunity and autonomy than they had as Southern sharecroppers.

The decades after World War II were also characterized by housing discrimination, the construction of new highways that tore through working-class urban neighborhoods, and federally subsidized White suburbanization. These trends contributed to the economic and social isolation of people of color in American "ghettos" (Anyon, 1997).

Economic shifts that occurred in the in the postwar years destabilized urban neighborhoods and—in conjunction with the economic crisis and emergence of a service economy in the 1970s—were root causes of the soon-to-emerge phenomenon of mass incarceration. These changes translated into the loss of millions of jobs. From 1967 to 1987, Philadelphia lost 64% of its manufacturing jobs and Chicago lost 60%. New York lost 58% of its manufacturing jobs, or 520,000 in absolute numbers (Wilson, 1996). Although jobs in service industries increased, their wages were considerably lower than manufacturing jobs. Unemployment rose and real wages have decreased—disproportionately effecting African Americans and Latinos (Wilson, 1996). In 1999, almost a *third* (29.5%) of Black men, almost *half* (40.7%) of Black women, almost *half* of Hispanic men (40.3%), and *more than half* of Hispanic women (51.8%) earned poverty wages working full-time, year-round (Anyon, forthcoming). If one calculates the individuals, rather than families, who made less than 200% of the poverty level in 2001 ($17.40/hour or $36,192/year), the results are as follows: 84.3% of Hispanic workers, 80% of Black workers, and 64.3% of White workers made wages at or under 200% of the official poverty line (Anyon, forthcoming).

Moreover, a smaller percentage of African American men are working now than in recent decades. Only 52% of young (aged 16 to 24), noninstitutionalized, out-of-school Black males with high school degrees or less were employed in 2002, compared to 62% 20 years ago (Anyon, forthcoming). In contrast, the labor-force activity of comparable White and Hispanic males has been steady over the last two decades, and employment among young Black women has increased significantly (Anyon, forthcoming).

The employment rate of young, less educated Black males is much lower in cities than in suburbs, and the gap widened over the last decade. The employment rate for young, less educated Black men living in central cities (46.99%) is now 16 percentage points lower than that for their suburban counterparts (63.09%) (Anyon, forthcoming, p. 4). The employment rate for young Black male high school graduates dropped by over four times as much in cities (9 percentage points) as in suburbs (2 percentage points) over the course of the 1990s (Anyon, forthcoming).

These economic shifts, coupled with dramatic cuts in social services in the 1980s and 1990s, led to dire material conditions and the social isolation of working-class African Americans and other people of color in inner-city areas (Wilson, 1996).

Other scholars complicate the notion of social isolation by expounding on the new economic and spatial arrangements found in urban areas as a result of globalization. They emphasize the interconnectedness between increased concentrations of poverty, immigration, processes of uneven development, gentrification, and the simultaneous creation of "hyper-anaesthetized bourgeois play zones" (Parenti, 2000), or "glamour zones" (Sassen, 1998)—such as SoHo in New York City. All of these, it is argued, are elements of the "global city" (Sassen, 2001).

Globalization is characterized by the worldwide primacy of financial and speculative capital, the creation and integration of flexible systems of production of goods and services, increased international mobility of workers, and the bifurcation of national economies into rich and poor (Sassen, 1998; see also Lipman, 2001).

Although many characteristics of globalization occur on the global scale, others are local—and it is the racial, class, and spatial arrangements that appear in urban neighborhoods and cities that are most important to this analysis. First, there has been a hardening of economic stratification due to changes in the labor market. Many cities have seen an increase in both high paying professional, managerial, and technical jobs on the one hand, and low-wage, informal, transient, and part-time employment in the service sector, on the other hand. This has created a polarization of class divisions along racial, ethnic, and gender lines (Sassen, 2001).

Second, globalization has changed urban geography through an intensified process of uneven local development. There have been both an increase in concentrated poverty and great increases in wealth in global cities like New York and Chicago, and in what Sassen calls "second tier" cities as well, creating high-income areas that abut very poor neighborhoods. Thus, everyday interactions between rich and poor may be increased. Low-income workers—who in most cities are people of color—traverse upscale commercial and entertainment zones as service workers or as consumers. And gentrification, the process by which the depreciation of property value in depressed urban areas makes investment profitable, coupled with the desire of some high-income professionals to live near financial centers, has created a situation where high-income workers increasingly move into poverty areas. This not only causes the displacement of low-income families, but heightens calls for increased surveillance and heavy policing of those who remain.

Parenti (2000) pointed to a major contradiction within the American economic system: "Capitalism always creates, needs, surplus populations [to keep wages down], yet faces the threat of political, aesthetic, or cultural disruption from those populations" (p. 239). The threat residing in an unruly reserve pool of labor is great, given the bifurcation of wages and the polarization of classes and races, uneven local development, and massive unemployment and underemployment in central cities across the country. Recent dramatic increases in the prison and criminal justice populations are attempts to manage this contradiction.

The sharp increases in poverty in American cities in the 1980s (Jargowsky, 1998) and cuts in social services were accompanied by a dramatic increase in the sale of drugs on inner-city streets in the form of crack cocaine. The "drug problem" gave politicians and pundits a way to respond to economic and social problems that were plaguing the city: Declare a "war on drugs." This is the most immediate cause of the explosion in the number of people incarcerated in the United States.

Some specific policy changes that accompanied the "war on crime" were the introduction of mandatory sentencing and three-strikes policies, and more stringent parole regulations. New York State's Rockefeller Drug Laws, passed in 1973, were considered among the toughest in the country (Mauer, 1999). Throughout the 1980s, many other states subsequently passed similar laws. These laws mandated mandatory prison terms and limits to plea bargaining. Federal legislation, such as the 1984 Sentencing Reform Act and the Anti-Drug Abuse Acts of 1986 and 1988, greatly expanded the use of mandatory minimum sentencing (Mauer, 1999; Zimring, 2001). Finally, the first three-strikes laws appeared in 1993 and the federal truth-in-sentencing law came in 1994.

These laws deeply weaken the social fabric of urban communities as hundreds of thousands of people of color enter the criminal justice system. A number of White rural communities, on the other hand, received somewhat of an economic stimulus, in the form of new prisons (Gilmore, 1998; Parenti, 2000).

Concomitant with changes in the political economy, by the 1970s the field of criminal justice had changed as well. The efficacy of the rehabilitation model dominant during the 1960s was questioned. In addition, many criminologists who were concerned about equity in sentencing contended that individualized treatment led to bias in sentencing, and therefore uniform sentencing procedures should be adopted (Garland, 2001). Soon the discourse of rehabilitation and the liberal emphasis on the individual treatment of the "disadvantaged" offender were replaced by discourses of retribution, punishment, and social pathology.

The current "tough on crime" rhetoric and focus on retribution can be seen as an extension of political maneuvers dating back to the 1960s—beginning perhaps with Richard Nixon's "law and order" discourse of 1968—which spoke to people's fears of growing racial tensions and social protest; this discourse was also aimed at feminists who were demanding safety on the streets (Mauer, 1999). By the 1970s, politicians had identified crime as an important political issue. Crime control became a "wedge issue," along with welfare, affirmative action, and immigration, used by conservative politicians to capture the vote of working-class Whites (Tonry, 1999).

Likewise, high taxes, inflation, and declining economic performance caused anxiety among the new middle classes, which triggered the major political realignment and shifts in public opinion around the issue of crime control just described (Garland, 2001).

The media have supported this new discourse through a dramatic increase in coverage of urban crime and the proliferation of representations of Black and Latino urban men as a "new class of superpredators." Although crime dropped by 20% from 1990 to 1998, crime news on network television increased 83%. Moreover, television networks overrepresent people of color as perpetrators and Whites as victims, and Black suspects are less likely than White suspects to be identified by name, consequently creating an image of the Black criminal as indistinct from other Black people (Dorfman & Shiraldi, 2001). Black youth, in particular, are perhaps constructed as the most dangerous element of the urban "underclass," as "young Black male" has become synonymous with crime in the media (Dorfman & Shiraldi, 2001).

Thus, the rationale provided by authorities and the media for mass incarceration does not implicate poverty or unemployment; it has become, instead, a "value rationale"—one that is expressive and moralistic (Garland, 2001). Young men of color (and teen-aged mothers on welfare) have come to represent the moral crisis in America, and young people of color in urban areas are blamed for the social and economic problems of our time. Increased levels of repression are justified on moral grounds, and control becomes a prevailing cultural theme (Garland, 2001).

The Urban School

In the 1970s, reproduction theorists who shaped radical educational theory demonstrated how schools, as predominantly ideological institutions, served to reproduce social class stratification (Althusser, 1971; Bourdieu & Passeron, 1977; Bowles & Gintis, 1976). Although these models were helpful in understanding the school's role in maintaining the class structure, they did not take into account human agency and the possibility of resistance (but see Anyon, 1980).

Willis's model of cultural reproduction offered a more dialectical notion of reproduction, in which students are not passive receptacles of the dominant ideology but play an active role in reproduction as they engage in shaping their own cultural responses to their conditions. Willis's working-class lads reject school culture because they see through the myth of meritocracy. They know that, as members of the working class, there is little chance that they will enter the middle class. Willis refers to these insights as "penetrations," or "impulses within a cultural form towards the penetration of the conditions of existence of its members and their class position within the social whole" (Willis, 1977, p. 119).

These penetrations, however, are only partial; they do not represent a critical working class consciousness. Here Willis uses the notion of limitations. That is, cultural penetrations are "repressed and prevented from going further (and in fact often paradoxically link the lads more fully to an unequal economy) by the contradictions built into [the lads'] actions" (Apple, 1995, p. 91). For example, the lads' celebration of manual labor and rejection of mental labor ultimately exclude them from middle-class jobs.

We argue that Willis's model is still relevant today. Nevertheless, within the context of globalization, urban impoverishment, and demographic polarization, the functions of schooling for working-class students of color have shifted. Thus, we ask: What is the function of schooling for Black students and other students of color in the current context of postindustrial impoverishment? And what is the relevance of Willis's model of cultural reproduction for these youth in the current context?

To answer the first question, we consider discursive shifts and policy changes that have occurred in the field of education in the past few decades. The changes in educational discourse have reflected discursive changes in the larger society and in fields "contiguous" to education, such as the criminal justice system. Liberal educational practices of the 1960s that acknowledged social inequalities and the need for civil rights had, by the 1980s, given way to discipline-oriented policies in the field of education that pathologized whole groups of people, as in criminal justice.

The 1980s saw a renewed emphasis on the Western canon and basic skills training, and fierce attacks on multicultural and bilingual education. Conservatives such as Charles Murray (1984) overtly advocated coercive policies—claiming that students, particularly working-class Blacks and other minorities, needed to be disciplined. Thinking behind these trends involved the stereotype that working-class people of color were culturally deprived.

In the 1990s, neo-liberal educational policies meshed with economic privatization and marketization tendencies, with similar and supporting results. In the new framework, the public must be convinced not only that the unregulated marketplace is the truest expression of individual freedom, but that the marketplace must be expanded into every sphere of life—including education—freeing it from the inefficient and dysfunctional public domain (Apple, 2001). The implementation of choice plans—vouchers, magnet schools, and privately owned charter schools—then becomes the commonsense approach to education reform.

However, privatization schemes ultimately have led to the intensification of social divisions along racial, ethnic, and class lines, and increased polarization of and in neighborhoods (Apple, 2001; Lipman, 2001, 2002). This happens as middle and upper-middle-class (typically White) parents—and some from the working class—that is, those with the social and cultural capital required to negotiate systems of choice—ensure that their children benefit from the new schools while leaving the most economically and socially disenfranchised students to languish in the poorest schools.

Moreover, the corporate logic embedded in privatizing enterprises has shifted the focus away from liberal education reform policies, such as decreasing class size and creating more culturally relevant curriculum, to a focus on increasing productivity while minimizing spending (House, 1998). Funding for enrichment programs has been cut while new systems of accountability, that is, the implementation of labor discipline practices, have moved the full burden for educational success onto students, teachers, and low-level administrators.

Today, one of the most significant policy initiatives is high-stakes standardized testing: standardized exams that students must pass in order to be promoted or graduate. High-stakes testing holds appeal for both conservatives and neo-liberals because on the one hand they help to carry out the conservative agenda by maintaining tight control over what constitutes "official knowledge," while on the other hand these exams fit nicely into the new corporate logic as they help to shift blame for school failure onto students, foster competition, and create new markets within the burgeoning testing industry.

Moreover, high-stakes testing has worked to maintain racial and economic inequality in America's cities by fostering highly regimented and superficial rote learning in schools serving students who have historically underachieved on standardized tests, that is, African Americans and other students of color (Apple, 2001; McNeil, 2000; Lipman, 2001). The requirement that poorly prepared students in urban schools pass these tests in order to graduate has been linked with increasing dropout rates. In some urban high schools, the dropout rate is as high as 70%, and those who drop out have increased chances of future incarceration (Coalition for Juvenile Justice, 2001).

Current education policy, then, aligned with the needs of the market, has reinforced and strengthened the school's role in the reproduction of social stratification, along class and racial lines, that was illustrated to us decades ago (Anyon, 1980). The heightened social stratification that results from current education policy does not establish a direct link between schools and the criminal justice system, but it certainly does create at least two distinct groups of students—those prepared for high-paying professional jobs, and those who must vie for the low-wage service jobs or enter the illegal economy. Not surprisingly, our prisons are full of young people who belong to the latter group—many of whom read well below grade level, do not have high school diplomas, have been placed on the lowest academic tracks, and have spent years in underfunded, underachieving schools (Coalition for Juvenile Justice, 2001).

The more direct link between schools in low-income urban neighborhoods and the criminal justice system is created by current "zero-tolerance" policies and practices. The term *zero tolerance*, which entered the public discourse in the early 1980s in relation to the new drug laws, found its way into educational policy rhetoric partly in response to a few highly publicized school shootings that occurred in middle-class White suburbs. In the mid 1990s, the federal government responded to public concern over what the media labeled "the national crisis of school violence" by implementing strict security guidelines for public schools. Zero-tolerance policies have since led to dramatic increases in exclusionary practices—suspensions and expulsions (Skiba, Michael, & Nardo, 2000). Moreover, zero-tolerance policies have increased the flow of some students into the juvenile or criminal justice system through the establishment of a close working relationship between school personnel and the police and the installation of high-tech security apparatus.

Other practices within school walls have led to the flow of students into the criminal justice system. Some studies identify the subjective views of White teachers and the cumulative effects of discriminatory, disciplinary action as major factors in the overrepresentation of students of color in school discipline cases (Ferguson, 2001; Skiba et al., 2000). Moreover, as in the criminal justice system itself, Black and Latino students are more likely to be punished than their White counterparts for the same offenses (McCarthy & Hoge, 1987; Skiba et al., 2000). Thus, Black and Latino students are more likely to enter the criminal justice system, as it has become increasingly common for disciplinary problems to be referred to the police.

Urban high schools, however, have not all witnessed the same levels of increased repression. For the most part, only large urban public high schools in poor areas have been prisonized through the use of security apparatus and police surveillance. Students in these schools, regardless of whether they have ever committed a crime, are at times subject to bodily searches, metal detectors, and referral to the police for small, nonviolent school infractions that were once handled internally. Thus, whole school populations are criminalized.

The school/prison continuum, however, does not rest solely on individual teachers' racist assumptions and new school discipline codes. The continuum is also supported by new intermediary institutions that manage the stages between school and prison. The establishment of alternative educational sites for students charged with certain disciplinary offenses in New York, and probationary schools for youth barred from regular high schools on release from incarceration in Philadelphia, are two such examples. Some of these intermediary institutions are private ventures, thus carrying out dual functions—educational exclusion and capitalist expansion. Intermediary institutions serve to solidify the connection between schools and prisons, creating a more totalizing system of control.

We are arguing, then, that although urban public schools have long been used, at least in part, to control the "dangerous classes," this historically repressive element of schools—that serves to physically contain and direct students' bodies—has now been for all intents and purposes "merged" with the criminal justice system.

Here, we have been most concerned with the atmosphere within those schools that have become prisonized—many of which were the large comprehensive high schools of a few decades ago from which each year cadres of workers would flow.

Willis's Model of Cultural Reproduction

One of Willis's most significant contributions to radical educational theory, his attention to the cultural level, is essential to an analysis of schooling today. Willis does not explicitly address the repressive elements of schooling; instead, his framework is consistent with the notion that schools are ideological institutions that serve to justify their own existence through a discourse of social mobility. However, his focus on the everyday lives and the cultural practices of youth can help to illuminate the repressive function of schooling we have been describing. Although schools today still maintain ideological functions, the everyday interactions between school officials and working-class students of color belong in the repressive realm. Bringing in security guards to handle disruptive behavior, walking through metal detectors, and police escorts of truant students to the principal's office are interactions that, in part, define many urban public schools today, and these daily events express the repressive nature of schools, not their ideological role.

Indeed, a new school culture has emerges in urban schools with a police presence, high-tech security apparatus, and zero-tolerance policies. Students become used to procedures like hallway sweeps, book-bag and locker searches, "pat down" and frisks, that treat them like criminals (McCormick, 2000). Prison metaphors used by teachers, administrators, and even students characterize a significant portion of the dialogue: "Students are on 'lockdown'" and "That one [referring to a third grade student] has a cell at Rikers with his name on it" (Nolan, unpublished research in progress).

Moreover, ongoing research by Kathleen Nolan indicates that some students, particularly the most marginalized ones who may already have experience in the criminal justice system, typically see little difference between prison and school. They describe both places as hostile environments where students gain nothing and teachers most often misunderstand them. The significant difference between school and prison for these youths are that they are able to leave the school building at 3:00 p.m., whereas in prison it is "24/7." In these ways, in this educational context, urban students are "learning to do time."

Willis's model of cultural reproduction—as it moves the theoretical lens onto the everyday cultural practices of youth—also offers a framework for understanding young people's own role in reproduction of their class positions. Like Willis's lads, many working class students of color, as we have mentioned, understand schools as out of touch with their lived experiences and irrelevant to their future lives. Nolan (ongoing research) has found, particularly as high-stakes tests such as the New York State Regents exams drive curriculum, that many working class students are dreadfully bored. Often at the mere mention of the exams, students' heads drop to their desks as they grumble their objections.

Sometimes, the students with the strongest critiques choose to dropout (Fine, 1991). At other times, students remain in school and find ways to cope. Like Willis's lads, many of our students attempt to win space from school and its rules by "having a laff." "Having a laff" can take on particular importance for today's students who find school not only irrelevant but hostile and prisonlike. So students find creative ways to interrupt the humdrum of exam preparation by telling jokes, cutting or walking out of class to roam the hallways, or passing around notes or magazines whose content is far more interesting to students than the drone of their teachers. Willis posits that the purpose of having a laff is to beat boredom and fear and overcome hardships, and we would argue that many of today's working-class youth of color, in the context of high-stakes testing, dismal employment prospects, and street violence, experience levels of boredom, fear, and hardship that far surpass the levels experienced by the lads.

Unfortunately, "having a laff" in an urban fortress such as a large comprehensive urban high school can get students labeled as troublemakers and send them down a slippery slope. This occurs when students engage in destructive pranks such as throwing other students' belongings out the window, as well as when students do something as minor as disrupt the teacher with an inappropriate comment. It is the school's overreaction to these minor offenses—often calling in the police—that has served to criminalize whole school populations. Thus it is that low-income students of color who engage in oppositional behavior—no matter how insignificant—

participate in the reproduction of themselves not as workers but as a probable criminalized class, subject to the possibility of incarceration and the exclusion from civilian jobs.

Willis notes that "having a laff" is not always an effective method of conquering boredom; violence, on the other hand, is the "ultimate way of breaking a flow of meanings" (p. 34). He posits that violence regulates a kind of honor among working-class youth, and is "the fullest if unspecified commitment to a blind or distorted form of revolt" (p. 34). Although violence has taken on quantitatively and qualitatively new forms in many urban American schools, the notion of violence as a means of claiming honor and a form of resistance is still prevalent in the more critical literature on school violence today (Dance, 2002; Giroux, 1983).

Indeed, in recent years, a growing number of ethnographies have been motivated by Willis's work, providing new analyses of students' oppositional behavior, school violence, and discipline in current U.S. circumstances. One such ethnography is *Tough Fronts* by Janelle Dance (2002). According to Dance, young African American boys and other youth of color who are not involved in illegal behavior often assume "tough fronts" anyway, as a temporary strategy for surviving the streets.

Postures of toughness assumed in the streets are then brought into schools—both for protection against peers and as a form of resistance to schooling. School officials and law enforcement agents may misinterpret tough fronts and engage youth as if they were troublemakers or criminals, excluding them from opportunities to enhance their academic performance (Dance) and often setting them on a track toward the criminal justice system.

In Dance's analysis, the image of the low-income urban Black male as tough "emanates from both mainstream society and the streets" (p. 5). Put another way, she argued that as low-income Black youth are bombarded with oppressive stereotypes of themselves as gangsters, some youth come to perceive themselves as tough, or in need of becoming tough, and assume gangsterlike postures—ultimately participating in their own alienation from the dominant school culture. Like Willis's work, then, Dance's ethnographic research illustrates the interplay between social structural forces and students' agency.

Dance's analysis, however, also reminds us that despite the significance of students' role in social reproduction, disruptive behavior and criminal activity are not necessary ingredients in the exclusion of working-class youth of color from educational opportunity and jobs. As Dance pointed out, the vast majority of working-class students of color are not violent. And students who do not appear tough—those with more academic demeanors—can be criminalized by school personnel. Just as Willis's lads demonstrated group solidarity through clothing choices, language use, and other cultural expressions, working-class youth of color today have also formed a collective identity, and, like oppositional behavior and "tough fronts," the cultural expressions of working-class youth of color, no matter how innocuous, have been associated with criminal behavior by people who are part of the dominant culture. A young Black man—even a studious one—who chooses to wear baggy jeans and a do-rag is often immediately perceived by teachers, prospective employers, or a police officer as a gang member or a drug dealer, thus—by his own manner of dress—participating in his exclusion from educational and employment opportunities.

There are also significant differences worth noting between Willis's and Dance's work. First, unlike Willis's lads, the working-class Black youths in Dance's study do have mainstream American dreams and aspirations, and she argues that counterschool cultural exploits are not linked to pride in working-class heritage as much as they are to the desire to maintain peer respect.

Second, although Dance emphasized structural forces and students' agency in her analysis, her major policy recommendation is a call for "down" teachers, that is, teachers who understand or are willing to learn about the pressures of street culture and do not devalue "the cultural assets necessary for surviving urban streets" (p. 145). Willis, on the other hand, is concerned with economic structures, students' agency and their own role in reproduction, and the possibility agency implies for resistance. Thus, his analysis does not lead to specific school-based policy recommendations, but instead suggests the importance of the political organization of the working class.

Another recent ethnography that examines the culture of working-class youth of color, as well as school violence and discipline, is John Devine's *Maximum Security* (1996). Although Dance focused on the fact that the majority of students who choose to assume gangsterlike postures are not criminals, John Devine, in his ethnography, emphasized the very real violence and criminal behavior that spills into schools from the streets. In fact, Devine critiqued Willis for framing violence as a form of resistance that can be characterized as "boisterous merry-making" during which no one actually gets hurt and no blood is ever shed (p. 139). He went on to argue that Willis fails to appreciate that street culture in school "possesses its own (de)formative power that is capable of transforming the student into an instrument of violence" (pp. 139–140).

Although Devine demonstrates great insight into the level to which street violence has escalated in some schools and the school's role in exacerbating violence, he neglects to acknowledge that Willis's study was conducted in a very different social and economic context. Perhaps Willis simply did not find the same level and forms of violence that Devine and his research assistants documented in an urban public high school in the United States in the early 1990s. Moreover, the acts of violence Willis describes did not typically lead a young person into incarceration as they so often do today.

Nevertheless, Devine's analysis is not completely inconsistent with Willis's, and in fact, he owes much to Willis's framework. That is, although Devine does not view violence as a form of resistance in the same way Willis does, his analysis remains on the cultural level and points to the students' role in social reproduction.

Thus, we argue that Devine's and Dance's books, along with other such books, owe a great deal to Willis's work, yet within the new economic, social, and cultural context, these books offer their own updated, or at least somewhat revised, analyses of oppositional behavior, violence, and resistance.

Up to this point, we have emphasized structural determinants and the interplay between institutional practices and students' own behavior in the production of a criminalized class. However, we would be remiss not to refer to the possibilities that Willis's model of cultural reproduction offers us. In an era marked by the unmitigated use of physical control, staggeringly high unemployment rates, deteriorated material conditions for people of color, and media representation of youth of color as criminals, rap and Hip Hop music, which more than anything else have helped to shape the new Black youth culture (Kitwana, 2002), offer a context within which creative identities and social critique can develop. For example, we see young people using Hip Hop texts and rap music "to construct locally validated selves and senses of community" (Dimitriadis, 2001, p. 5). In other words, young people are using rap in creative ways, to define themselves and make meaning of their worlds. This helps them cope with their difficult material conditions and provides a forum for the development of social critique. For example, although not without serious contradictions, rap music is replete with social commentaries on the irrelevance of schools and police brutality. This focus on the cultural productions of youth and their creative uses challenges nihilistic and fatalistic depictions of working-class Black youth and, as Willis suggests, points to the possibility of resistance.

Bakari Kitwana moves beyond an analysis of the cultural productions of Black youth and other youth of color to examine the activism of what he calls the "Hip Hop generation." He argues that there are some significant differences between the activism of the civil rights generation and the activism of today's youth, which finds its form within the postindustrial context we have described. That is, youth in general and Black working-class youth specifically lack the mass political movement that characterized their parents' activism. Instead, they tend to organize themselves on smaller scales around single issues that are indicative of today's political and economic reality—police brutality, the death penalty, college tuition hikes, and mandatory minimum sentencing, to name a few.

Although these single-issue movements are not often rooted in a broader radical agenda, they certainly cannot be overlooked for their radicalizing potential. Although the insights of today's working-class youth of color, like Willis's lads, are often partial and do not constitute a collective working-class consciousness leading to (radical) political action, some working-class youth of color today, particularly ones with experience in the criminal justice system, may be closer than ever to the articulation of a radical social critique and political action. Young people in organizations such as Youth Force or the Prison Moratorium Project often appear to understand the connections between the increased investment in prisons, defunded urban schools, and staggeringly high unemployment rates in communities of color. And as working-class youth of color continue to experience both the exclusion from economic and educational opportunities and the heavy weight of the repressive hand of the state, there is perhaps an even greater chance that the cultural penetrations of youth will lead to a critical class (and race) consciousness and political action than Willis had ever imagined for his lads.

References

Althusser, L. (1971). *Lenin and philosophy.* New York: Monthly Press Review.

Anyon, J. (1997). *Ghetto schooling: A political economy of urban educational reform.* New York: Teachers College Press.

Anyon, J. (1980). Social class and the hidden curriculum of work. *Journal of Education, 162,* 67–92.

Anyon, J. (forthcoming). *Social policy, urban education, and a new civil rights movement.* New York: Teachers College Press.

Apple, M. (1995). *Education and power.* New York: Routledge.

Apple, M. (2001). *Educating the "right way": Markets, standards, god, and inequality.* New York: Routledge Falmer.

Bourdieu, P., & Passeron, J. C. (1977). *Reproduction in education, society and culture.* Beverly Hills, CA: Sage.

Bowles, S., & Gintis, H. (1976). *Schooling in capitalist America: Educational reform and the contradictions of economic life.* New York: Basic Books.

Coalition for Juvenile Justice. (2001). *Abandoned in the back row: New lessons in education and delinquency prevention.* CJJ 2001 Annual Report. Washington DC.

Dance, L. J. (2002). *Tough fronts: The impact of street culture on schooling.* New York: Routledge Falmer.

Devine, J. (1996). *Maximum security: The culture of violence in inner-city schools.* Chicago: University of Chicago Press.

Dimitriadis, G. (2001). *Performing identity/ performing culture: Hip hop as text, pedagogy, and lived practice.* New York: Peter Lang.

Dorfman, L., & Shiraldi, V. (2001, April). Off balance: Youth, race, and crime in the news. *Building Blocks for Youth.* Washington, DC: Justice Policy Institute.

Ferguson, A. A. (2001). *Bad boys: Public schools in the making of Black masculinity.* Ann Arbor: University of Michigan Press.

Fine, M. (1991). *Framing dropouts: Notes on the politics of an urban public high school.* Albany: State University of New York Press.

Garland, D. (2001). *The culture of control: Crime and social order in contemporary society.* Chicago: University of Chicago Press.

Gilmore, R. W. (1998). Globalisation and U.S. prison growth: from military Keynesianism to post-Keynesian militarism. *Race and Class, 40*, 2–3.

Giroux, H. (1983). *Theory and resistance in education: A pedagogy for the opposition.* South Hadley, MA: Bergin and Garvey.

House, E. R. (1998). *Schools for sale: Why free market policies won't improve America's schools and what will.* New York: Teachers College Press.

Jargowsky, P. A. (1998). *Poverty and place: Ghettos, barrios, and the American city.* New York: Russell Sage Foundation.

Justice Policy Institute. (2000, August). *Cellblocks or classrooms? The funding of higher education and corrections and its impact on African American men.* Washington, DC: Author.

Kitwana, B. (2002). *The Hip Hop generation: Young Blacks and the crisis in African-American culture.* New York: BasicCivitas Books.

Lipman, P. (2001). Bush's education plan, globalization, and the politics of race. *Cultural Logic: An Electronic Journal of Marxist Theory and Practice, 4*(1). Available online at http://eserver.org/clogic/4–1/lipman.html.

Lipman, P. (2002). Making the global city, making inequality: The political economy and cultural politics of Chicago School Policy. *American Educational Research Journal, 39*(2).

Mauer, M. (1999). *Race to incarcerate: The sentencing project.* New York: New Press.

McCarthy, J. D., & Hoge, D. R. (1987). The social construction of school punishment: Racial disadvantage out of the universalistic process. *Social Forces, 65*, 1101–1120.

McCormick, J. (2000). Aesthetic safety zones: Surveillance and sanctuary in poetry by young women. In L. Weis & M. Fine (Eds.), *Construction sites: Excavating race, class, and gender among urban youth* (pp. 180–195). New York: Teachers College Press.

McNeil, L. (2000). *Contradictions of school reform: Educational costs of standardized testing.* New York: Routledge.

Murray, C. (1984). *Losing ground: American social policy, 1950–1980.* New York: Basic Books.

Parenti, C. (2000). *Lockdown America: Police and prisons in the age of crisis.* New York: Verso.

Poe-Yamagata, E., & Jones, M. (2000, October). *And justice for some.* Building Blocks for Youth Initiative. Washington, DC: Justice Policy Institute.

Sassen, S. (1998). *Globalization and its discontents.* New York: New Press.

Sassen, S. (2001). *The global city: New York, London, Tokyo* (2nd Ed.). Princeton, NJ: Princeton University Press.

Skiba, R., Michael, R., & Nardo, A. C. (2000, June). *The color of discipline: Sources of racial and gender disproportionality in school punishment* (Report No. SR1). Research Policy Report.

Tonry, M. (1999, October). Why are U.S. Incarceration rates so high? *Crime and Delinquency, 45*(4).

Wacquant, L. (2001). Deadly symbiosis: When ghetto and prison meet and mesh. *Punishment and Society, 3*(1), 95–134.

Wacquant, L. (2002, January/February). From slavery to mass incarceration: Rethinking the "race question" in the United States. *The New Left Review, 13*, 41–60.

Willis, P. (1977). *Learning to labour: How working class kids get working class jobs.* New York: Columbia University Press.

Wilson, W. J. (1996). *When work disappears: The world of the new urban poor.* New York: Knopf Books.

Zimring, F. (2001, March). The new politics of criminal justice: Of "three strikes," truth in sentencing, and Megan's Laws. *Perspectives on Crime and Justice: 1999–2000 Lecture Series.* NCJ 184245. Washington, DC: National Institute of Justice.

CHAPTER 9

Thinking About the Cultural Studies of Education in a Time of Recession

Learning to Labor *and the Work of Aesthetics in Modern Life*

CAMERON McCARTHY

> What strikes me is the fact that in our society, art has become
> something which is related only to objects and not to individuals
> or to life. . . . But couldn't everyone's life become a work of art?
> (Michel Foucault, quoted in Sarup, 1996, p. 87)

In this essay I call attention to a specific thematic dimension of the concep-
tualization of work and reproduction in modern life raised (but also
repressed) in Paul Willis's germinal ethnography *Learning to Labor,* (first
published as *Learning to Labour,* 1977) and in the cultural studies of education research literature that Willis's now legendary volume precipitated.
This aspect of work and reproduction concerns the role of the imagination
and aesthetics in critical cultural and economic processes central to modern
existence: that is, the mobilization and organization of capitalism and its
late-20th century and new millennial global transformations, as well as the
historically variable counterhegemonic response of the working-class poor
of both the metropole and the periphery to these developments. This essay
engages Willis's *Learning to Labor* as a critical point of departure for
thinking about the work of aesthetics in the fates and fortunes of the
marginalized proletariat in the peripheries of the First and the Third

Worlds.

Indeed, nowadays, when I think of *Learning to Labor*, I cannot help thinking of the rising tide of denunciations of cultural studies both from the Left and the Right, particularly Judith Williamson's extraordinarily blunt rejection of "Left-wing academics picking out strands of subversion in every piece of pop culture from Street Style to Soap Opera" (Williamson, 1986, pp. 14–15). Of course, the radical academic world is saturated with bad-faith punditry, soothsaying, and the empiricist declarations of Cassandras. As, perhaps, a compensatory reflex, we are genre prone. No sooner is a new theoretical line of inquiry announced than a whole new congregation gathers, a field of affiliation is declared, even as its enemies, theorists on the other side, gather, lying in wait in the shadows. Well, the end is always near, at the closest "post." Reading/writing/researching radicals live precarious lives, and so forth. But there is something nagging in Williamson's statement; it concerns the attack on texts and textualism, the opposition of that fatal couplet "text" versus "experience," and the attendant cynicism about the politics of everyday life and popular investments in taste and style. These are all issues that are raised directly or obliquely in Willis's work, particularly his recent *The Ethnographic Imagination* (2000).

It is therefore not my purpose to defend cultural studies on these grounds here. I do, however, want to take up the matter of aesthetics, not simply in terms of the narrow scenario of what its conceptual status or place might be vis-à-vis the economic and so forth. Neither, certainly, am I speaking of aesthetics as elite or maverick practices of creativity, refinement, or taste. What I wish to discuss is something else altogether. I want to talk about a central energy in modern life associated with the production, reception, and circulation of representations and images and the diffusion of knowledge and information. I want to talk about the rising importance of the materiality of immateriality. I want to speak about the centrality rather than marginality of the diffusion of practices of self–fashioning in life sustaining processes and objectives. I am speaking about the work of the imagination in ordinary life. Here imaginary practices are understood as social practices of meaning production in the context of modern life, defined as it is by time–space compression, disembeddedness, disjunctures, and radical flows consequent upon the intensification of globalization and the separation of culture from place (Giddens, 1990). The idea here is to link the aesthetics of existence to economy and power—to think of these dynamics, in the context of globalization, as coarticulated. I want to maintain that the worlds of the metonymic Pakis, Jamaicans, and the Lads—the working-class youth protagonists of *Learning to Labor*—are deeply related, integrated into the processes of globalization in which the work of the imagination plays a pivotal role, co-coordinating the fragments of the materials of everyday life, even in their industrial strength. I want to extend the discussion of aesthetics to speak of an anthropology of politics, pulling the whole ascetic firmament of Marxist politics down to the everyday.

Customarily, cultural studies and neo-Marxist scholars of education writing on urban life have tended to place aesthetics on the boundaries of critical practices, treating aesthetics as a surplus set of practices that could only be made fully relevant when added on to a more concentrated attention to economy and politics. I argue here against this tradition. Instead, I maintain that aesthetic practices now underwrite the fiber of everyday modern life. As Arjun Appadurai (1996) usefully pointed out in *Modernity at Large*, aesthetic practices are no longer to be simply understood as the practices exclusive to the artist, a maverick citizen creating images about the past, present, and the future of human existence. Rather, aesthetic practices are linked to the work of the imagination of ordinary people and connected even more earnestly to the work of capitalism and its organization and reorganization on a global scale. Contrary to the neo-Marxist thinking, aesthetic practices are at the epicenter of lived experience and commodified and institutional processes of modern societies. These practices of performing and shaping self and community are now broadly diffused throughout society. These practices provide the language of cultural translation and revivification of identities. And they cultivate, provoke, and register the turbulent rearticulation of difference and multiplicity in our age. Our lives are now (self-)governed in concert with massive processes of textual production and simulation associated with media and educational systems and other institutional apparatuses of the state and global capital. Theses processes work in tandem to produce technologies of truth and identification that serve to transform concrete individuals into cultural citizens whose lines of loyalty and affiliation now exceed the territory and social geography of the nation-state (Miller, 1998).

As C. L. R. James (1993) alerted us in *American Civilization*, popular aesthetic practices constitute a great window on contemporary life, revealing central societal contradictions, tensions, and discontinuities between the individual and community:

> To put it more harshly still, it is in the serious study of, above all, Charles Chaplin, Dick Tracy, Gasoline Alley, James Cagney, Edward G. Robinson, Rita Hayworth, Humphrey Bogart, genuinely popular novels like those of Frank Yerby (*Foxes of Harrow, The Golden Hawk, The Vixen, Pride's Castle*), men like David Selsnick, Cecil deMille, and Henry Luce, that you find the clearest ideological

expression of the sentiments and deepest feelings of the American people and a great window into the future of the modern world. This insight is *not* to be found in the works of T. S. Eliot, of Hemingway, of Joyce, of famous directors like John Ford or Rene Clair. (James, 1993, p. 119)

In the 20th century, modern aesthetic practices received their full amplification in popular forms of life—particularly in the emergence of television, film, radio, newspaper, and new genres of music like jazz—and not so much in the classical or establishment cultures that are now valorized in the selective tradition that informs the organization of aesthetic knowledge in schooling. Of course, postcolonial intellectuals have been making this argument for sometime. This, after all, was the burden of the Latin American and Caribbean writers' forum of Intellectual and Cultural Workers (George Lamming, Gabriel Garcia Marquez, and others) who had very publicly opposed the Reagan government invasion of Grenada in 1983. They insisted, as did Arnaldo Roche-Rabell of Puerto Rico, that aesthetics were imbricated in economy and politics and that artistic militancy is critical to production of democracy (Roche-Rabell, 1996). This, too, is the critique of Reinaldo Arenas of the excesses of communist government in Cuba in the film *Before the Night Falls* (2000). The work of aesthetics is crucial to any formula for democratic transformation, as Derek Walcott maintains in "What the Twilight Says" (1970).

I want to speak on these matters, not from the heroic status and point of view of the Lads, but from the perspective of the, perhaps, antiheroic, postcolonial subjects—the West Indians and Asians, the metonymic "Pakis" and "Jamaicans," the petrified Third World spectators of metropolitan subcultural lore—witnesses to the birthing of the White working class into the modern industrial society as bricoleurs, flaneurs, and the like.

First, I want to discuss the entanglement of aesthetic discourses in the diffusion of modernization and developmentalism to the Third World. Second, I want to point as well to the deepening role of aesthetics in the organization of capitalism in the new millennium in which we live. Third, I discuss briefly the crisis of language that the aestheticization of everyday life has precipitated in neo-Marxist efforts to grasp the central dynamics of contemporary societies. The latter development has led to a depreciation of the value and insightfulness of neo-Marxist analysis in our time. We live in an era in which old metaphors associated with Marxism—concepts such as "class," "economy," "state," "production," "reproduction," "resistance," "the labor/capital contradiction," "reality" and "fiction," "ideology" versus "truth," "materiality" and "immateriality"—are being worn down by the transformations of the past decades in which the saturation of economic and political practices in aesthetic mediations has proceeded full pace (Klein, 2000). Let me now turn to a discussion of the historical context of the integration of aesthetics into commerce.

The Marriage of Aesthetics and Economy

The long shadow of the integration of aesthetics and economics in the elaboration of the capitalist order can be tracked back to before the turn of the 20th century in the production of new markets for the ever-expanding range of capitalist goods and services and the generation of consumer durables. These "luxuries" of personal style were in their everyday utility, if not necessity, expanding middle-class consumption patterns to the working class. A growing market in cheap *luxury* items allowed others (the lower and working classes) to purchase the symbolic accoutrements of status (Ewen, 1988, p. 59). Within this set of developments, deepening patterns of aestheticization of advertising, the imbuement of commercial products with sensuality, flair, and feeling, and so forth generated a leveling effect in the processes of class representation and helped to transform agrarian and immigrant actors into the new acquisitive urban subjects. The working class could try on the uniforms of the upper classes, explore their ways of life through the illumination of bric-a-brac, and, through consumer credit and loans, acquire the imitation furniture, jewelry, and items of leisure that mirrored aristocratic existence. Aesthetic practices integrated into economic form were now performing the pedagogy of molding the new subjectivities of the modern age—less in collision with capital in the classical 19th-century sense identified by Friedrich Engels in *The Condition of the Working Class in England* (1845/1987) but more in the besotted communion with the spectacular array of consumer products capitalism had strewn in their wake. "Progress," the narrative of one's life trajectories and imagined futures of linear accumulation, would now be marked by the range and capacity of one's consumption. To be a true citizen in the modern society was to be a dedicated consumer.

This model of progress, proletarianized and internationalized by the middle of the 20th century, would be taken full scale to underdeveloped countries around the globe, embodied in Coke and Pepsi ads, the family-size Coca Cola drink, the cultural translation performed by the films, musicals, popular songs, and so on that entered the Third World through cinema houses, and especially radio and newspaper, cartoons, and the lure of the new sleek-looking surfaces of the consumer durables and household appliances. Here, retail and hire purchase practices of the lower orders summarized the needs of the masses for something more than material want. These practices of borrowing today and paying tomorrow underlined a fueled working-class interest in comparative affluence, taste, and leisure—a desire to expand and materialize freedom by codifying taste and style and by integrating the aesthetic and erotic, leisure and pleasure practices into their rigorously subordinated lives defined by industrial parks and in agrarian obligation.

Musicals such as *The King and I* (1956) and *The Sound of Music* (1965) and soap operas such as *Portia Faces Life* (a radio soap opera that was started in 1940s and later taken up for television broadcasting by CBS in the 1950s) offered aesthetic solutions to the problems of necessity and want in the Third World. These popular cultural productions propagated ideas such as the inviolability of contract and the value equivalence involved in the process of exchange of labor power for wages. They extended a shimmering imaginary plane of existence linking the metropolis to the periphery latent with needs and saturated with unfulfilled desires. These aesthetic works suggested that Third World life, linked to tradition and agrarian organization and imagination, was flawed, oppressive, backward (a neo-Marxist claim as well!). This type of enlightenment narrative was propagated, for example, in highly popularized musicals such as the *The King and I*. Circulated through radio and television, *The King and I* made popular the modernization dilemma of the old traditions of Siam (what is now Thailand) versus the suppressed wish fulfillment of Siam's people, particularly their capacity for individual action and choice. *The King and I* ultimately set the capriciousness of the absolutist state against the visions of constitutional democratic nation-state. The way out of cultural miasma and backwardness to enlightenment was provided in the person of an English schoolteacher, Anna, who would carry out the work of cultural incorporation and translation. The cultural and philosophical forms of modernization—the right to private property, the capacity of the workers to sell their labor power, and the deification of Western democratic traditions—are all underscored in this musical in which a half-naked king, with Anna's help, must reconstitute his relations to his subjects and retool himself as a comprador agent of capitalism's expansion in southeast Asia.

The aestheticization of the economic—capitalism with a human face—sold the Third World on the modernization theories of Western policy intellectuals such as Daniel Lerner, Harold Lasswell, and William W. Rustow. The "passing of traditional society," as Lerner (1958) called it, involved that fearful asymmetry of contractual agreement to exploitation and excavation of the resources of the native and her land, along with state-enforced guarantee of the privileged status of the right to private property that multinationals and mercantile local elites so intensely craved. The development gap between the Third World and the First could be jumped by the expansion of the consumerist culture of possessive individualism and the infrastructure of industrialized production to "overseas" territories. Just as new streets were being paved for industrialization by invitation in Puerto Rico and Barbados, the sweet middle-class life of the "Brady Bunch" and later the "Partridge Family" presented itself through television as the embodiment of the one and only true heaven, as the buoyant end game in the struggle for happiness (Lasch, 1991). Why couldn't a woman be more like a man (*My Fair Lady*, 1964)? Why couldn't we Third World Siams be more like the enlightened West?

It was, in part, this logic of modernization, the embeddedness of the developmentalist project, the dream of plenitude and progress, the work of the imagination of ordinary Third World people that delivered the Pakis and the Jamaicans to the land of the Lads in pursuit of the Holy Grail of the better life and the material rewards of capitalism. What we confront in the ocular opposition of the immigrant other to the Lads in *Learning to Labor* is this abridgement of a continuous line or movement of disembeddedness, displacement, and transformation in an imaginative and spatial geography that extends the aspirations of the Jamaicans, the West Indians, the Pakis, the Indians and Bangladeshis from the periphery to beachheads in Brixton and Manchester, and elsewhere in England. The full significance of what this movement would mean in the changing terms of globalization was indeed far more fully recognized in the popular films *The Full Monty* (1997) and *Billy Eliot* (2000). To understand these dynamics more clearly, we must now turn to a consideration of the role of aesthetics in everyday life.

Aesthetics and Everyday Life

The role of aesthetics in everyday life has deepened in the last few decades with the rising importance of computerization and media-driven technologies. The work of aesthetics is not simply now embodied in the selling of messages and images but in the very construction of products and constituencies of affiliation in the new millennium. It is that whole area of stylization of the self, self-regulation, surveillance, and the self-management of everyday life, that Foucault discusses in his *History of Sexuality* volumes. But the processes of aestheticization also reach deeper into the marketing and circulation of goods and services, the proliferation of labels and the redirection of difference and diversity towards the new vending machines of choice. As the author of *No Logo* (2000) Naomi Klein insisted, it is the aesthetics of entrepreneurial identities and labels, logos and brands, that has displaced the manufacture of products as the heart and soul of what makes post-Fordist capitalism tick:

> The astronomical growth in the wealth and cultural influence of multinational corporations over the last fifteen years can arguably be traced back to a single, seemingly innocuous idea developed by management theorists in the mid-1980s: that successful corporations must primarily produce brands, not products. (Klein, 2000, p. 3)

Everywhere, smart capital is running away from the materialization of dense product inventories, costly overheads, and static models of factory organization, and opting instead for the cultivation of new bonds of consumer affiliation and labeling, relying on the faithful consumer to spawn markets by parading the labels of branded distinction in their natural habitats. The consumer's body has become the canvas of commodity fetishism. And it is in this framework of cultural oversupply that the modern consumer tries on new identities and directs and redirects practices of self-correction and self-modulation. Transnational corporations such as Starbucks, Borders, and Nike now brand new ecumenical communities with their labels, like so many tattoos on the social/global body. And so, ethnic, class, and gendered communities are now coalescing around practices of consumption and patterns of taste rather than around production relations or ancestry, or geography, or biology (Bourdieu, 1984; Dolby, 2001). The language of the new aesthetically branded world now registers the new ecumenical orders of feeling and the organization of affect and taste. As Manuel Castells tells us in *The Rise of the Network Society* (2000), these ecumenical orders overlap with the traditional collectivities of class or race or gender, but in the most frenetic and unpredictable of ways. This new aestheticism has generated a new cannibalism as the modern actor seeks refuge in ever more savage intensities and hybridities. Attachments to subject positions are now more precariously saturated. The old authenticities of class and race rooted in place, ancestry, economy, and so forth have been swept away by the new developments associated with electronic mediation, mass migration, and the rapid movement of economic and cultural capital across borders.

This has meant, for example, the end of the auratic status of race. That is to say, for instance, that the notion of race as residing in origins or in "biological" or "cultural" unity has been broken, overwhelmed by the immense processes of hybridity unleashed in contemporary life. These processes of migration, electronic mediation, and globalization have had the effect of separating culture from place. Difference has therefore become an abstract value that can be dirempted from specific ("authentic") groups and settings in ways that combine and recombine, narrate and renarrate cultural forms and passionate attachments. For example, clothing designer magnates like Tommy Hilfiger, drawing on the critical disciplinary expertise in demography, ethnography, semiotics, social psychology, art, and design, now appropriate elements of, say, inner-city Hip Hop culture and style, reordering and infusing these styles into a broad-banded appeal to a new ecumenical community of hip youth from a wide array of class and ethnic backgrounds. In the process, Hilfiger shamelessly sells a version of the inner city back to the inner city itself. Aestheticization breaks down the symbolic realms of insulation separating Black youth from White ones and so forth, cracking the codes of youth desires and elaborating a new community of Pepsi drinkers, Gap hipsters, and Nike shoe devotees among a wide array of ethnic cross-dressers. These new ecumenical communities are themselves dynamic and unstable, constantly changing as new aesthetic resources, systems of ready-made representation, and over-the-counter personas can now be used to generate very new and different genres and lines of affiliation. We are living in a new context in which aestheticization as a strategy of existence has spread throughout the body politic. One in which the oblique powers of capital and the state work toward the reordering of identities, uprooting stabilities associated with the labor process as well as private and public spaces beyond the shop floor. Capitalists, and some right-wing strategists, may now understand these logics of multiplicity better than the Left, deploying multiculturalism and integrating difference into the division of labor and the labor process at warped speed and appropriating new sources of value from the Lads and their adversaries in new asymmetries and alliances of production and consumption. W. E. B. Dubois's psychological wage is now spread around the world, indexing ever new avenues of difference and intraclass subordination in the stratification of taste and culture among the lowest of the low. All of this has placed a special interpretive strain and test of relevance on the analytical powers of neo-Marxist scholarship in education.

Neo-Marxist Scholarship and the Shifting Terrain

This shifting terrain of identity and affiliation has overtaken neo-Marxist scholarship in education. Categories and metaphors that had been relied on in the past to unscramble social relations and dynamics now seem challenged by the new circumstances of contemporary education, work, and leisure. The formation of interests, distinctions, needs, and desires seems now to be so susceptible to an endless array of permutations. The framework of analysis that linked education to capitalist employers, to factories, to the nation-state, and so forth is no longer serviceable, as the coordination of economic and symbolic production is now rearticulated along multiple sites in a global process of marketing, branding, and outsourcing of goods and services. Much of the limitation of contemporary neo-Marxist discourses in addressing the dynamic movement of cultural and economic capital today has to do with a tendency toward a residual structuralist realism that both reifies and privileges notions of an authentic working class, a territorially bounded nation-state and an economy understood in terms of the language of commodity production and accumulation. What these theorists need to recognize, as Naomi Klein (2000) suggested, are the new trends that point to a deepening reorganization of capital. Within these developments, symbolic mobilization is now an ascendant practice. Capitalist industries are divesting in inventories of commodities and investing in cultivating label affiliation, brand loyalty, and esprit de corps among the consuming population. Style and taste are now driving the economic as ecumenical communities are fabricated in the uniforms of Nike or Gap or Hilfiger. It is the royal consumer whose newly dressed body serves as a mobile billboard for the corporate enterprise of Nike, Starbucks, Borders, Adidas, and others. The new consumer is the new citizen, whose aesthetics of existence are now ever more deeply imbricated in a universalization of the entrepreneurial spirit and the propagation of the redemptive neoliberal value of choice. Nowhere do we see this cultural morphing of capital and the citizen more than in schooling. Students now approach their school and university curricula as the savvy consumer shopping for courses. And courses are weighted by educational administrations on the basis of their "drawing power"—the numbers of enrollees per class (Miyoshi, 1998).

We have reached a stage in this new millennium where the old "conflict" versus "consensus" metaphors do not seem to apply. Instead of models based on conflict and resistance, social groups are being increasingly defined by overwhelming patterns of transnational hybridities, new forms of association and affiliation that seem to flash on the surface of life rather than to plunge deeper down into some neo-Marxist substructure. Paul Willis's nationally and geographically inscribed Lads are now being replaced by Jenny Kelly's Afro-Canadian youth, who are patching together their identities from the surfeit of signs and symbols crossing the border in the electronic relays of U.S. television, popular music and cyber culture (Kelly, 2003). Postapartheid South African youth now assign more value to markers of taste—Levi and Gap jeans, Nikes or Adidas, rap or rave—than ancestry and place in their elaboration of the new criteria of ethnic affiliation (Dolby, 2001). All these developments are turning the old materialism versus idealism debate on its head. It is the frenetic application of forms of existence, forms of life, the dynamic circulation of and strategic deployment of style, the application of social aesthetics that now governs political rationalities and corporate mobilization in our times. The new representational technologies are the centers of public instruction providing the forum for the work of the imagination of the great masses of the people to order their pasts and present and plot their futures. The massive work of textual production is a socially extended project producing the cultural citizen in the new international division of labor.

Conclusion

Ultimately, then, the issues I am exploring here go beyond a consideration of *Learning to Labor*, they reach out into a new field of questions. How should we understand the dynamics affecting the separation of culture from place in modern life? How do we understand the heightened and intensifying role of aesthetics practices in the everyday lives and fortunes of people? How can we intervene in the ever-changing present? Some of the answers to these questions lie at the frontera of a negotiation of neo-Gramscian and Foucauldian perspectives on the work of culture in modern life and the expanding networks of knowledge and power that circulate in the new information technologies and their central involvement in popular identity formation, agency, and transgression. Here, too, the narrow nationalistic project that has defined cultural studies to this date needs a retooling in postcolonialism and transnationalism to remind us that the everyday lives and fortunes of people in the metropolitan center are now fully articulated to the peripheries of the modern world—Kingston to Brixton, Lahore to Oldham, Kabul to New York. I am framing my responses this way because I think we are confronting the way in which neo-Marxist, even cultural Marxist, scholarship has looked at questions of culture and power: that is, within the fatal couplets of base/superstructure or production/consumption. Within the latter frame of reference, aesthetics of everyday life always seem to be linked to "consumption" understood as a crass, unthinking activity. And consumption seems always to be doing the work of dissipating the agency and emancipatory promise of the oppressed. Even when neo-Marxists theorized consumption through notions of lived and commodified culture emphasizing "resistance," that resistance always seemed marginal or a poor substitute or proxy for production-driven politics. This is in part why the perpetrators of 9/11 surprised both the Left and the Right, organizing beneath our noses and rearticulating the tools, symbols, and technologies of the everyday with devastating effect: Box cutters, fax machines, crop dusters, tap water, commercial flights, a pair of fundamentalist shoes, matches, all now harbor new terrors and uncertainties, as Greg Dimitriadis and I have argued elsewhere (Dimitriadis & McCarthy, 2002). It reminds me of having conducted a war of maneuver with the Barbados health care system regarding my father's health care by phone, e-mail, and letters. Here, deploying the politics of diplomacy within my large family in getting decent care for 86-year-old Dad enlarged both my sense of family and my opposition to the Barbados bureaucracy.

Marxists have always advanced notions of resistance to power, notions of transformation, that involve a bulldozing masculinist logic that targets the state, the shop floor, and the commanding heights of capital as the indisputable markers of radical action. This is a model of change that projects onto the working class a status of folk other, the noble savage of rebellious middle-class fantasies of capturing power as an object of repression and seizure. This formula of change read from the economy onto culture and subculture ignores the enormous transitional costs that will be borne by the working class within this transformative regime. This model of politics and change speaks the language of vanguardism and edicts, assigning to the subaltern a very limited degree of reflexivity and creativity. I am arguing instead for the vital need to anthropologize Marxist politics as C. L. R. James suggested in his book *American Civilization* (1993).

Thinking about power in these terms involves thinking about change within the terms of modulation, rearticulating and redirecting the terms of the center–periphery thesis that dominates neo-Marxist optics on social formation toward envisioning the materialization of new communities and investment in the work of the imagination, working with and against constraint, in the struggle for happiness. Ultimately, then, the pursuit of aesthetics of everyday life calls our attention to latent possibilities in modern social spaces and points to the negotiation of constraint in modern life. It calls attention to the enormous pedagogical role that can and must be undertaken in the domain of the popular arts and textual production and within the field of the active imagination of the broad masses of the people across the divide of center and periphery.

References

Appadurai, A. (1996). *Modernity at large: The cultural dimensions of globalization.* Minneapolis: University of Minnesota Press.

Bourdieu, P. (1984). *Distinction.* Cambridge, MA: Harvard University Press.

Castells, M. (2000). *The rise of the network society* (2nd ed.). Oxford: Blackwell.

Dimitriadis, G., & McCarthy, C. (2002). Urban renewal: Gordon Bennett's *Notes to Basquiat* (9/11). In G. Bennett (Ed.), *Notes to Basquiat* (pp. 1–4). Adelaide, Australia: Greenaway Art Gallery.

Dolby, N. (2001).*Constructing race: Youth, identity, and popular culture in South Africa.* Albany, NY: SUNY Press.

Engels, F. (1987). *The condition of the working class in England.* London: Penguin. (Original work published 1845).

Ewen, S. (1988). *All consuming images.* New York: Basic Books.

Giddens, A. (1990). *The consequences of modernity.* Cambridge, UK: Polity Press.

James, C. L. R. (1993). *American civilization.* London: Blackwell.

Kelly, J. (2003). *Borrowed identities.* New York: Peter Lang.

Klein, N. (2000). *No logo*. London: Flamingo.

Lasch, C. (1991). *The true and only heaven: Progress and its critics*. New York: W. W. Norton.

Lerner, D. (1958). *The passing of traditional society: Modernizing the Middle East*. New York: Free Press.

Miller, T. (1998). *Technologies of truth*. Minneapolis: University of Minnesota Press.

Miyoshi, M. (1998). "Globalization," culture and the university. In F. Jameson & M. Miyoshi (Eds.), *The cultures of globalization* (pp. 247–272). Durham, NC: Duke University.

Roche-Rabell, A. (1996). Under a total eclipse of the sun. In R. Hobbs (Ed.), *Arnaldo Roche-Rabell—The uncommonwealth* (p. 44). Seattle: University of Washington Press.

Sarup, M. (1996). *Identity, culture and the postmodern world*. Athens: University of Georgia Press.

Walcott, D. (1970). What the twilight says. In D. Walcott (Ed.), *Dream on Monkey Mountain and other plays* (pp. 3–40). New York: Farrar, Straus and Giroux.

Williamson, J. (1986, September). The problems of being popular. *New Socialist*, pp. 14–15.

Willis, P. (1977). *Learning to labour*. Westmead: Saxon House.

Willis, P. (2000). *The ethnographic imagination*. Cambridge, UK: Polity Press.

Critical Ethnography, Culture, and Schooling:
Paul Willis reflects on *Learning to Labor*

CHAPTER 10

Twenty-Five Years On
Old Books, New Times

PAUL WILLIS

I owe many thanks to Nadine Dolby and Greg Dimitriadis, who spotted a couple of years ago the looming 25th anniversary of the publication of *Learning to Labor* and have put so much work, effort, and good will into organizing, editing, compiling, and publishing this excellent volume. Thank you! I cannot say that I had noticed the approach of this milestone[1] until Nadine sent me an email suggesting the possibility of the AERA panels. My immediate thought was, "Christ, we are ageing at the same pace, 25 years . . . what kind of an old codger does that make me?" But the idea was excellent. The panels gave me much food for thought, and I am delighted that this book sees the light of day with its many wonderful contributions from people whose work I have long admired or am happy to learn from now.

It has been something of a salutary experience, though, as well as a privilege, to focus on writing a response to the chapters of this volume and to try to survey 25 years of my own chaotic life as somehow "intellectual development." In a way, the book has led its own strange and often schizophrenic public life variously separate from my own private wanderings, which have included a long period away from academe in practical policy engagements (see Appendix). How could I make sense of the dizzying range of responses to the book over the last 25 years and relayed here now? What, anyway, was the purpose of such an exercise? In the event, rather than try to respond to individual positions or chapters, or to attempt thorough academic surveys (painstakingly accomplished any way in many of the chapters), or to attempt an implausible "developmental" periodization of my own life and times, I have plumbed for a very personal route of trying to reclaim, develop, and apply some of the themes and emphases of *Learning to Labor* that, at the risk of idiosyncracy and self-referentiality, seem to me as of most use for understanding the current conjuncture. In doing this I do not write within any one discipline—education, sociology, cultural studies, anthropology— but in a spirit of multi- or postdisciplinarity. This is essential, in my view, to the future of ethnography and its continued vigour. The journal, *Ethnography*,[2] that I jointly founded and jointly edit is also devoted to breaking down and transcending barriers between the disciplines, especially sociology and anthropology. It is focused on connecting and encouraging the work of ethnographers worldwide, no matter what their disciplinary homes.

Although I do not refer to them in detail, I have the chapters published here very much in my thoughts as I write, and have learned from them as well as finding constructive disagreements. Often, actually especially in disagreement, they have reminded me of what it is that I really want to communicate to a new generation of scholars. Nor do I pass up the opportunity of replying to critics more generally, not as a settling of accounts, names, chapters, verses, but in the spirit of more fully developing positions, which are of use, I hope, to future ethnographers. I have divided my comments into two basic sections; the first pursues a theoretical clarification of perspectives essential to the ethnographic enterprise, and the second is devoted to grappling with the complexities of the new situation, in many ways so profoundly changed since "back in the day" when I did the research for *Learning to Labor*.

I have not devoted a specific section to a discussion of the family of methods that constitute the practice of ethnography, but, in different ways, the whole piece is aimed at showing the irreplaceable importance of ethnography to understanding various dimensions of the new situation of crisis and epochal change effecting not only schooling but societies quite generally. Very much in mind I have the hope of encouraging researchers, Ph.D. students in particular from across the disciplines, to attempt the unnerving task of the ethnographic evocation of the experiences and cultures of others, so carrying on and enhancing a very important tradition. My comments are meant to give them heart and focus.

The Ethnographic Theoretical Sensibility

Cultures and Class: A Three-Stage Model

First of all, prefacing the complexity of the theoretical model I outline next, what I take from all of the chapters and very much roll forward from

Learning to Labor, what I ask all ethnographers to take renewed heart in, is the importance of the embattled term and concept of "culture." The more it is criticized, the more we need it. Why do we need this portmanteau term? Because it designates materially symbolic patterns and associated practices of human meaning making in context, which cannot be reduced to a reflex of something else—individual psychology, "discourses," or the economy. It is its own thing. In one way I am a simple empiricist: Write down what happens, take notes about what people do and say, how they use objects, artifacts, and symbolic forms in situ. Do not worry too much about the endless debates concerning ethnographic authority and the slippages of discursive meaning understood from an abstract post structuralism. Tell me something—I know all the method problems—tell me, tell your readers, something about the world. We launched the journal *Ethnography* in part addressed to an old-fashioned notion of ethnography and ethnographic articles having some empirical data in them, rather than endless methodological discussions where we learn everything about the sacred bourgeois formation of the writer and nothing about the profane formation of the subject. I seem to hear subjects screaming silently from the margins of the page, "but what the hell about us?"

Since I wrote *Learning to Labor*, the importance of culture, understood as just outlined, has become even more important. No sociological, anthropological, educational, or cultural studies research project, no policy initiative can make sense without asking in some form or another: "What is the culture of the people with whom we are dealing?" "How do they make sense?" "How does the world look to them?" "What do they make of us looking at them?" So, culture is worth recording in its own right but, *pace* my apparent empiricism, enjoys a further purchase because it also is a theoretical site. If your problem is understanding the relation of structure and agency; if your problem is understanding new formations of the social order; if you are looking at the new social functions of schooling; if you are looking at reproduction, how classes get replaced over time; if you are looking at the formation of labor power, how the subjective capacities of individuals are formed up and applied to productive processes: All these things require a cultural moment and analysis. An ethnographic sensibility implies a theoretical sensitivity to the importance of culture and human experience in human affairs.

At the heart of the concerns of *Learning to Labor* and coming rapidly up the agenda again and what I would like to focus on specifically here is the complex theoretical relations of culture(s) to social class (see Nadine Dolby & Greg Dimitriadis's Introduction, the chapter by Michael Apple, and Peter McLaren & Valerie Scatamburlo-D'Annibale's chapter). All the preceding questions conceal associated questions of class: How are those without power taken up into positions where power is exercised over them? How do social agents "see" and embody the structured world of power, both resisting and reproducing it in complex ways. For me, these things are achieved in and through the radical unprefigurability of culture, which, because things are not fixed, also gives an option for politics and hopes for making a difference, for making it different next time. So for me, questions of culture and class and politics are inextricably interwoven.

That is saying a lot. Let us pause a little, take a good breath, and step back to unravel this complexity somewhat.

What do I mean more precisely by class and how it relates to culture? The issues are complex and it is necessary to play a little game, a three-stage construction in our thought processes. This is not to attempt to paint a picture of the world more accurately, explaining its workings better than others. It is to try to provide a glimpse of the kind of underscaffolding that might make for the possibility of better three-dimensional picture painting. Patience is required; the early stages of the construction are meant to be tools for thinking, not mighty foundations for a better model. The whole construction only has a hope of being put to work usefully when all stages are finally put together in their unified, interconnected, and therefore continuously interdependent and self-modifying operations.

Stage 1. For analytic purchase, the first theoretical construction, it is important to be able to locate certain "basic" class elements as being, so to speak, "precultural"—again, it must be stressed, not as putative reflections of the way "things really are" but as a provisional analytic device in thought. How can we think of a "precultural" world? For a moment let us exercise our imaginations, hit an imaginary button to freeze the world so that its complex and dialectical relations of parts, normally in ceaseless and relativised motion, are stopped in our thoughts. Let us begin to unpack the complexity by blowing up the frozen elements in a splay diagram. What are the elements in our blown up diagram that relate to class? We are ignoring, for a moment, all the "color de rose" of the individual participants: the colors, smells, and passions of their everyday practices and cultures. In the gray and economistic world that remains, *class* for me designates the *positions* of agents in groups and their *relationships* to each other in systematic groups. What separates the groups is the possession of power and/or capital. Working class subjects are in subordinate *positions*: They have no power and capital. Their *relationships* with those who do have power are ones of domination through the exercise of this power: crudely, being told what to do—most notably and importantly in production (the subsumption of labor power in capitalist labor processes overseen by owners or managers) but also across a wide swathe of institutions, educational ones not least, where some form of "necessity" (direction) reigns. This "economistic" or "precultural" level of analysis is necessary, although actually quite limited in its own terms (most of the "moving" picture of human affairs has been frozen), in order to guard against *everything* being elided into the notion of culture and its horizontal differences. For "culture" to be effective as a notion, to give it some "go" and to show the *social* work that it accomplishes, there must be some things that are "not culture"; this is actually to show precisely the *autonomy* of culture, that is, *the manner of its autonomy with respect to something else.* Of course I know that "in reality" culture not only conditions economic relations but actually dynamically and transformingly embody them to bring about a fully human living system—what happens when we finally hit the button to start everything moving again. But unless there is a moment in our analysis that separates larger forces and relations we are in danger of presenting a depthless view of the world, which is not saved by a radical patina added to cultural descriptions rhetorically invoking emancipation and liberation.

Stage 2. Still the economistic level of analysis *is* only of limited value. So let us hit our imaginary button again, the second stage, to set the working class agents in motion, holding the rest of the picture still frozen. Let us restore the color and irreducible humanness to subordinated and dominated groups and focus on what is specific about the *cultural* elements of our splay diagram. What I want to focus on here is the specificity of culture as the active process of "meaning-making" of social agents, their "making sense." But of what? Of many things possibly, but I would argue in particular of their economic *positions* and *relationships.*[3] At least in part, cultural practices are about forging viable identities and strategies for human dignity, development, and becoming in relationship to and through their conditions of existence, in so doing at their own level making sense of economistic *positions* and *relations*[4] (so renewing them, changed, in their always already-ness). But these practices do not operate in the abstract or conjure up meanings from thin air. They need symbolic materials; the processes and activities do not proceed only as electric currents within individual brains. There is a production process at the cultural level, a *cultural production,*[5] that you could say is similar to material production in the labor process whereby humans engage in sensuous practices working on raw materials to produce new or refashioned things fit for useful human purpose. In this case the "products" are meanings and expressions useful in themselves but also, in one way or another, useful for making sense of economistic *positions* and *relations,* those things first isolated in our splay diagram.

In trying to really focus on this *cultural production* of our second stage, comprehend the way in which it relates to the still frozen elements of structure, I find it useful to deploy, again, the notion of *penetration.* The cultural practices of *cultural production*, I argue, function to "penetrate" or "see into" their conditions of existence (*positions* and *relations*) as part of the cultural calibration of how identities and actions can be best developed in their light, the constraints and enablements they supply. I take forward from *Learning to Labor*, therefore, the notion of "penetration," after all these years still troublesome for its masculinist associations but, for lack of alternative, used again here and in my recent *The Ethnographic Imagination*. Especially in relation to the difficulties of setting aside its sexist connotations, I am grateful for Madeleine Arnot's clear exposition and treatment of the term in her chapter. The term tries to capture, at one moment of analysis, the impetus to reveal the structural elements on which cultures depend, their conditions of existence. These are the "insights" of embedded folk knowledges, of common sense, of what I have sometimes referred to as "grounded aesthetics." Lois Weis refers to it in her chapter as "critical moments of critique," Michael Apple as "good sense." The results of the *work* of cultural production can never be prefigured in advance.

Here is the radical source of the creativity and unprefigurability of cultural practices and forms. It is agents, not academics, who make the *penetrations*. So academics can never come up with fully adequate "outside" explanations. It is not possible in advance and from "objectivist" outside surveys of, or armchair theories about, the "determination" of structural forces or cultural systems to deduce the forms of these *penetrations*, either of what or how (both very possibly pointing toward "undiscovered" aspects of structure) they focus on or the lived forms of their embodiments and practices. Here is indicated, again, of course, the supreme importance of "being there," of ethnographic witness and an associated theoretical sensibility. Cultural forms are of intense interest for the postdisciplinary ethnographer not because they preserve a set of quaint customs and hypostasised self-maintaining values to be recorded for ethological and historical record but because they contain a certain cruciality in context, embedded and lived insights with respect to their own conditions of existence. To be interested in an ethnographic account of subculture, for instance, is to make some kind of an epistemological break. If you believed some kinds of Marxism or post-structuralism, you would not bother going to the field. If you believed institutional, ideological accounts of what kids do, you would not bother going to the field. If you were interested in "discourses" and their internal instabilities, you would not go to the field. The whole point of doing so is to try to understand how particular subjects are making sense of themselves and their situations in ways that cannot be prefigured and that might "surprise" you.[6] And that making sense must be of something, not of the moon, not of the stars, but of their daily life and the conditions of existence of their daily life, of their own situation and its possibilities. This is the very business of ethnography for me. What sense is this culture making of its situation? What sense are you making of that sense making, recognizing that there is a possibility of a break, a difference, a form of local knowledge, created by actors upon conditions of course but, nevertheless, never reducible to what is supplied from outside, ideologically. Through the mediations of the counterschool culture, "the lads" of *Learning to Labor,* for instance, *penetrate* the individualism and meritocracy of the school with a group logic that shows that certification and testing will never lift the whole working class, only inflate the currency of qualifications and legitimize middle-class privilege. They frame the giving of their labor power in wearing circumstances without "career" illusions, judging the minimum that is necessary, so avoiding the double indignity of living their practical subordination twice, once really and again in ideology. Cultural and psychic capacities so released are made available for other uses: fun, diversion, "having a laff."

The "raw materials" for processes of *cultural production* and their attendant *penetrations* come in a wide variety of forms, plastic, oral, textual, musical, and from a wide variety of sources, historical and contemporary, local and mediated, commoditized and non-commoditized. The textual "treasure troves" of history should not be underestimated, nor the funds of oral history and advice passed on from elders. Ideological accounts and texts also play a variable part. Many of the symbolic resources used in cultural production have not been named yet by social science classification but are the interstitial stuff of ethnographic accounts of real lives in progress. But the particular traditions and continuities provided by social inheritances in the well-trodden classifications of sex, gender, race, ethnicity, and age are of the most particular importance. They both organize other kinds of symbolic material and supply their own symbolic meanings.[7] Because they are subject to the work of *cultural production,* all of these resources can be made into new shapes and put into new articulations producing new hybrid forms. Again it is a supremely ethnographic question to ask how resources are combined, through what practices, for what purposes.

Stage 3. Let us come to the third and final stage of our mental constructions, hitting the button again to put structure and culture in dynamic and connected motion again. A further crucial point about the cultural level for me is that processes of "making sense" of structural location not only "reveal" aspects of them but also act to reproduce them in supplying the living, moving, embodied forms through which they (*positions* and *relations* structured according to power) are maintained and reproduced. In the case of "the lads," for instance, the forms in which their very penetrations were made also prepared them, ironically, for insertion into the lower orders of the economic structure. Although highly relevant in opposing and penetrating the demands of the school, the antimental animus of the counterschool culture also becomes a kind of second nature for "the lads" that continues to orient bodily style, attitudes, and values during the transition from school to work and long after. This pattern impels them toward a certain kind of culturally mediated and experiential form of meaning making throughout their lives. The danger is that this antimental attitude leads to the whole world being divided into two—the mental and the manual. It makes all jobs involving mental work, now and for the future, seem to be simply boring paperwork—"Who wants to spend their day pushing paper around?" This makes hope for a "second-chance" return to higher education much more difficult and unlikely. The lads' antimentalism reconciles them and those like them to manual work and often to job hopping between dead-end jobs—now interspersed with long spells of unemployment, or even permanent unemployment—for the rest of their lives.

Although the "precultural" relations of power may be profoundly modified by their cultural embodiment, they continue in some form within basic limits set by the necessary maintenance of basic *positions* and *relations*. They live again to structure the next round of human "meaning-making" which in turn helps to reproduce structural relations and positions, and so on and so on.[8] It is in this continuous dialectic of renewal and the reformation of the old (tout ça change, tout c'est la même chose) that social structures should be understood from an ethnographic point of view, leaving far behind the static "economistic" stage with which we started.[9] Key ethnographic questions, therefore, concern not only how far cultural practices "make sense" of structural location but also how far these same practices ironically contribute toward the maintenance through time of those very power relations and interests. These questions also raise in their train political questions of the broadest hue: In future circles of these mutual relations, how might the balance be switched more to the advantage of the dominated, and under what conditions might the *penetrations* of cultural production be turned into outright political opposition and radical interruption of the reproduction of inherited structural relations?

Theoretical Integrity in a Postdisciplinary World

Above all other methodologies, ethnography invites in a postdisciplinary perspective. Ethnographic data needs a dialectical relation to theory, broadly considered, in order to bring out its sinews in relation to urgent issues and nitty-gritty questions. We should be eclectic in considering the possible relevance of all theories. But even in a postdisciplinary world not *all* theories are equal with respect to the tasks and dilemmas of ethnography. Beware of ethnographers who never met a theory they did not like! What I want to say about *penetrations* and culture is not ecumenical, not infinitely plastic. There are positions, in my view, that are not compatible with an ethnographic view of culture as meaning making from below. I often feel that *Learning to Labor* and my work generally are pushed around rather too much, considered without respect to its context and ends, unfairly critiqued for not doing, and sometimes strangely praised for doing, what it cannot do and does not attempt.

This not the same thing as asking for disciplinary consistency. Often the same issues and difficulties are approached in similar or usefully complementary ways from quite different disciplines; often within the same discipline can be deeply contradictory perspectives. Perhaps ethnographic practice will lead the way to new formations of intellectual practice focused on coherency of approach, explanation, and object, rather than academic schools.

My position is that, in general, ethnography needs *generative* not outside explanatory theory (see Michael Apple's chapter). The tiresome debates between the "culturalists" and the "structuralists," between so-called populists and political economists, pivot not on whether the former are without theory but on the differences in type between their theories, implicit or explicit. Although I see it as important to include structural factors, along the lines just outlined, there is nevertheless a line of radical indeterminacy necessary to ethnographic perspectives. In ever-decreasing circles, structural and structuralist theoretical social scientists of one kind or another run themselves ragged trying to track down cascading chains of determination to explain the relations of all levels, often bracketing out all possibility of creativity at the "lowest" levels of their models. In so doing they produce, knowingly or not, "objectivist" and "outside" accounts, because any recognition by them of an indeterminate subjective element allowing elements of agentive choice, except as an illusion to be "explained," would defeat the purpose of prediction and explanation. Ethnography and qualitative work then become simply a hunt for exemplifications of what it has already been decided should be there, no "surprises." In my view, some theoretical appreciation of a few simple and open-ended *generative* mechanisms (creativity, penetration, reproduction) implanted, not in the analyst's head but in the "real" world, repeating over and over for different groups with different although not unpatterned outcomes, is enough to encompass myriads of observable results that madden the objectivists to further theoretical involutions but that lead the ethnographer out to the field to be "surprised."

What I am arguing is a severe qualification on some Marxist notions of ideology, which see meaning as coming from outside to "interpellate" their subjectivity. My position almost inverts aspects of such Marxism. If you like, ideology can also flow in the other direction, with subjugated subjects and positions of subjugation enjoying epistemological resources, through their cultural forms, to seek contradictions in ideology or to retell its stories in somewhat different ways from a subordinate interest and point of view.

What I am arguing is also not compatible with many versions of post-structuralism. As Madeleine Arnot's chapter points out so deftly and as I have learned from her, it is interesting to note that in some ways *Learning to Labor* shares with poststructuralism, almost precursively, some interests in the workings and reworkings of symbolic articulations (see next section also). But for me they are produced in living and active ways rather than internally and textually. Ethnography is about observing the use of objects and artifacts and the conjunctions of discourses and being "surprised" about their new articulations, not in textual forms but as they are worked on, used, shaken and stirred for purpose in living ways through practices on the profane grounds of history. Intersections, reversals, unexpected combinations, repositioning within unlikely context, inappropriate exaggerations in inappropriate contexts, reversals in polarity, monitoring others for affects of enacting particular discourses and their recombinations and reordering in that light—all these practice-based workings of discourses are the stuff of ethnography and can yield contents, meanings, ideas of difference just hanging in the air that exploit the always slipping, never properly to be known relations between signifier and signified. Meanings so produced are not assimilable back to relations of dominance or the contents and "subject positions" of any one discourse "structured in dominance." Here is perhaps an unlikely field of cooperation between "humanist" ethnographic practices and "antihumanist" poststructuralisms. But the ethnography must keep paramount the practices of *cultural production* in concrete situated context. Practice bends all kinds of symbolic resources, recalcitrant as they may be and following whatever internal "grammars," to perform not their own internal scripts but some kind of referentiality in context as use for social purpose. Isolated discourses considered in the abstract, even if they are considered in hybrid relations, always have a dominant reference, implicit collusions with the mental/manual divide rendering as mental constructions and representations what are crucial conjunctions where it is practice that makes the difference for subordinated groups. In the end, ethnography is concerned with acting subjects and their "surprises"; otherwise, everything could be read out from discursive forms. Without an ethnographic anchor, poststructuralism can advocate a diversity and a creativity altogether without a subject. I am absolutely for showing the complexity and variability of the subject with respect to the forming up of symbolic systems, but, nevertheless, I still posit some kind of social subject formed enough to act and to have a hand in shaping their own culture.

Of course, the trump card of poststructuralism is its critique of essentialism. Humanist positions and perhaps especially ethnographic writings are seen as assuming, in one way or another, that meanings and senses of the self, self-identities, arise "expressively" and automatically from centered human beings. Although accepting the strictures against essentialism, I do not accept that ethnographic approaches must automatically fall prey to them. Indeed, against the poststructuralists, it could be argued that they can fall prey, in their turn, to a discursive essentialism where meaning is reduced to the internal operations and slippages of symbolic systems, at best mutely "performed," rather than arising from their articulations with context and practice, often utterly changing the import of their internal codes. Discursive approaches attempt to locate "genes" of information in symbolic forms, but they are as far off as genetic biology is from producing or comprehending the flows of human life and living human beings as they commit the flat packs of genetic information to the sensuous concourses and confluences of material life, profane, lived, real.

My position is simply that we do not need to go to the internal relations of the arbitrary signifiers of discourse to confound a presocial scientific essentialism. The argument about the *penetrations* of cultural forms is not that they come from fully formed preexisting unified subjects, making individual cognitions directly intended to reveal their conditions of existence. *Penetrations* come about almost randomly in the profane, corporeal, and un-prefigurable operations of cultural forms as they reconnoiter the land in a de facto kind of way, scraping it in the pursuit of their own fullest development in their own terms and for their own potentials and objectives. "Identities" do not predate this but are formed and re-formed in practice. The ways in which structural positionality is *penetrated*, explored, exposed, by "the lads" in *Learning to Labor* do not constitute the direct purpose or function of the counterculture, nor are they the referents of the discourses through which it works. Very often, working-class cultural forms expose aspects of social structure "unconsciously." Because of the subordinated historic positions and relations that working-class agents occupy, they cannot call forth their own necessary and self-determined "pure," "class-expressive" culture. They work on and through a variety of discourses and "found" symbolic resources, exposing in them *through practice* surprising potentials, previously unimagined "double edges," meanings never meant to be there and certainly not marked through like writing in seaside candy rock "working-class culture" (see endnote 5). In surviving and working through, making the best of, imposed conditions, living cultures expose aspects of social structure basically eccentrically and indirectly, almost accidentally. The immediate objectives of "the lads," for instance, is not to further the class struggle but to pursue fun, diversion, "the laff," and "having a go" at disliked figures or restrictive aspects of the specific and concrete regime of the school as it faces them. They are not trying to be good class warriors; they are trying to be good "lads." In pursuit of that some sort of "lived penetrations" of individualism and meritocracy and the nature of labor, power and laboring under capitalism are accomplished, but these are still only *cultural* revelations. They are not verbally articulated and have to be analyzed almost as the hidden premises on which cultures depend, unconscious assumptions that their members make about how the world works as far as they are concerned. *Penetrations* need a whole other stage of decreasing likely political and intellectual work and the mediations and preconditionality of a working class political party in order to become *political* entities (a gap in the otherwise excellent commentary in the chapter by Peter McLaren & Valerie Scatamburlo-D'Annibale).

All that said, it is absolutely part of my argument that relevant and socially generative *penetration*s, once formed by whatever hidden process of logic, help to determine the vivacity and longevity of cultures and are extended, continuously "reselected" if you like, in their operations for reasons quite different from the randomness of their causation. They socially "mark" a culture as producing a social as well as a cultural effectivity, helping them thereby to make better "sense"—in the way of the viability of identities and practices, freeing up psychic and real space—than other available cultural or official options. This "marking" also makes them more likely to be pitched into social antagonisms and is also fuel for negative stereotyping and social prejudice against them. Again, though, it is important to emphasize that this is a social "marking," not a Marxist or pure class marking, not a branding (as some have taken me as saying) as "working-class hero culture." A working-class hero may well be something to be, but it is an essentialist construction of discourse not one of ethnographic presentation and analysis. If *penetrations* were indeed straight and true then we would not be condemned to the parochial analysis of ironic reproductions. We could proceed straight to emancipation.

There is a further antiecumene point with respect to poststructuralist and postmodernist positions on methodology and "reflexivity." The formulations and prescriptions I am giving now require some responsibility to be taken on by the analyst, a responsibility to undertake an interpretative stage for which all parties to the fieldwork relationship are not equally prepared. Against fully reflexive positions I argue that fieldwork relationships are necessarily asymmetric and that the responsible ethical and intellectual recognition and response to this should be not a faux equalitarianism but a responsible working through of the advantages, training, and wider perspectives that the analyst brings. For me, this responsibility entails some degree of the provisional adoption of an epistemological realism in portraying how cultures are materially placed (stage one of my construction). What are the conditions of existence on which cultures depend and that they are attempting to *penetrate*? What external ideologies are being *penetrated*? If you go wholly down the self-reflexive road, if you go down a complete dialogical relativism in methodology—everybody's account is equal—you cannot generate such contextual accounts of culture. Every form would be equal, every text equal. You would not be able to indicate which are *penetrations*, which are *reproductions*, and you would not be able to identify which of the governing conditions of existence in a particular area are important for those *penetrations* and *reproductions*.

This is not to argue against reflexivity as a theoretical and political self-consciousness. We must always engage "points of view" on our own "points of view," be aware that collected data and associated theoretical advances are specific outcomes of our research questions and starting out theoretical orientations. Different research questions and different theoretical orientations would produce different analyses and findings. This is reflexivity not as a personal confession but as the awareness of the productivity of our research questions and theoretical resources. It is a quality of "rich" ethnographic texts, though, that they offer and contain capaciousness, reflecting the indeterminacy of their cultural subject matter. They present forms of life, "unnecessary" detail and contexts beyond what is relevant to any particular theory about them, so allowing other or even contradictory theories to utilize their data. This is a further reminder that we are not observing the world directly but in a particular universe of concern. The researcher is situated in context just as surely as are the agents they researchers observe.

Gender

Gender relations and associated symbolic meanings and practices are crucial to the full understanding of any cultural form. In terms of the articulation of symbolic systems, the shared concerns of ethnographic and poststructuralist perspectives, perhaps the two most important systems, with race/ethnicity a close third, to be explored for the specific manner of their interrelations are those of gender and class. The ways in which gender relations, the male/female division, map on to other kinds of divisions are at the heart of *Learning to Labor*. I did think, 25 years ago, that this was perhaps one of the main "scientific" findings of the book, that gender categories overlaid and changed the meaning of capitalist categories, particularly the mental/manual divide, and that the latter, in turn, conditioned the meanings of gender forms. This was, if you like, again, a very early poststructuralism in precisely arguing, against subsequent major misunderstandings of the book, that this form of working class culture was not inevitable and arising in some essential way from the "nature" or genetic culture of those working-class lads, but that it was precisely a construct, a particular form of masculinity in relation to a particular division of labor and in relation to a particular mental/manual division and in relation to a particular state formation at a particular time. Of course, where I part company from post-structuralism, these articulations did not take place in the abstract or from an internal discursive causation or motor. Masculinity was mobilized in a class context because of the work it could accomplish for "the lads" in relation to the urgent issues facing them as they saw them. Symbolic structures of masculinity help to embody and give an extra force to their school resistance. Masculinity gives them an axis of power over women, but it also gives them a realistic basis for feeling at least some ambiguous superiority over other less successful males, such as teachers and "ear'oles" (conformists). This response has a definite logic and is effective against the attempted domination of the school, and it gives alternative nonmental grounds for valuing the self and a whole solid, sometimes formidable, presence to resist belittling. But just as practice in context precedes the articulations of gender and class, so real social effects follow in train. As I argue in *Learning to Labor,* once formed, "hard" or "tough" masculine identities and the patterning of social relations that follow prove highly inflexible, intractable, and durable (see Lois Weis's chapter). Masculinity and its reflexes henceforth help to organize the same repertoire of defensive/offensive responses no matter what the situation. Furthermore, the antimentalism generated in the school and the masculinity of the lads become intertwined with their sense of themselves and their own vital powers. For "the lads," a manual way of acting in the world is a manly way, whereas a mental way is effeminate. These gendered associations reinforce and lock each other, producing a disposition and sensibility that may, quite literally, last a lifetime. In a final sealing of their subordinate fate, mental work becomes not only pointless "paper pushing" but also "sissy" work for "the lads." Even higher paid mental work is considered "sissy" from "the lads'" point of view. Exhausting, exploited, and increasingly low paid, manual work can somehow be seen in a masculine register, which prevents its true brutality from showing through.

It is still the case that students are forced into the unnatural atmospherics of the school, which pressure cooks together different social and symbolic relations regardless of how individuals are supposed to survive psychically, although through their very suffering gathering symbolic resources around them in order to build some kind of viable cultural identity, not least in gender terms and as bulletproof as possible—storing up particular trouble for working-class males mismatched for available jobs (see the chapter by Jane Kenway & Anna Kraack). But none of this is ordered in the genes or in the lap of the historical or economic gods. In different circumstances, all of these articulations could be ordered differently. That opens up a contingent cultural politics.

So, it was and still is a bit surprising and disappointing to be attacked so comprehensively by some feminists (for details, see Nadine Dolby & Greg Dimitriadis's Introduction and Madeleine Arnot's chapter). Of course, they have attacked what they see as uncritical reproduction of the insulting terms and behavior of "the lads" as well as or as part of an attack on my supposed essentialism. I accept that I could have shown more reflexivity in how sexist behaviors were presented in the book, but my point here is that the analysis was, overall, deeply gendered, especially for a class-based treatment of social relations. I am not trying to award myself full retrospective feminist credentials. I reproduced sexist terms too unconsciously and I think it is probably right that I "discovered" (was "surprised" by) a sexed class on the ethnographic way to trying to understand more fully, more humanistically, the brutality of capitalist relations. My object was to try to understand how capitalism works at a human level, how male labor power was inserted into factory production in concrete detail under the economic conditions and social relations prevailing then. But along the way, responding to the data and in order to get a more robust analysis, I took up seriously the whole question of the symbolic articulations of gender relations. In this the book foresaw and perhaps in a small way helped to inititiate the academic field of masculinity studies. I welcome that with one important caveat. The whole point of my analysis in Learning to Labor was to highlight the articulation of gender forms to other forms, not least to class, the mental/manual divide, and the institution of the school. It seems to me that it might become a blind alley to look at masculinity only for its own sake. Although floated off into a separate academic realm, masculinities cannot be seen as making themselves in a vacuum. They form always in some institutional, class, and power context and in relation to other discourses and symbolic resources. So, if you like, the gender dimension needs to come on home, back to structured contexts and its articulations with other kinds of symbolic relations in order to really make progress. Not least, as we see a resurgence of interest in class analysis it is vital for a full ethnographic understanding and presentation to see class categories as always inseparably intertwined with and conditioned by gender and that gender, in turn, is profoundly shaped by class.

Culture and Schooling in the 21st Century: New Times

As all the chapters of this volume evidence, things have certainly changed in the United Kingdom, the United States, and worldwide since Learning to Labor was published. The papers in this volume demonstrate a whole host of changes very clearly. Perhaps the most dramatic change has been in the material conditions of the working class (see particularly the chapters by Jane Kenway & Anna Kraack, and Kathleen Nolan & Jean Anyon). Within the so-called "core" countries there has been a deep and profound worsening of their economic position. It is perfectly possible that I caught "the lads" at the last gasp of a certain kind of real, if always subordinated, working-class power and celebration in England; almost from the moment the book was published, the conditions got worse. In the late 1970s and early 1980s the United Kingdom became the first industrialized country to experience massive losses of the manual industrial work that had previously been available to the working classes. This trend is now firmly established across the old industrialized world. In the United Kingdom over half of the manufacturing jobs that existed in the 1970s have been destroyed, with a slightly larger reduction in related trade union membership. At the same time, there has been a virtually epochal restructuring of the kind of work available. Taken together, the new customer service call centers and the hotel and catering industries now employ more than double the number of workers as the old "smokestack" industries—cars, ship building, steel, engineering, coal mining.

The whole working class has been badly affected by the diminution in both the quality and quantity of jobs available, especially young people, older workers, and ethnic minorities. Perhaps especially in the United States, where the minorities now make the majority of the working class in some major cities, race stereotyping and prejudice increase the likelihood of economic exclusion for Black and Latino groups as well as adding extra barbs of stigma to the condition of unemployment. From the point of view of the working class and from all its age and ethnic constituencies, work opportunities have shifted away from relatively abundant, well to reasonably paid skilled or semiskilled industrial work, to much lower paid service and out-of-reach white-collar work. For reasons of culture and disposition only too well analyzed in *Learning to Labor*, the new high-tech jobs and the higher level training and educational programs designed to fill them are irrelevant to most of the displaced and to be displaced manual industrial workers. A new and developing feature is that the state has also intervened much more massively in the operations of the labor market and a reregulation of collapsing traditional transitions from school to work. For many working-class youth, the choice is now workfare, being forced into low-wage labor, or street survival with jail as the likely terminus. This is a state-mandated attempt to regulate and reform the labor power of the working class wholesale, attempting to make "idleness" impossible just as work disappears.

The objective probabilities of a reliable and decent wage through manual work have been radically decreased, then, for substantial parts of the working class, and the threat of its removal has become a permanent condition for all workers. I would argue that the old expectations often continue in some form but have been thrown into permanent crisis. There are still plenty of male working-class kids, like "the lads," who are perhaps more willing than ever to take on exploited manual work in traditional masculine and antimentalist ways (see the chapter by Jane Kenway & Anna Kraack), but there is not enough work to go around, and many are left in suspended animation on varieties of state schemes and dead end training programs. Many simply disappear from the radar screens. These dramatic changes have destroyed or substantially weakened working-class paths from school to work and have shaken the material foundations of traditional working-class cultural forms.

In many ways we are now entering an epochal and possibly catastrophic social void.[10] We are seeing in the current "postindustrial revolution" a shake out of especially male industrial labor on a scale similar to that of the shake out of agricultural labor in the first industrial revolution. In England, the first country to experience the industrial revolution, this shake out was accompanied by mass internal migration from the country to the city. Although lived through suffering, massive dislocation, and countless personal tragedies, this constituted, ultimately, a way out of the "void" as it faced displaced peoples then. Displaced "landless laborers" moved to the new cities, forming there new urban relations and cultures, through struggle and possibility finding and making new psychic, cultural, institutional, and material homes. But when you are displaced from the city, where do you go? What cities are the new mostly male "workless workers" bound for? If you have just arrived with diasporic bags unpacked, where do you go? Cities of the sky? Derelict cities of dead and alienated souls hovering over the decaying city centers where once they were welcome? Falling into its cracks and crannies, making new cities of the sidewalk? Cities of vastly expanded penal institutions? Signed "Training Centers," cities of state warehouses for the unemployed? Schooling as we know it was developed for the expanding Victorian cities of the first industrial revolution; what of schooling now for the new ghostly cities of the postindustrial revolution?

Apace with these profound material changes effecting the world of work has been a profound social recomposition of working class communities and of "labor supply" for the vastly different (or disappearing) kinds of jobs available. In some ways inversely reflecting the decline in demand for male manual labor power, women across all classes are achieving higher education levels and rates of labor force participation. Continued waves of migration, now politically driven as well as economically, flow into the metropolitan centers, cumulatively changing and forever their race/ethnic compositions and expanding labor supply even as the "proper jobs" dry up. Britain also now has a very substantial third generation of predominantly Asian British and African Caribbean British youth who, even though now facing actually a tougher labor market unless very well qualified, do not willingly accept the conditions their grandparents suffered in silence, and who contest every day ignorant presuppositions and insulting stereotypes about their "outsideness" and supposedly homogeneous racial identities (see Fazal Rizvi's chapter in particular). With newfound ethnic confidence and in new ways they exploit electronically freed-up resources of global diasporic networks and often commodity-borne postcolonial hybrid and syncretic forms to adapt to and explore their current conditions, not least original and creative ways of occupying and surviving the new cities of the mind and institution.

In some ways the scale and direct effects of the mass movement of people across the globe are often exaggerated. Over 97% of people live and work in countries where they were born.[11] But for the majorities, even if they are still, symbolic borders pass them. Not least this redraws the cultural map for the White working class, for those such as "the lads" of Learning to Labor. They are having to recognize themselves, often unwillingly or with resentments, as a newly "marked" ethnic group as they lose or can no longer automatically take for granted the advantages conferred by colonialism and participation in the durable formations of the first industrial revolution and its (White) proletarian inheritances of a decent industrial wage. Economic leveling, especially in the light of renewed ethnic confidence among non-Whites, brings a whole set of visible comparative and relational issues: cultural questions of otherness and difference, similarity and solidarity, for identities no longer resting on what they took unconsciously to be categorical, historical and economic advantages. Now they are revealed to be similarly subject to the much larger relations of subordination that always trapped those on whom they so recently looked down. Here lie potentials for new forms of White antiracism, for racial solidarity, for racial cultural borrowing in diverse forms of White ethnicity, as well as for possible pits of resentment to fuel more conscious and virulent forms of racism replacing the old unconscious and taken-for-granted forms of superiority.

Alongside these material and social changes, further complicating their own internal dynamics, has been an accelerating epochal change at the specifically cultural level whereby symbolic resources, from whereever derived, have been commoditized and their communicative and useful potentials subject to fetishisation. Of course, commercialized cultural forms were of great interest to the lads of Learning to Labor, so this is not a new development. But the sheer weight of commercial provision, the massive increase in broadcast TV channels, the faltering of public service, or at least of its ethic, accumulate to render quantitative into qualitative change. Commoditization of objects, artifacts, and cultural services has become the norm. New global electronic forms of communication are sidelining old sensuous communities—face-to-face interactions with known others—with now literally hundreds of TV channels available through digitalization. This is furthered by the huge growth of commercial leisure forms. The post-modern cultural epoch is characterized by this qualitative expansion of commodity relations from the meeting of physical needs—food, warmth, and shelter—to the meeting and inflaming of mental, emotional, expressive, and spiritual needs and aspirations. You could say that the predatory productive forces of capitalism are now unleashed globally not only on nature but also on human nature.

At the level of culture, young people are becoming less defined by neighborhood and class and more defined by these new relations of commodity and electronic culture. Even as their economic conditions of existence falter, most young working-class people in the United Kingdom would not thank you now for describing them as working class. They find more passion and acceptable self-identity through music on MTV, wearing baseball caps, branded sneakers and designer shirts, and socializing in fast-food joints than they do through traditional class-based cultural forms.

You could say that the commodization and electrification of culture has produced a double articulated crisis of "the void": Not only are the material conditions of the working class profoundly changed, but the cultural resources and forms through which that crisis may have been understood and responded to have been eroded and devalued. Fetishism has removed the "ghostly cities" further into the spectral. Although exaggerated and sometimes mythologized now, too easily forgiven for their racism and sexism, the traditional forms of British working class culture, for instance, did at least give a corporeal and embedded sense of the self in relation to a larger group and a logic for understanding the relations of that larger group to other groups, not least dominating ones. Just as this domination deepens dramatically and material conditions change profoundly for the worse, the means for placing the self and understanding are plunged into crisis as well. It is certainly conceivable that if the old cultural forms, and their institutional extensions and expressions, had held there would have been much stiffer resistance to, or much better collective settlements made within, the multiple crises now engulfing the working class. As it is, market-led processes of individuation have helped to render structural change and deepened subjugation apparently into matters merely of personal misfortune.

Understanding New Times

So we are faced with a bewildering new world of contradictory influences, a profound crisis of the old and faltering births of the new. The collapse of industrial employment in the core countries continues apace with the postmodern separation of time, place, and culture. The commodified aestheticization of everyday existence and materials accompanies the mass movement of peoples across the globe. New postcolonial diasporic social relations and the development of "new ethnicities" in the "core" economies accompany gravely worsened economic conditions for all those, Black or White, with only their manual labor power to sell. I recognize all of these trends, but if it is immodest, forgive me, I still see ethnographic practices with *Learning to Labor* as a model and *The Ethnographic Imagination* as some sort of guide as providing highly relevant ways of proceeding.

Unsurprisingly given the diversity and complexity, the different facets of the new situation are considered in fragmented ways with different disciplines highlighting different fragments. Cultural studies has developed to highlight the creativities of consumption and the new possibilities for postcolonial identities. "Boring" sociology focuses on broken transitions and the destroyed inheritances of the working class and working-class culture. What is needed is a bringing together again of sociology and cultural studies, anthropology too, although in some ways the latter has always fared better from an interdisciplinary point of view. Although cultural studies has celebrated freedoms in the realm of choice and identified fluidities and possibilities in the making of new ethnic identities, these identities and formations, for the most part (although see the chapters by Kathleen Nolan & Jean Anyon and Jane Kenway & Anna Kraack), have not been grounded with respect to their articulations and productiveness within realms that are still determined by necessity, especially, for instance, school, work, and/or state schemes. The question for me is: How does the necessary connect with the voluntary under new conditions?

Ethnography shows the grounds on which this consolidation might take place. At a minimum, and as a precondition, it stresses agency and insists always on a role for subordinated groups producing their own cultures and understandings. Crudely, ethnographers always ask, what is the meaning-making from below? Too often, profound changes are seen as passive processes, described in gerund terms from above—nobody, no acting subjects are really responsible. Globalization, who does it, who suffers, who cares, it's *globalization*, stupid. Downsizing—nobody is doing the sacking, it's just a process—nobody knows where it comes from. Restructuration? "Oh yeah, it's a modern condition of the world." As Tony Blair is fond of saying on hearing of the latest factory closure, "It's sad but that's the nature of the modern world we live in, isn't it?" There is no agency there, it is just happening. In my hometown of Wolverhampton, "relicization" is the most recent word I have heard used to describe what is happening to our industrial inheritance—whole sectors of the city have become industrial relics, empty wastelands apparently only because another dratted "-ization" has been on the loose. These are all top-down views. Desperately, urgently, we need the view from underneath. What does it feel like for the working class to be "relicized"? What are the subjective understandings on the shop floor for those who teeter on the edge of "relicization," who remain for the moment in the old but now sped up, globalized, and Japanized factories?

Ethnography further reminds us that real social agents live simultaneously, and in the same life space, the dislocations of "the void" together with the recompositions of the social together with the commoditization of communicative social relations. Ethnographic work must encompass the interpenetrations of these too often separated worlds as they constitute the practical field on which agents live and act. How is "relicization" understood through and in relation to new social representations and identities, through a world of commodity communication whose materials are out of reach for the new workless, barely in reach for the new armies of the working poor keeping their heads just above water in seas of symbolic plenty?

Against the gloom, cultural theorists, my part, too, are right to emphasize that in the train of the new commodity relations and their erosion of traditional cultural forms have come new possibilities, emergent forms that although so far promising much less for institutional development than the old forms of solidarity must be scrutinized for their social possibilities, clues to social becoming. Among these is the emergence of an, albeit damagingly individualized, "expressive subject" (see the chapter by Peter McLaren and Valerie Scatamburlo-D'Annibale for an excellent exegisis as well as critique!). This concerns individuals taking for themselves—on the alien and profane grounds of the commodity—something that only the elite has enjoyed as part of their sacred privilege. This privilege entails the formation of sensibilities to mark oneself culturally as a certain kind of person—rather than simply an unconscious carrier of traditional markers of class, race, and gender—or to "choose" to belong to these categories in transformative, distinctive, mannered, celebratory, or self-conscious ways. This is to take part in self-formation on relatively autonomous expressive grounds, rather than to be formed from outside on automatically ascribed grounds. The connection of the "given self" to *variable* external symbolic forms reflects the desire not just to take up social or material space in a way governed by others, but also to *matter* culturally. Of course, these *cultural productions* are subject to future rounds of commoditization as market researchers scour the streets for the next inner-city fashion to sell to the inner city. But there is an inescapable moment of meaning-making from below here that, through the very promiscuity of the restless commodity, also aids processes of change, hybridity, and syncretism. The changes of race and gender composition and especially the new assertiveness and confidence of previously "invisible" or "representationally fixed" groups produce complex changes for all representations of social difference, multiple opportunities for ethnic, gender, and class "cross-dressing" (see Cameron McCarthy's chapter) as ordinary possibilities for social agents to intervene in the symbolic orders of their own social universes.

But for me the urgency remains. How are the new orders of symbolic experience related to structural features of contemporary experience, to the *positions* and *relations* of a deepening oppression that seem oddly to be have been made invisible by the new surface diversity of social and cultural forms? I propose that an indispensable tool here is class analysis as explored in the first part of this chapter.

The issue is not one of the "objective" disappearance of class, but one of the disappearance of the once relatively clear lines of connection, shown in *Learning to Labor*, for instance, between class positions, class cultures, and class identities. There are no longer, if there ever were, totalizing systems of representation (see Fazal Rizvi's chapter). And there are simply more groups, so to speak, within the working class, and, mostly depending on luck (but also perceptions about them in the labor market), very divergent economic prospects for them. Within the different groups are very many more discursive, symbolic, and socially symbolic resources feeding into their *cultural productions*. But an important feature of the latter continues to be the effectiveness with which they explore and exploit their conditions of existence. What is needed, what was unified in *Learning to Labor,* is the bringing together of class perspectives with the focus on culture, albeit now less centered and more diverse.

Diversities and creativities are celebrated too often for themselves and for their apparently free-floating ontologies. They are connected up only horizontally and in the abstract through loose associations of similarities in form and potential. My argument is that within the different forms we need to ask: What are their *penetrations* and *reproductions*? What *positions* and *relations* lie beneath the diverse surface forms that might share convergent *penetrations* about them? How do they all converge in a social reproduction of polarizing structures that depress the prospects for all subordinated groups? What are the hopeful mismatches and ragged edges between *penetrations* and *reproductions* in situated context?

In the first section of this chapter I argued that the old working-class cultural forms were nothing like as solid, homogeneous, purposive, or class-expressive as they are now held to be, portrayed in mythic, if surpassed, form, with *Learning to Labor* sometimes held up (thereby suppressing its current theoretical and political messages) as a nostalgic and sentimental icon. Against that, I say, again, that the *penetrations* of "the lads" were not essentialist or directly "class-expressive." They worked indirectly and eccentrically with respect to the direct purposes and phenomenal flows of their culture. So it should be no surprise now that current forms do not declare themselves on their foreheads to be "working-class culture" but are nevertheless speaking to and revealing of class-related contexts of subordination. It is therefore no big step to analyze them in the same way as I analyzed the counterschool culture of "the lads."

Of course, class processes, impulses and responses may be clothed and coded in other ways. Not least in the U.S. context, for instance, racism adds weight and form to structural oppression, but race and ethnic belongings and traditions also supply the phenomenal forms and symbolic resources for survival and expressions, including resistant ones, for Black and Latino groups. These as well as other oppositional themes are commodified and through the mediations of popular culture (see endnote 5) put into capitalist circuits both of accumulation *and* of the spread of ideas and symbols, many subversive, thus supplying materials for the *cultural production* of much wider groups. So, there is certainly much more grist to the mill of the *cultural production* of young people and all social agents, but the questions remain the same: What is articulated and *penetrated* and *reproduced* with respect to their structural *positions* and *relations*; are the cultures under question *socially marked* in any way, and if so, what is the social work they accomplish?

Here is a broad agenda for ethnographic cultural research and one in which we should have real confidence in the likely productivity of our findings. How are *positions* and *relations* lived and understood? How are the requirements of economic and state systems met? What kinds of labor power or withdrawal of labor power are required? What are the new relations of exploitation and how are they actually embodied in living, breathing, and cultured, clothed bodies? What happens *culturally* in the welfare offices? What happens *culturally* in work placement and training schemes? What happens *culturally* in McDonalds? What happens culturally in the still existing but sped up Fordist factories?

Schools

From a general point of view of understanding social change through to the pedagogic interest, schools are important sites for ethnographic investigation. Along with work and state-mandated sites of labor market regulation, they constitute a very important and continuing realm of necessity where diverse cultural forms and a whole range of identities are brought together by force to face inescapable and urgent questions structured in one concrete site. Schooling continues to supply its own set of forces and contradictions that school-based cultures must survive and work through, thus further profoundly effecting identities within them. Students are thrust into a realm of necessity with little or no control over the terms of their presence or participation, but with greater "choices" than ever over how they register and understand the possibilities and confinements of school. The contradictions of individualism and meritocracy carry over, actually in much deeper ways, from the days of *Learning to Labor*. The "new" floating resources of the imaginary world of commodity culture, changing gender relations and identities, diasporic cultural networks, postcolonial cultural topographies, syncretic and hybrid combinations of all these, are here located in very anchored "old" situations. Added now to the complexity of school is an extra layer of difficulties and contradictions to be made sense of, those produced by the disappearance of manual industrial work. Are schools training for work, for the dole, or for endless state schemes to follow, and what sense do any of them make from which student points of view? The impulses of cultural response, old and new—conformism through instrumentality through disassociation, through resistance— are likely to show some continuity with previous cultural forms, but are also likely to be clothed and articulated in some new ways with attendant and specific forms of *penetration* and *reproduction* (see the chapter by Kathleen Nolan & Jean Anyon).

The ethnographic impulse forces you to be broad empirically if not entirely ecumenical theoretically. In the pursuit of the ethnographic presentation and understanding of school-based cultures, I would certainly add many more symbolic resources to the mix, discourses new and old, symbolic relations ushered in by the mass movement of peoples, and the increased range of possible articulations between class forms, gender, and ethnicity, not least those brokered through the now dominant relations of the commodity. But the project for understanding the complexities is kind of similar: to repeat, what are the *cultural productions* within the specific site, what the *penetrations,* what the *reproductions,* what the ragged edges?

In the new context, it is more difficult than ever to outline positive programs for schooling and pedagogic strategies for the betterment of subordinate groups. Compared with the old Victorian schools with one roof over one purpose, the roofing of schooling now covers a multitude of different trajectories, arrivals, departures. Schools are continuously buffeted by changes, internal and external to their operations, continuously cutting their sails to differently blowing storms. They are having to become more "marketized," focusing on high-status testing preparing labor power for jobs in the new "weightless economy" (see Michael Apple's chapter), but, in working-class and inner-city neighbourhoods they are also having to grapple with a variety of cultural responses from those who are excluded or exclude themselves from these opportunities, as well as attempting to deal, although ever more unsuited to welfare roles, with pathological manifestations of the profound dislocations of community, poverty, and suffering associated with unemployment. Caught between these objectives, it is harder than ever to see schooling, in an earlier modernist liberal way, as a unified force for the emancipation of the whole working class. Are schools to train working-class students to compete with each other ever more vociferously for the ever diminishing supply of "proper jobs?" Are they to prepare them, or some of them (which ones?) for coping with a hostile state in a life without work? Are they to prepare them for contractual submission to an ever-extending succession of training schemes? Prepare the rest for jail?

There are many interesting guides in this volume to the new functions and formations of schooling, bleak additions to the traditional functions of preparation of industrial labor power where schools also provide fodder for jails (see the chapter by Kathleen Nolan & Jean Anyon) and permanent unemployment (see the chapter by Jane Kenway & Anna Kraack). We need more studies showing the cultural complexities of schooling, particularly of the new roles of cultural consumption in school.[12]

What of pedagogy? What is to be done now on Monday mornings? Often I am seen as too pessimistic and concentrating on resistant or, in one way or another, deviant pupils. Of course my belief is that we should not underestimate the continuing importance and potentials of school for all students and that we should continue to protect its freedoms and necessities as a site at least partly removed from the deeper necessities, exploitations, and exclusions of the world of work and now unemployment. Although we must never underestimate the complexity of how schools function differentially and for whom and to what purpose, it is still the case that schools are the major source of skills necessary in the labor market and the main avenue for student chances of a "proper job." Through all the contradictions and counter forces, schools must continue to offer all working-class students the best possible individual opportunities and highest expectations for educational advance, ignoring all provocations and rejections. Maximum possible resources—the more difficult the school, the higher the budget—should be mobilized to support teachers in their heavy tasks, giving them maximum time out of class and in sociologically informed and literate support groups to maintain a social as well as a pedagogic professionalism that refuels their ability to see behind the insults often thrown at them.

In any particular student there is likely to be a conflict between horizontal cultural influence and individualized aspiration. Bracketing out the ambiguities of seminar debate, in the classroom teachers must seek to supply safety, inducements, and appropriate contexts to encourage the students to take and keep to the individualistic routes and what they offer, not only for upward mobility, but increasingly, through evidence of conformist attitudes, for the very possibility of a decent permanent job. Actually, many students from working-class backgrounds still lean instinctively toward the school, especially in their early years, and pursue its individualistic promises even at the cost of some local cultural embarrassment, rejection, lack of belonging, or complex "double-agent" dealing. There have to be safeguards, protections, and supports for those who take this sometimes rocky road. For the resistant or disaffected, traditional and experimental attempts to explore and lay bare (in sympathetic, not damning frustrated, prediction) likely future reproductions may reconnect some students to an individualistic path. Within the fluidity and dynamic tensions of the new articulations of race and gender, fractures in the formations of subordinate culture (e.g., White lads ethnically disaffected, perhaps, from the resistant White culture) may throw up groups for whom there is real subjective point in and objective possibilities for meritocratic advance, less solidaristic cultural roadblocks in the way. They should be identified and supported, for schooling may be their only hope.

To be clear, my position has never been against schooling, against learning, or against personal intellectual development. It should never be forgotten that the problem with knowledge and mental activity in schools is not that there is something "wrong" with knowledge and mental activity or that students from subordinated backgrounds are not interested in them— in their own ways and through their own practices they clearly are. "Dumbness" is celebrated nowhere. The problem is that the current social and institutional contexts and arrangements for the transmission of knowledge and mental skills produce fields of social opposition against them. The "ideal" productions of "educated selves" are targets rather than models for subjectivities produced through general experiences of surviving everyday subordination. Although often given its instrumental dues, mental work is hobbled for many because it is articulated so closely with indiviualism and meritocracy within the compulsory school, complicit with hierarchized labor markets and oppressive capitalist labor processes. But once students find a bridge across institutional and cultural hazards, they can find a world of knowledge, mental development, and expression that can be appropriated and appreciated in autonomous ways. It is these destinations that always have to be borne in mind, all bridges kept open, built anew and multiplied. They are not only crossings to disclose, they also install whole new landscapes.

I know that I will be in trouble here with some readers and even with some coauthors. So far my discussion of pedagogy deals only with individualistic forms of knowledge and does not meet, in like terms, those culturally articulated forms that proceed with a social or collective knowledge and guide many students. This continuing mismatch is indeed an ironic condition for guaranteeing the renewal of nonconformist cultures. But our societies, certainly in Britain and America, are further off than ever from operating public and economic policies that protect collective interests and guarantee safety, security, and development for all. Educational institutions are absolutely not wired into such collective horizons. They are thoroughly and for the moment inextricably mired in the capitalist relations of the market economy and capitalist labor market. Falling off the meritocratic academic ladder now is to risk falling a very long way indeed, possibly into the spectral cracks of the miserable cities of the postindustrial revolution. Neither I nor you, the likely professional readers of this book, would contemplate that possibility as an alternative in our own lives, nor for the futures of our own children. Do we owe anything less to the children of others? It is not the role of teachers to stand by while students culturally grease up the bottom rungs of the only ladders that might save them. We must put our weight and feet on that bottom rung to help them up and stabilize it for them.

At the same time, for all the difficulties and respecting student abilities to handle contradiction, just as we do, and recognizing that the school is not just a pedagogic instrument but a field of *cultural production*, I argue strongly that along with the maximum attempts to keep students on individualized tracks should run curricular and extracurricular provision for exploring collective logics, programs that deal with social justice, not least exposing schooling's role in the reproduction of deepening class divisions in capitalist societies. This may open fields of mental life that can be developed for themselves, ironically also for individualistic advance. But their purpose is to explore the however distant prospects of social advance towards emancipation and a world free from the unequal *positions* and *relations* which restrict the free expressive and cultural development of all. For all the reasons discussed throughout this chapter, this may seem utopian given all the forces buffeting the school. Even where allowed, the formal and systematic teaching of systematic critical perspectives may fare no better among those who really need it than does the mainstream curriculum. I am absolutely for demands for radical streams within the main curriculum but would also ask for, possibly in relation to and as feeders for them, some lifelines into informal cultures. What are the ways of finding a way through here, not by building bridges over the cultural "blocks" but by going through them, utilizing them, the mental life of their *penetrations*? An important feature of the class analysis I proposed in the first half of this chapter is that *penetrations* are never fully assimilated back into social reproduction. There is what I have called throughout a "ragged edge," precisely a mental contents to be experimentally mined and recovered and then connected to systematic critical thought. The working-class distrust of meritocracy and un-illusioned appropriation of what it is to give manual labor power continues. New formations of ethnicity are, in part, adapted to the conditions and possibilities of their new locations, what do their cultural and identity politics say about the ideological architecture and *positions* and *relations* of modern capitalism. What is the nature of their social "marking"? Can it be so hard to break open the "secrets" of cultural reproduction when reproduction in general now proceeds in so many brutal, coercive, and open ways compared to the days of *Learning to Labor?* Can it be so difficult to make connections?

I do not have any magic "social pedagogy" bullets to offer. I will close, though, with two modest suggestions. What is usually referred to as the field of "popular culture" offers many possibilities. For all their individualizing and fetishizing tendencies, commodity communication and expressive forms reflect crucial features of the cultural universes of the young including oppositional themes, if sometimes liminal. They also bring new hybrid and ethnic resources to the lived and creative rearticulations of received social representations, not least in sites such as the school. A recent special issue of the *Harvard Educational Review* (see endnote 12) is devoted to exploring the pedagogic potentials of popular culture and contains many useful ideas and possible lines of approach. Cultural commodity forms and their uses in context are sites of intense interest for most young people and offer, both the texts and their appropriation, fields for imaginative pedagogic practices to connect up their relevance with lived *penetrations* and with wider critical perspectives and analyses. Further, informal education sites can offer access to cultural commodities on terms controllable by young people, maintaining a critical difference from private sites of consumption in their recognition of informal *cultural production* and in their attempts to connect it with more formal expression: speaking, writing, singing, recording, and filming.

Second, I would recommend new or further use of critical ethnographic texts, or fragments of texts, or performances related to texts, in school settings. Exposing similar, although not copresent, cultural forms to them can pique even resistant student interest and show the commonality of separated cultures, drawing together a cultural membership in to an awareness of a wider social membership indicating interests in common. Reading or hearing cultural texts in more formalized contexts can produce an othering and distance that dignifies and releases popular cultural practices from invisibility in the everyday, (see endnote 5) so aiding the prospects of a more systematic analysis of *cultural production,* exposing their critical impulses for connection up to wider critical perspectives.

Here is where I end as I began, beating the drum for ethnography. Knowing that the tasks I set myself are difficult and incomplete, I pass the baton to others, stressing again as I did at the beginning of the chapter the broad impact and importance of ethnography. This is what I hope to be the legacy of *Learning to Labor*, that critical ethnography should play an expanded part in registering and analyzing the profound changes we are living through and provide useful tools for social and cultural understanding and emancipation in these "new times" so distant from when the book was published.

Notes

1. Mention should also be made of a parallel though slightly later and unconnected approach by Wiel Veuglers of the Dutch organization SISWO that also resulted in an excellent day conference, *Learning to Labour: Twenty-Five Year Anniversary Symposium*, in Holland in October 2002, the proceeds of which have not been published but that have also informed my reflections here.
2. For a full description of the mission of the journal, see P. Willis and M. Trondman (2000). Manifesto for ethnography. *Ethnography 1*(1), (5–16).
3. I do not discount aspects of the directly constraining and determining power of structural forces not only over *positions* and *relations*, but also how they are understood. My essential point here is that I do not see the relationship of structure to culture as only one of *direct determination*, structures are also things to be explained and discovered, so to speak, in the reverse direction. There is a convoluted, inconclusive, and extensive debate on whether *positions* or *relations* should predominate in class analysis; how to define and measure them in relation to production (Marxist perspectives) or to wider market, social and status considerations (Weberian approaches); and on how far economic class entities determine or correlate with cultural, voting, and attitudinal "outcomes." My position is that many of the difficulties and dead ends of this debate can be seen to arise in trying to scientifically locate as real entities what are for me only notional "precultural" elements. I would argue that the unpredictable ways and measures in which cultural relations and cultural productions take up, embody, change, and reproduce which (never actually existing) "precultural" forms are themselves determining factors and not simply dependent variables or "outcomes" so imparting a "spirit" to the machine, which will always confound "machine mathematics." For a comprehensive review of the class analysis debate, see Mike Savage, *Class Analysis and Social Transformation* (Buckingham: Open University Press, 2000).
4. For clarity of exposition I am focusing here on the cultural practices of subordinated and dominated groups (for short, working-class culture[s]). But of course the middle class or powerful groups "move" within their own cultural production and with the power to legitimize their own positions, relations, and cultures through institutional power. So we have to bear in mind that subordinate groups "make sense" not only of economic positions and relationships but also of a variety of cultural and ideological ways in which these and the cultures of others are fleshed, justified, and represented, if you like also making sense of ideological relations.
5. See *The Ethnographic Imagination* (Polity, 2000) for a fuller exploration.
6. For a discussion of "surprise," see P. Willis, "Notes on Method" in S. Hall, D. Hobson, A. Lowed & P. Willis (eds.), *Culture, Media, Language* (London: Hutchinson, 1980), pp. 88–95.
7. I know that these categories constitute not only repertoires of possible symbolic meaning but also sources of *position* and *relation* with respect to their own symbolic stakes and often material interest. The valiancy of these symbolic resources and how their availability over time has been continuously reproduced come from active contestation of meanings and identity within their own terms and boundaries. As I explore in the section on gender, the "full picture" needs to show a complex dynamic of the interrelationship of different kinds of relationships. It would also be perfectly reasonable to posit a feminist version, for instance, of structural *positions* and *relationships* where class traditions could be seen as supplying

symbolic raw materials for "making sense" of gender. Why do I prioritize class? The basic social classifications of gender, and race as well, do in some sense have more importance than class categories, say more empirically about a person. But for me they are more "inert" than categories of class; the latter change them more than they change it. The organizing drive of the capitalist world system comes from an imperative of class organization at bottom derived from economic motives and organization. In the end, in order to better understand the formations of race and gender (locating what may well be most of human experience), or more precisely to comprehend their direction of change and source of internal tension, we need to locate them with respect to *more dynamic* class relations that work through them.

8. Although it is only tangentially the focus of this volume, frequent criticisms of *Common Culture* (P. Willis et al., Open University, 1990) accuse it of "cultural populism": a celebration of the creativities of common culture unrestricted by a consideration of structural forces and constraints. Indeed, that book does more or less restrict itself to a consideration of informal cultures in "sites of choice" rather than "sites of necessity," and this does dispose analysis toward a horizontal plane, limiting its ability to show the cycles presented here. This was in large measure determined by its (policy addressed) funding from the Gulbenkian Foundation, heterogeneous range of fieldwork, and aim to intervene in policy debates (much clearer in its sister volume, *Moving Culture*, P. Willis, Gulbenkian Foundation, London, 1990) concerning youth's creativity in order to widen arts funding opportunities for youth groups beyond their traditional focus on the received and legitimate arts. The book gives an over-reading to the autonomies of culture, but, against the critics, I would argue that it in no way contradicts the possibility of the analysis of the cultural exploration of social and economic conditions of existence and their ironic reproduction. It certainly shows the diversity, complexity, and nonreducibility of the cultural forms through which this has to be understood.

9. This is why those criticisms of *Learning to Labor* that complain about my use of "off-the-shelf" Marxism are wide of the mark. Of course there have to be provisional starting points where views are "borrowed" (no analysis springs fully formed either from the analyst's head or from the empirical world), but these are then modified or refined and put in better working order through the practice of fieldwork, its "surprises," and successive rounds of dialectical and mutual influence between theory and evidence. (see "Manifesto for Ethnography" for a fuller account of this process).

10. I thank Mats Trondman for introducing this term to me in our long discussions about the current crisis.

11. See: Humanity on the move: The myths and realities of international migration." *Financial Times,* July 7, 2003, p. 9.

12. See the Special Issue, "Popular culture and education," *Harvard Educational Review, 73*(3), Fall 2003.

"Centre" and Periphery— An Interview with Paul Willis[*]

DAVID MILLS AND ROBERT GIBB

Paul Willis was a student and research fellow at the Centre for Contemporary Cultural Studies in Birmingham from 1969 to 1981, publishing his doctoral research on Hippy and Biker subcultures as *Profane Culture* (1978). He is best known for his book *Learning to Labour* (1977), a ground-breaking ethnographic study of the shaping of working-class masculinities within a British classroom. He has also worked and published extensively in the field of youth policy (1986, 1988, 1990a, 1990b). His most recent work is *The Ethnographic Imagination* (2000), and he is also senior founding editor of the new journal *Ethnography*.

As students of anthropology, our motivation for the interview was primarily undisciplined curiosity. What had given rise to the studied ignorance displayed by British anthropology towards the politicised deployment of "its" methodologies within cognate disciplines? And why, everywhere else, had a set of debates that began within a small prefab hut outside the Arts building at the University of Birmingham remained so mythologised? The interview helped us answer both these questions. More importantly, it provides a historicised sense of the everyday administrative and intellectual

---

*Centre and Periphery—An Interview with Paul Willis, by David Mills and Robert Gibb, was originally published in *Cultural Anthropology*, 16(3), 2001. Reprinted with permission of the American Anthropological Association.

routines that lay behind the Centre's published work. The pedagogic practices developed within the Centre—such as a postgraduate-led, collaborative working environment—are rarely acknowledged as the precursor to the subsequent theoretical innovations. For as long as classroom power relations and the politics of learning remain an under–examined aspect of academic life this situation is likely to remain—some labours are less easily learnt.

We met with Paul Willis in his hometown of Wolverhampton in the so-called "Black Country" (named from the sooty legacy of its role as a cradle of the industrial revolution) over a day in May 2000, and this co–written transcript is taken from our wide-ranging conversations. These ranged from personal reflections on his own life-narrative, through an optimistic discussion of the possibilities of shaping local government policy, to some trenchant comments on contemporary trends within anthropology and academia. We have edited and arranged it under three broad headings—"Childhood and Education," "Teaching and Research" and "Ethnography and Theory." Paul recently described himself as an "intellectual vandal," and his own iconoclasm looms large in this dialogue. This is a highly consistent iconoclasm nonetheless. His unwavering insistence on a model of humanistic creativity, regardless of the vagaries of intellectual fashion, together with his commitment to linking theory to policy and practice, mark out a courageous model for an engaged academic career.

Part 1: Childhood and Education

School Days

Following the example of Learning to Labour, *can we start with your childhood and school experiences? How formative were these for your subsequent career and intellectual projects?*

I was born in 1945 in Wolverhampton where I still live, an industrial town not far from Birmingham in the English Midlands. I guess my cultural background was working-class, perhaps *petit bourgeois*. My father was a carpenter who became a "general foreman" and went on to work for the local authority as a building inspector. He then developed his own small property business.

My mother died when I was very young, nine. My father was an incredible engine of competence, production and responsibility: a single parent looking after two kids, myself and my brother who was four years older than me, and going flat out to make an economic success of his life. We were a very close if depleted nuclear family unit, very masculine ambience and bonding. He, my father, was both very ambitious for his family, "I'm doing what's good for the Willis's," and very optimistic in a classically "modernist from below" kind of way, viewing life through a rational lens of everything-was-getting-better-through-the-powers-of-science-and-labour. Academically ambitious for his kids, that didn't stop him forcing us out to work with him onto building-sites from very shortly after my mother died. "Forced," that's the wrong word, it was simply expected. In the family was a sense—typical of that period—of rising expectations, a gathering sense of control over nature, of the world, of your future—perhaps in our case a very masculine and vigorous sense of these things. In school too, a rational and practical application was all. . . . In different ways all of our activity was practical and scientific and in everything we were encouraged to work hard, not least at school.

I went to a co–ed "grammar school." These were the days of the "11+ exam," a selective exam taken by all at age 11 where 15 percent or so were selected to go on to elite grammar schools. My father backed up my grammar school selection and relatively elite education. He felt it was all part of the plan [laughs], things working out perfectly. So what's my back-ground? A very particular version of upward aspiration: a classic Hoggartian "scholarship boy" story of being selected through a grammar school system to go into a good, privileged education. I was in fact the only boy ever from my grammar school then to go on to Cambridge.

Did that make you, in the language you describe as employed by "the lads" in Learning to Labour, *an "ear-'ole"?*

Looking back on it, it was clear that I had to make the best of a contra-dictory situation. There was a very high emphasis on achievement and doing well, and at the same time this school was overwhelmingly working-class. There were tough cultures, and clear divisions between those who were exceptionally hard-working and those who were rather less so. I was often frightened in school. I was so embarrassed when the French teacher picked on me and forced me to try to say things in French which I simply thought I couldn't, to derision from the teacher and other pupils. It put me off languages *for life*. I used to be quaking behind the desk—would I be picked on next?

Later on I enjoyed school, or at least found it more manageable, partly because of sport, particularly Rugby Union Football. The school had switched from soccer to rugby in an attempt to improve its image, look posh like a Public School (the British title for privately-funded schools), to get fixtures with them, hoping something would rub off on us. I was big and athletic, well strong anyway, and was selected for the first team when I was only fifteen. This was unusual, playing with eighteen year olds, a big differ-ence at that age. It felt like a massive breakthrough, especially when the extremely strict and frightening and over-bearing gym teacher, Mr Jones, suddenly started calling me by my nick-name, which was "Will." Of course for the teachers you were just "Willis." Suddenly, evidently because of the surprise promotion to the first team, there I was being called in front of mates, in front of girls, women, "*Will,* I'll see you on Saturday then!" I was a man amongst the other boys of my age. I think sport and especially physical-contact sports were and still are a very big area where you can have subcultural kudos *and* academic kudos. Teachers could play on that. Deviance was contained, even given an acceptable masculine register that made conformism, or over-conformism, seem effeminate. Throughout my early career Rugby was an important vehicle for the expression of a certain kind of independence, muscularity, for not being an ear-'ole, but in a way which didn't jeopardise my academic standing.

You decided to specialise in the sciences at A-level?

I was good at the sciences throughout my school career, and got the school prize for physics after "O"-level (oddly enough, choosing *The Rubaiyat* by Omar Khayyam as my prize). I guess in some way the scientists were also the rugby-players, and the Arts were for the girls. And it was *definitely* sissy to be interested in poetry and drama. I remember, quite by chance, an old auntie died and I had a book of Byron's poetry, an antique Victorian bound issue, bequeathed, or at least passed on to me. Dad brought it home one night, this was when I was sixteen or so, and I started reading it at bedtime. I remember being thoroughly moved by Romantic poetry. I had a major crisis half-way through the lower-sixth, whilst I was doing Physics, Maths and Chemistry. I was *quite* a good physicist and I think it's still in me a bit; there are certain kinds of theorising I like if they are elegant and successful and cut through stuff. But I just wasn't *that* interested. Meanwhile I was really moved by the Romantic poetry which seemed to speak to *me* in my adolescent uncertainties as well as in my struggles over identity: was I a big masculine, rugby-playing scientist or a budding entrepreneur still forced out at weekends to work on the building sites with my father ... ?

Or a poet?

Well, yes, I was trying to write poetry. I have to give my father credit: once I explained my dilemma to him, he was open and he didn't force me. He found it odd and he didn't know what was going to become of me, and the school didn't like it much. Anyway, after consultations all around and something of a family crisis, I switched to the arts: literature, history, geography. It was a wafer-thin decision, I could easily have thought "I'm being silly" and stuck with the Physics and the Chemistry. And you know, it would have been a different life-course to say the very least. But it suddenly seemed to suit me and within eighteen months I'd got an "A" in English and within twenty months I was sitting in Cambridge studying literature.

Cambridge

It was my father's fault! After the "A"-level results he said: "You know you've got these "A"s, so why aren't you going to Oxford or Cambridge?" But our school had no tradition of Oxbridge entry which is still a highly specialist route, so during the summer of 1963 I wrote around to all the Oxford and Cambridge colleges—including the women's colleges because I didn't know which were which—asking if there was a chance of sneaking in at the last minute? Both St. Peter's of Oxford and Peterhouse of Cambridge offered me places within the space of four or five weeks. I chose Peterhouse.

Was Cambridge a shock?

Yeah, I guess so. It had all been rather sudden but my actual experience of Cambridge on an intellectual level was *extremely* and almost immediately disappointing. I very quickly realised that I just didn't know what was happening. I didn't understand the lectures, the famous Oxbridge tutorial system just didn't work for me. I quickly formed the impression that the tutors thought I was a Black Country, working-class "oik" who had wandered into the place by some terrible mistake, perhaps from a training programme for the unemployed up the road or something. Within weeks there was a comment in the Junior Common Room (JCR) suggestions book from an old Oxbridge, public-school twit saying that the "JCR had noticeably deteriorated this term with the arrival of people who seem unable to speak the King's English." And I was quite sure that it was for me. Still, I don't know quite how I managed to wind up in Peterhouse, which continues to be a bastion of old right-wing Tories and Whig historians. Why on earth? I don't know. I've never asked, I never questioned. I *was* an ingénu, an innocent wandering into an old, privileged bastion both in the social life of the college and, oddly, in the subject, which, within a term of going, had lost me. . . .

Because of its scholasticism?

Yes, though at the time I experienced it simply as my inadequacy. I just felt inadequate. After feeling that I'd almost magically found the centre of things, me at the centre, I was out on the edge again. The small group seminars and close reading sessions were both a revelation and source of total depression. We'd get an unseen piece of poetry or literature and you'd have to comment on it and try to place it. The historical knowledge, in depth, of literature and verbal confidence and polish which the public school kids had was simply frightening. The truth is I just knew about Shakespeare and the Romantic Poets. I couldn't have even sat down and given you a period, a periodicity, a schema of the different stages, genres and types of English. I was just completely out of my depth and worse, frightened to open my mouth. And I couldn't see rhyme or reason in how the lecture system worked. I just couldn't link up the lectures with the weekly essays I was supposed to be writing and with the close reading sessions. Again, this is reading *back in* a social scientific category: I now see all of those difficulties as related to my relative lack of cultural capital. I must have been a bright working-class kid to have got there, and aspiring to something or other, but basically got flattened by English. Having had a sense of myself as rather literate and rather intelligent, I began to think I was a bit of an idiot basically.

I got a third in my first year, which was embarrassing given that I was supposed to be grooming myself for a glittering career. I didn't want to go back after the summer vacation. I was far happier in my home town where my friends were. However, I stuck with literature, partly thinking it was a question of work to try to develop the knowledges others had. Slowly I got better, finally ending up with a 2:2. Trying to jump through their hoops but not knowing quite what the hoops were.

As it was, rugby saved me again socially. I got into the College team as "pack leader," even had a trial for the University, scoring a try which was reported in the local press of my home town and proudly reported at the Speech Day of my old school. I still preferred coming home to Wolverhampton. I missed the bustle, the double decker buses, the lack of pretension, I missed the disco, I missed a wide range of friends as well as my girlfriend, Val, who subsequently became my first wife.

Did your friends change their attitude towards you after Cambridge?

I don't think so, because my immediate friends were also scholarship kids off to University too. My immediate group was classic working-class, grammar-school selected, upwardly-aspirant, many of whom I still know and see. At the same time, of course, part of the advantage of the town and one of the reasons why I've stopped here is that I knew and know a whole variety of other groups: neighbourhood-based, through my father, school friends who didn't spiral up, etc. Within those groups I think I was seen as changing, even now people say to me that my accent has changed, become posh even though I still speak with an evident Midlands lilt. I never attempted to change my accent, but nor was I politically above it, it was just something that happened.

Birmingham

How did you come across the Centre for Contemporary Cultural Studies at Birmingham? What made you want to go to do post–graduate work?

Having decided I wasn't a particularly academic person, I had in mind my father's trajectory—going from working-class to small businessman—so I applied to Manchester Business School and got in there with a bursary.

Along with accountancy, operational research, business planning I also studied industrial sociology and industrial social-psychology. I remember being impressed with Tom Lupton and a psychologist there. Suddenly I was bright and clever and top of the class again which was wonderful.

I began to think that I'd found a métier in social science. I was offered a grant to continue to do a Ph.D. in Manchester. But because my Wolver-hampton girl-friend of the time was finishing college in London, I applied to the London School of Economics and from there came a bursary for an M.Sc in Industrial Relations. I'd become a bit of a hippy, shoulder length hair, interested in things, "the revolution in the air," interested in social science but seeing it as basically manipulative, telling the bosses how to kick the asses of the workers but in more sophisticated and clever ways. I became interested in "culture" in a general kind of way, not least because of the ferment around me, and wondered if I could re-tune my re-awakened academic abilities to my *real* interests. I don't quite know how I found out about Birmingham, and the newly launched Centre for Contemporary Cultural Studies (CCCS) which was looking at contemporary culture. Even then it had a *very* trendy image, well for me anyway. Probably through the staff at LSE, or maybe the lecturers at Manchester.

So you were one of the first students when you started?

Yes, maybe the third or fourth year of students, a very early crop, a fledg-ling class. I had no chance of a grant. But I went down, was interviewed and accepted by Stuart Hall as a self-financing part-time student. I wanted to do serious work on cultural change, cultural development, cultural resistances to old forms of working. Though I had enjoyed my return to Wolver-hampton, I also saw in the Centre a way of getting out of my previous class, cultural restrictions and experiences in Wolverhampton, or of finding a new relation to them. Within any biography there's the terrific role of sheer acci-dent, what you hear about and when. Happenstance explains a lot. Negative "avoidance factors" also play a role. I just didn't want a "proper job."

I was also *very* attracted by Stuart and by Stuart's emphasis on multi-disciplinarity. "I'm not interested whether you're a sociologist or an English person or whatever, Paul. What I *am* interested in is that you want to look at youth culture and music and at how young people live now." And that seemed like a liberation compared with the very restrictive experiences I'd had at a number of institutions as well as Cambridge.

What was the working culture like, amongst the students and the staff at the Centre? Were your peers more important than your supervisors?

I was actually Richard Hoggart's student for the first year, 1968–9. Then he went off to UNESCO. He was very busy, and we had our first supervision

204 • David Mills and Robert Gibb

over lunch. I remember him saying, in the lunch queue I think: "Paul, it's very important to immerse yourself in the destructive element, and don't rush into anything too quickly. Unless you feel very confused you can't then put together a new thing. So I'm not going to ask you exactly what you're going to do or what your theory is." That was good. Keats called it "negative capability," being able to live with uncertainty but still have a sense of direction. I think it's such an important thing, you know, in a good research project, a tolerance for chaos whilst willing coherence, living on that edge. If you know exactly what you want or what you're going to prove, then you go to the field for a few exemplifications and you write what you always knew. But if you are willing to get disoriented and confused, which can feel, well, disorienting and confusing, it's not necessarily a bad thing, out of it can come real gems. Of course, if you carry on just being confused [laughs] it's a bad thing, but at a certain stage and grappling with a new topic it's vital. So that was an early impression for a then 23 year old: "Immerse yourself in the destructive element, Paul, don't formulate. . . ."

Did you have to justify your approach or topic or style of work?

No, not at the beginning. No, I just did it. A very important reason for that was of course that I was paying for myself, I was part-time, forking out hard earned cash, after tax, to pay the fees. So coming from what seemed like a very elongated, privileged existence at Cambridge, Manchester and London with good grants, by the time I got to the Centre I was teaching in four different places to support my studies. You could easily pick up part-time teaching in those days: "Communications" at Aston University; "English for Business" at Birmingham College of Commerce; and "English as a Second Language" at Handsworth Tech, and Wolverhampton Poly teaching "General studies." And I was selling ice-cream from an ice-cream van during Easter and summer vac's, weekends. I was really working very hard, not at all a full-time student floating around the Centre. I was unusual at the Centre, for I was a local boy. I used to drive over from Wolverhampton (14 miles away)—and didn't feel particularly elite or special in terms of my conditions of life and types of daily social contacts. By my second year at the Centre I was married with a newborn baby, with all the pressures that brings. I didn't feel like an elite person. I hadn't done well at Cambridge and I'd been a bit of a vagrant, carpet bagging full-time student afterwards. I had to be *very* effectively organised to get around all my different teaching, and *very* practically organised to be in the field. I wasn't in the Centre anything like 100% of the time. I was there when I wanted to be, to benefit directly from especially Stuart Hall, or when I had to be, for the so-called Theory Seminar for instance.

Part 2: Teaching and Research

1968 and the CCCS

Did you get involved in the student uprising at Birmingham?

I wasn't directly involved with the eruptions at LSE during 1967–68. I left LSE in the Summer of 1968. The big Birmingham sit-in was Autumn '68 which I *was* involved in. I had a feeling, a bit like the original feeling for Keats and Byron, but social now, that there was something in the air, something happening in everyday culture and social relations. Things would never be the same again. I joined in the occupation of the Great Hall of the University, sat in on planning meetings, relished the atmosphere. Centre students, were leading lights of the sit-in. Especially Jack Hayward, and Larry Grossberg, both American students at the Centre for a year. Larry, I remember, pony tail right down his denimed back, opinionated, was a *major* instigator. My recollections of the actual events are dim. I was rushing around teaching everywhere to earn a living, selling ice-cream, getting back to Wolverhampton, so I was a part-time student revolutionary, popping in and out to do my teaching and to keep my own private life together. Stuart, most *definitely* in a contradictory position as a full-time employee of the University, was a major figure in the sit-in, a memorable and major speaker in front of huge masses of students and exciting rallies. The Centre and that group of students who had just arrived were very involved. Courses were cancelled, the entire proceedings of the Centre were suspended, all time and energy was given over to arguments over strategy and political discussions of what the demands were or should be or could be. A very exciting period. Richard telling me to be confused and now the world was really turned upside down. Embarrassingly I think for Richard Hoggart, always down to earth and courteous, his baby, the Centre, had become the think-tank for the student revolution.

How much lasting change was there within universities? From the institution's viewpoint, didn't it all blow over, to a certain extent?

Well, I don't know, I forget some of the specific demands now. But there was certainly student representation, student councils were instituted and there was *far* more student in-put into curriculum development, although how long-lasting that was is debatable. In terms of the Centre, "blow over," *absolutely not!* We were the permanent revolutionary council of the sit-in extended indefinitely—in our minds at least. Stuart was very brave, as well as conditioned in a certain degree of paranoia, in coping over a very long period with the feeling that he was camping out in an enemy institution. But from that moment, especially after Richard left, the Centre was very clearly a pioneer in a different kind of pedagogical relation. *I* was perfectly clear that Stuart felt that he was protecting us from the institution and that the Centre was some kind of experiment—although we all thought it was an experiment that would expand and take over the world. Somehow I was simultaneously centre and periphery. Against what I said just about feeling "normal," non-privileged, you could say that along with other students I also shared some sense of the importance of being at the centre of things. A failed "scholarship boy," I was now recruited to the revolution, being groomed for something or other returned now in radical guise. Whereas before I thought I'd be joining the establishment, then this happened, and through accidents of history, personal inertias against other kinds of future as much as anything else, I moved into a radicalised position. I felt that I was really part of some important movement in those years and Stuart was *the* charismatic leader, taking great risks with his own career trying to put into practice within our tiny, micro-institution many of the feelings and principles of the student movement, *especially* the notion of being open in terms of disciplinary areas and being led by student interests, connected *outwards*.

To what extent did Stuart Hall define the focus of the Centre?

In a remote control kind of way perhaps, also, of course controlling and maintaining the general parameters and political ambience. Not substantively. Collectively we really did control most of the administrative processes, certainly the areas of work, reading and research. There was no question but that it was a collectively-controlled process. We certainly felt that. Though looking back on it, we probably did exactly what Stuart wanted a lot of the time. This arrangement was a secret from the university: if the administration knew, there would be dire consequences, such as being closed down, especially after Richard Hoggart had gone. That first year was a very strange inter-regnum. After the sit-in and after '68, Richard went. I have no evidence but I wonder whether Richard went *because* of the sit-in. He could see he'd got this nest of radicals, the nest that he's never known what to do with since. In one way he must have been pleased, for his entrepreneurial actions in setting up the Centre led to the formation of cultural studies—and *The Uses of Literacy* was and is a very important book in that. But I think he must have felt cause for alarm when it ran in to a kind of continuation of New Left battles in different form.

After Richard, Stuart took on a new kind of institutional role; rather than just the archival, professorial relations that Richard was used to, he was attempting to foment academic revolution from below. Business meetings were every Monday, where Stuart would open the books and say what was happening, what the University was on about to him. All the crucial issues and processes of admissions were collectivised. Admission criteria were discussed as rationally as possible, political, subject area, academic. Groups of students interviewed candidates. Curriculum-wise students chose areas, topics and texts collectively, though with advice from Stuart. I remember him advising caution about getting seriously into Marxism because it was not something you could easily get out of again or readily adapt to an eclectic frame. I also remember him saying, many times, that quality was essential, depth of understanding and rigour of argument were to be the weapons of persuasion, not political assertion.

Has the subsequent fetishisation of that period surprised you? The way in which it's been mythologised?

I don't know. The real lessons may have been entirely forgotten. I think it still carries lessons around pedagogy, and around how we might organise intellectual work, lessons from a long-lasting academic experiment in genuinely collective work. Oddly there is most to learn from what were experienced as the failures within a stuttering but still continued experiment.

What was the "Theory Seminar"?

Our early attempts to define "culture," to find relevant disciplines and methods and approaches developed into what we called the Theory Seminar, where we went through intellectual traditions in a reasonably systematic way. After the impetus of the student sit-in, we tried to carry some of the principles of collective work into this Theory Seminar. I don't remember exactly, but I think we started off with literary theory, structuralism, then sociology, I remember Berger and Luckmann, moving eventually into an engagement with Marxism. But it hit the buffers and basically failed. The attempt to really work through a coherent position on what culture was and what a method was, and adapting them to a radical programme, just proved impossible. People couldn't agree, and there wasn't a coherent heart to it all. Compromising, we moved from what we called a "tight collective" to a "loose collective." We split into working-groups, we called them Work Groups. So those who were interested in literature and the Humanities went into the Literature Group; heavy-weight theorists went into the Ideology Group; later feminism, "race" groups and so on. We just couldn't all agree.

Were these political differences, or theoretical differences?

The principal problem, as I recall, was that we couldn't agree on a central theoretical core, but as you can well imagine, theoretical differences were associated with political differences, which were associated with different political positions, in some cases sectarian positions. At times things were quite tense, or I experienced them so. These devolved work groups met often without a member of staff for a whole year and were, of course, self-directed. But something very important remained from the "tight collective." You had to report back at what we termed the Centre Presentations, every summer, on what the hell you'd been up to. The place still had that sense of, you know, this ambition, some sense of a major project. Only now it was really focussed and productive. You would be *judged* at the Centre Presentations, so you pulled your finger out, stopped up all night preparing and writing. People used to get absolutely *terrified* about making their presentation, both to show that they'd been up to something—which of course they had been—and perhaps more importantly to in some way justify it as part of the project, to justify it with respect to other positions. And, looking back, it is simply extraordinary how many of those presentations from working-groups, which might have been working with only a few students, subsequently became books or issues of *Working Papers in Cultural Studies*. So I think we stumbled upon a fantastically productive way of working. Some framework of overall direction and commitment, substantial autonomy; collective pooling of ideas and critique, and terror motivating individuals to work to a deadline. Odd combinations of centre and periphery again. A stable instability of collectivism and rampant individualism.

Learning to Labour

How was your own work, both with the hippies and the "lads," received in the working groups of the Centre?

I felt throughout that my fieldwork was seen as unscientific, humanistic and rather subjective. The major area where I felt a palpable, sometimes personal, sense of critique was in a Marxist attack on agency and subjectivity, almost an orthodoxy on the inadequacy of humanistic positions. I felt that I had to justify myself, take the issues seriously. In another place, you would have been allowed to continue in the humanist track of your own concerns. At the Centre there was, through the continuing plenary sessions in every summer term, a sense of trying to bring things back together in some co-ordinated and central, critical, cultural studies approach. But still I felt sectored off.

None-the-less in terms of my development it was very important that I was in a Centre which had some central collective purpose together with a space for autonomous work. Although there wasn't really a strong ethnographic tradition at the Centre, that particular mix of autonomy and purpose was what kept me at my last. The Centre presentations posed question after question for me, trenchant questions which I couldn't ignore. I was at the periphery taking the centre very seriously.

Did you carry on defending your own project as these critiques developed? Did you feel you had to keep defending your way of "squaring the circle"?

Well, I was accused of working with a banal or un-theorised sense of subjectivity and agency, and that I was kind of assuming an answer without stating the main puzzle. By assuming a sense of subjectivity and creativity I was short-circuiting, deliberately ignoring or simply altogether overlooking the Althusserian position on interpellation. I was working from the assumption that "the lads" were creative, rather than trying to explain the conundrum that they felt so against all the contrary evidence. I felt that hanging on to that creativity was the main concern, and I still think it is, although the terms of the argument have undoubtedly changed. I don't know whether I defended my position so much as stuck with it *sotto voce*. I do remember Stuart, in response to a Work Group presentation I was involved in, saying "What Paul calls creativity I call survival."

There is a very strong continuity throughout your work in your ideas around creativity.

I suppose that's my story. I had an initial interest in individual artistic activity, feeling that was at the centre of things, but drew a blank in the boring, aesthete, refined textual version of that. It continued as an impetus to find the same thing in ordinary life: some form of holding the centre and the periphery again perhaps. And there is a longer-term politics to seeing some spark of creativity or aspiration or aesthetic motivation within absolutely, everyday, common experience. Rather than it being a continuous, visible, presence, this is routinely lost, distorted or alienated or turned into reified forms, folding back in oddly repressive ways according to circumstance in different sites, institutions and situations. Never quite lost though, always recoverable, that's the point. I think in every intellectual work, one tries to preserve the core, an impetus, a subconscious stream of the will to know or to state or to argue for.

The lesson of the Centre was that the humanistic assertion of human creativity had to live in those same four walls of the Centre with *very* tough Marxist notions around reproduction and class continuities. And then *certainly* there was the feminist critique of me at the Centre. How I'd ignored patriarchal divisions, reduced them to class ones. And especially some sense of my under-estimating the importance of the home: as the factory was the site of capital conflicts, that the home too might be the site of gender conflicts, that my own methods were mostly related to work and schools and didn't take enough account of domestic relations. There was a move in one of the feminist Centre Presentations to critique, even outlaw, naturalistic ethnography like *Learning to Labour* because it was seen as uncritically reproducing rather than condemning and deconstructing sexist conventions, forms and prejudices.

Actually, in *Learning to Labour* I did think I was working in a way that took account of patriarchal categories and feminist critiques. This was another pressure I felt I was working against, not by refusal, but by creative internal extension, invention and appropriation. I still feel that some of what I'd been trying to argue hasn't been taken seriously by feminists, which was an attempt to see how gender divisions overlapped onto especially manual-mental divisions within capitalism. I wasn't arguing that a certain working-class male masculinity was forever linking manualism and masculinity, but that these were different binary systems with their own histories, and that in other situations you might have different articulations of gender, patriarchal and capitalist categories. There is a real instability in the way that gender systems and capital systems or capital relations are articulated with each other.

Right now there is a terrific disruption in the apprenticeship model, reshaping modes of social reproduction formed over a very long period of industrialisation. And we are seeing a crisis or reformulation of how important binary systems of thought relating to gender and relating to class and relating to location are *re*combining. I would very much argue that some of that ethnographic, theoretical Marxism continues to be relevant, not in an all-time depiction of a certain working-class masculinity, but precisely in freeing up the terms of the analysis, so that different articulations and combinations are possible. So that there might be a gentler, working-class masculinity, or there might be a masculinity which is freed from proletarianism. And to my mind, I had taken the feminist point about systems of patriarchy. Whether I've taken it properly methodologically back into the home or quite what a method is for the home I don't know.

It must have been quite hard for you—you had to be brave to defend your position again and again?

Yeah, though you shouldn't get too heroic a notion of how I defended myself. Throughout the period I lived in Wolverhampton and drove over to Birmingham: in the early part of the period I was working in four institutions and selling ice cream; in the second part where I was a Research Fellow working on *Learning to Labour* I was out doing fieldwork, or I was in Wolverhampton having a *very* normal life. And all of those were supports for an alternative subjectivity, one which I didn't have to sustain or fight for in the Centre. There was always a centre of gravity or base or some lead in my bottom which was related to other identities. And you *could* argue that this maintained a certain humanism as well as a certain interest in field practice. I wasn't an active, discursively and intellectually fully-armed, fully-referenced, fully kitted-out, Centre warrior fighting in each of those Marxist, feminist and anti–racist revolutions. I understood the implications for subjectivity of the arguments around interpellation, around gender, around "race." I could see all that, but I *also* had, and it's embarrassing to say it, a "common sense" view which knew that your identity was always *more* than class, gender or ethnicity, involving a whole set of points about the way you lived, how you fitted in, who you knew, what the myriad of your personal and domestic relations were: these things were separate from the theories that I picked up specifying obvious binary divisions. If you're in the field and trying to understand the way a pub works or a factory works, then there's a million other things going on around humour, around language, around personality types, around taking-the-piss—and where you're just not clever enough to have worked out all the binaries, all the binaries producing other terms or still other binaries. A good fieldworker *knows* something's important without being able to say: "This is an example of class. This is an example of gender. This is an example of "race."

How do you feel about Learning to Labour's subsequent reception?

Learning to Labour is, in many ways, an odd book. I didn't think it would travel very far, I thought it was "only" a monograph which I was very relieved to get published. I got a poor deal out of the publishers, but it was very surprising how quickly it succeeded and sold a lot of copies. It was a bit of an accident, perhaps, that it hit a certain time in academic history, a certain time in Marxism, in cultural studies, educational sociology, a certain time in educational politics around an emerging disillusionment and disenchantment with the promises of comprehensive schooling. It's gone to several editions now and numerous translations. It is selling more than ever, certainly in Japan, Germany, the U.S. of course. I was recently in Korea, where there was a briskly selling pirate edition. I saw the book as an ethnography of creativity and social consequence in unexpected place. It continues to hit a variety of debates, issues and interests, travelling out of Cultural Studies altogether. Perhaps its natural home has become anthropology which is both odd and gratifying.

Amongst anthropologists, do you think Learning to Labour was more influential in America, because of its broader and more inclusive anthropological tradition, in comparison to Britain?

I don't know. I can't speak authoritatively about anthropology. Certainly in the U.S. the book registered early on in anthropology. I had several take-ups and invites from U.S. anthropology departments, and that was not the case until recently in British anthropology. In the British case now this may be a partly paranoid, partly justified reaction to the advance of cultural studies. Maybe they've opened their doors to me to protect themselves from other sources. Perhaps my work is discussed as a reverse Trojan horse within cultural studies, to indicate that the best part of the enemy has been doing exactly the same anyway!

Policy, Politics and the University

Can you tell us about how you got involved in working for Wolverhampton council, and how The Youth Review *(1986) came about?*

During the Thatcher cuts and contractions of the early 1980s I lost my research fellowship at the CCCS and was unemployed for about a year. I was involved with the local Labour party here in Wolverhampton and they asked me to do a review of youth unemployment. Their idea was to try to formulate and implement effective policies for the enormous crisis engulfing the town, we were falling into the yawning gap of mass unemployment—this town has lost half of its manufacturing jobs since 1979. Thatcher's strategy was to use monetarism, the high pound and international capital to outflank and discipline workers and trade-unions. The closure of British Steel and other plants hit this town very hard. There was a particular concern about youth unemployment. I used that opening to try to do a thorough account of the local impact of unemployment in a whole variety of ways, with a sample survey and ethnographic studies of social groups of young men, young women, African–Caribbeans and Asians. I had three research assistants paid for by the council: the research grew and grew. I also did a review of all the main local agency departments, ten I think, in relation to what I called the "new social condition" of youth. I believe that this was the first comprehensive review of the local impact of post–industrial mass unemployment in developed context.

Rather than start with the usual internal departmental reviews, we were trying to show the crisis from the point of view of youth and *then* move on to how the local authority departments might adapt to the new situation and the new needs of youth. Don't forget that the Black Country was the Silicon valley of the Industrial revolution. You could say that in 1979 and the early 1980s it saw the beginning of the post–industrial revolution, that vacuum still waiting to be filled. Other places saw the new industrial revolutions. This is a crisis that we are *absolutely* still working through. A region and a population that over 200 hundred years had adapted to the rhythms and exploitations and disciplines and powers of the industrial wage, suddenly lost its centre. Relatively settled patterns of social and cultural reproduction were thrown into crisis. It was almost as if Mrs. Thatcher wanted to push areas like this quite literally over the brink.

What was your experience of engaging with policy-makers? Did you try and define an agenda, or argue that policy-work should make a space for what you call "sensuous creativity"?

I can't say that I talked about "sensuous creativity" but that was the resource from which I was working and hoped to liberate. Politics is to some extent a dirty business. From the point of view of getting change at the local level and perhaps feeding something through to the national level, I felt it was important to have a big slab of evidence to give to local politicians. The *Youth Review* was a very chunky document, containing hard and soft data. I stressed the importance of taking the perspective of young people against departmental and professional perspectives and inertias, and for building in systematic forms of youth representation. In terms of making changes happen it was important to work politically, seek alliances, open up new channels of political influence. I helped form a youth council. Involved in distributing funds for cultural activities, it also supplied representatives of a new political committee called the Youth Affairs Committee. This political committee wasn't just interested in what's normally at the *bottom* of usually the education committee's agenda, ie. youth clubs and youth leisure and sporting activities, but it also took reports on housing, policing, social services, education and so on. The Youth Affairs Committee and the youth council still exist. The fundamental spirit of *The Youth Review* was to re-orient the local state to the needs and problems of youth, rather than what has predominated since, which is to use the state to reform youth as more useable and low priced labour power for internationalised capitalist labour markets.

I tried to suggest to the voluntary sector as well as to the state that policies could be derived from the actual existing condition of the youth, rather than from the view of the powerful as to how they should change or be formed. It is wrong to think that there is a right royal road that connects through from ethnography to policy. I think it can play an important role, but the question of politics, in so far as you are involved in politics when you are doing fieldwork, is a very broad front indeed. We used all kinds of methods. One of them was certainly to do sample surveys, so you could show in big numbers what was happening. This was combined with qualitative work, so you could begin to try and develop an agenda that was made by the needs of young people. You can't simply stick a microphone in a seminar and ask them what they want; by the fact of their structural situation they are confused and disoriented when it comes to formulating public positions. Nevertheless you can use an ethnographic technique to look at the forms of their lives and to an extent speak on their behalf. There continue to be whole sets of issues around training and education, cultural provision, housing, for many working-class youth on very low wages. For example, whether they have low-paid jobs or no jobs they find it impossible to get into an increasingly privatised flat market. Why the hell isn't the state dealing with that issue?

How did you feel about using ethnography in this new setting?

I'm not claiming wonderful successes, but I am claiming some direct communication of real needs and that the youth affairs perspective has, for example, registered housing needs as central to the youth condition and has met at least some housing needs of young people in special singles developments.

To try to focus a bit, in my view the work for *The Youth Review* was almost the opposite of the colonial encounter which spawned anthropological ethnography. Now don't forget my accidental drop into anthropological methods relieved me, as I see it, almost entirely of colonial bad faith and guilt. On the other hand it has saddled me with a humanist urge, perhaps a white working-class or petit bourgeois take on whatever human creativity is supposed to be. Far from being associated with colonial agency, trying nostalgically to preserve, in a dis-connected backwards-looking and elite kind of way, a threatened or perhaps imagined past, I thought I was helping the "people" in their current struggles to formulate their position in order to make demands on the local state in an emergent set of social relations. I was *within* the circuit of as a contending force rather than trailing its dominant elements.

I don't know though, it's complicated. You could say that I was concerned with a disappearing way of life and I was paid for by the colonial administration—though is the Labour party really a similar organisation? It is also true that there was a situation of fear after the 1981 riots and there was a worry all over the country about youth rebellion. As with the colonial paymaster, there was an issue of intelligence for social control.

But there was a very genuine feeling in the Labour Party that we were spending a lot of money on local services, youth provision and education and that it could be made more relevant to "*our* kids." There was a sense of the whole region being set against wider powers. If you genuinely take in feeling from below, even with a reformist programme, there are definitely changes that are worth making to make structures, provisions and services more in line with real and emergent conditions as experienced and lived.

If you look back now, what difference do you think you've made? This is a question partly about your vision, your ways of seeing. In your new book, you describe yourself at one point as an "intellectual vandal." At another, you say that there are no large projects any more, only cultural gardening jobs. Looking back on your different projects, would you want to say that one has had more impact than another? Has Learning to Labour *been more influential than* The Youth Review?

It is very difficult for me to bill myself as having been effective in any particular way. Think back to some of the idealistic self-promotions of ourselves at the Centre—that we were organic intellectuals about to change the world! In fact we moved within a short tight circuit of influencing each other and ultimately perhaps some other intellectuals, but not really the real world. I would be embarrassed about claiming identifiable effects on anything other than what I've done in immediate contexts and circumstances. You can certainly bear in mind possible longer range effects and argue for certain versions of them, but it's by no means obvious how things will work out. There are the struggles within intellectual practice which are well worth having, and then there are the consequences of how we see the world within our own practices.

My work has been about trying to grasp in an ethnographic way what it means to live and act out structurally given conditions of existence and changed structural positions. A lot of kids won't be in permanent work now. They'll be in a mosaic of study-schemes and very low-paid part-time work, sometimes scrounging off parents then back into another state scheme. That's a whole new role, or much extended regular role, for the state. The state sector is going to become a whole terrain of experience, not as a part of a transition, as an early part, but as a continuing condition of experience. Blair has also talking about 50% of 18 year-olds going on into Higher Education. There is developing a whole new type of student body. Surprisingly, perhaps, because in this country now students have to pay their own way and their own fees, there continues to be a strong demand for sociology, media studies and cultural studies as well as or instead of vocational studies, training for IT etc. It's hard to see the meal tickets at the end of social studies, but there is still this clear demand. Socially relevant ethnography, my own work included, can offer very useful curricular and project materials for these new spaces, allowing students to recognise, dignify and analyse their own private experiences and cultural practices—often a motive, sometimes mis-recognised, for an interest in social studies. Ethnography can help in developing a certain kind of self-reflexivity, not so much in being aware of oneself, as being aware of the conditions of possibility of the self, the self as an historical as well as existential construct. I have a history of letters from workers and others who had read *Learning to Labour* in various contexts, who had already encountered it in classes, or by accident, one in a prison library, and who have re-understood their own experiences of ten years and more before, and become more mentally and socially attuned. There is a diffuseness about intellectual work which we simply shouldn't underestimate: texts do take on their own lives. There is a special poignancy in ethnography, about reported experience which can make itself live again, or re-ignite in different ways, elements within the experiences of the reader, in the experience of reading. This is a way of digging out the relations between selves and their mediated conditions of existence; of contemplating the possible meanings of living *changed* conditions of existence. It's a way of identifying what may be controllable as well as identifying the continuing power of cultural anachronisms even when we don't know what the "synchronisms" might be.

Do you think this sort of work is still possible in Blairite, sound-bite, focus-group Britain?

The general policy framework, structurally, has been moving against the left, and against a kind of radical policies that try and understand issues systematically from below. The Labour party, which was a major hope for connecting through to influences or interests from below, has become detached from the working class. In many ways it is continuing a kind of Thatcherite project, connecting with the masses through advertising techniques. But Blairism, focus group-ism and political marketing doesn't exhaust the political or policy field. In all kinds of ways the state is and will be involved with managing the population, and there are huge issues for everyone, not least state agents of one kind or another, about how this is done—intellectually, culturally, personally politically. What is the state's role to be in managing explosive new developments in: new technologies; exploding communications; floods of cheap or without cost information; nano-technologies and new manufacturing; exponential rises in computer power and artificial intelligence; micro-biological control of genetic make-up. What is to be the shape of the *inevitable* state involvement in the interactions of these things with commercial interests and the commodisation of all kinds of human provision? Even more important still, what will be the state's involvement in managing the social relations of the emergent trends of this brave new world, especially in managing those left out, economically and culturally, but who could still ruin the party for the rest? There *could* be liberating dimensions of a new governance in so far as *practical* aspects of feelings from below are registered and become part of the operation of power, and can mine, twist and develop from there. Whereas under New Labour, it's hard to see how we're not just a branch of multi-national capital with the state trying, without fully knowing what it's doing, to train workers to attract international capital. But there are many dimensions. Don't forget that state sectors are still hugely important—45 pence in every pound spent in this country is spent by the state, mostly locally or through the local state. Questions of politics and governance at a local level—of how the population is enrolled under these conditions—are very important topics indeed, especially with the increased importance of culture and subjective experience. There is a feeling that you have to take into account peoples' views. Even if you do manipulate them in the end, you can't do it in old top-down ways, especially in face to face service and institutional locations. There are new discourses around, of human rights, which are in part an articulation of the way people really have changed. People aren't prepared to be ascribed identities, I'm a worker, she's a whatever. Everyone, in a very incoherent way, is struggling for their own piece of action. How are these cultural trends and the technical/economic trends to collide? Economic disenfranchisement is juxtaposed with strange cultural enfranchisements. That is where critical ethnography can be very important, to get more thought-out, integrated policy options, especially in local government; options which both attend to the cultural impetus and keep the redistributive questions alive.

You talked of the implications of 50% of 18-year-olds being in higher education, and of people staying in state-sector provision throughout their lives. What are your feelings about the potentials and risks of these changes for the future of the university?

A lot of the educational/training discourses in the U.K. about attracting inward investment to Britain are very instrumentalist. Improving our "human capital," "competitive advantage" etc., etc. The global situation has changed the parameters within which the game is played out: within the official discourses there is a never-ending game enforced of apparently increasing the value of labour power to multi-national capital. Meanwhile in local areas, the situations of people going into HE (higher education) are far more diverse. It still amazes me that working class middle-aged women will sign up to do sociology and cultural studies, with very few apparent employment prospects, rather than IT or personnel management, the skills from which they might expect to have 20 years reasonable income and material security. They are doing it for personal development, doing it to make sense of their previous personal and cultural history, and doing it, to use my old humanistic terms, in search of some sort of creativity in their own lives and possible futures in ways which aren't entirely linked to labour market outcomes. I think this whole area can be a huge opportunity for sociological studies, cultural studies and anthropology, using critical ethnography as a live action research project to understand what the new transitions/destinations/mosaics and possibilities are within the logic of cultural practice and experience, so that involvement in higher education is intrinsically interesting and enjoyable, and relates to forms of consciousness raising and development which needn't be vacuous or rely on the worn-out old cliches of "race, class and gender." If cultural studies had developed in a different way, through the early fermenting period had fashioned a cultural studies ethnography, rather than splintering into several idealist camps, cultural studies might really have become *the* form of adult education.

Anyway, the current situation. Education is enmeshed in an unequal struggle between contending views of labour power, you might call them instrumental vs. expressive, with the former calling all the shots. Peoples' experiences and motivations, especially on a local level, might however relate more readily to an expressive labour power, and if you were clever enough you might be able to combine them all up, because developed expressive labour power may be a very valuable resource for many employers.

How to play the future? I don't know. Defend institutional positions, defend subject positions, try to argue that expressive labour power is an economic resource, all of those are possibilities. The sector will undoubtedly further fragment between the "elite" and the "new" universities, and "e-unis" will rise. We are going to head more towards an American situation. But my own view on local universities is that they should be real universities, and that they shouldn't be glorified further education colleges, intellectually franchised only to teach other peoples' research. Part of that local relevance must be in, by any standards, high quality work, where policy and ethnographic interests can come in and combine.

Part 3: Ethnography and Theory

"Being There": Tape-Recorders and Ethnographic "Data"

I caught I think the first technological wave of ethnographic work. I was very short of time (this is 1968, with everything else that was happening in my life), and I was desperate to get out into the world to see what was happening. It was the classic, first-time, cold contact ethnographic encounter. There was a famous pub right in the centre of the hippy scene in Birmingham and I asked the bartender who were the big hippies, the people who were on the hippie scene. And he told me, he introduced me to some of them, saying I was doing a project for a Ph.D. on music and hippy culture, and needed more information. I hadn't done any methods courses, I didn't see myself as an anthropologist, I knew I just had to have data. So I said do you mind if I record the discussions? They didn't have portable tape-recorders and cassettes at this period at all, or not that I knew about anyway. The Centre had just spent a small fortune on a massive, top quality reel to reel tape-recorder which was like a suitcase, and I carried this huge suitcase around the hippy pads, stuck it on the table, unpacking great spools of tape. Talk about unobtrusive methods! I saw it at the time as "For god's sake get something, get some data!" I'd got so little time, I wanted to have a form of working where I could get data and use it, do it quickly.

Did you not feel you could just take notes? Did you feel you had to have some tapes?

Yes. To have data for some confidence that I'd got something, the feeling of being in the field and filling up with data as efficiently as possible. A store of data, a bit like a store of money, against the rainy theoretical day. You could figure out how to use it later, though you didn't know how to use it then, in the future you would have a store of data. Making hay when you could. I was taking notes as well, and making notes, especially early stabs at theoretical explanation. Though I also remember having piles of notes from the field, the hippies, and looking through and thinking "God, I haven't got enough! What am I going to say about this?" Haven't you had that feeling in the field? It arose from a real insecurity that I didn't have enough, the importance of getting a store of data that you could go through later was simply crucial to me. I think it would be a very interesting line to figure out when tapes came in, and whether they change field practice, or make people lazy? I think I'm partly responsible for cultural studies' over-reliance on verbal responses, and on a cultural studies notion of a very quick, dirty raid which is discursively based. First of all you turn to the tape-recorder, and you've got a project if you've got an hour's conversation. Then if you are just going to use a few words anyway, why not just remember a few things that somebody said to you in the pub [laughs]. So you could imagine it as the beginning of the corrosion of serious fieldwork.

But at the same time, I think it's a very good example of how technology can be fantastically useful. We are very poor now at exploiting modern technology: visuals, moving images and video you know. Sometimes the fly-on-the-wall documentaries, docu-soaps and much of popular culture is about using visual means to represent everyday experience, whereas with the professionals, if you're not using your pen and your notebook, you're still not a real anthropologist.

But the problem there is that the tape-recording becomes ethnography per se. That somehow a tape stands for fieldwork.

Yeah, I think that is a negative thing, duplicating the limits of the docu-soaps in a way. Though you can also fall down by mistaking the notebook for the field, or its meanings. The antidote to all of this is the flexible and open use of theory. Of all of the questions about how theory relates to ethnography, I think the crucial point of ethnography is its flexibility; that you can, almost unconsciously, test theories and hypotheses as you go through in the field. But it's also the case that some form of that takes place afterwards in your own data analysis, so that listening to your tape and seeing what main categories develop out of your tapes, how they relate to your existing thinking, is a way of getting onto something, getting traction.

It's nice when you're able to go back to the field to refine this, but even within the data there is a similar dialectic going on, where even if you can't go back to the field, you nevertheless go back to other bits of data, or you look through fieldnotes with a new sensitivity to issues that you didn't have at the time you wrote the data. Data should never be a congealed block simply waiting to be turned over to readers like toppling a concrete slab their way.

This is another route back to the importance of an open notion of what's relevant in the field and an open theoretical notion so that you record things that seem to you to be interesting and important, even if at that point you can't say why. It may well be that at a later stage in/of the data processing and analysis, you do know why you had a hunch that this was important, but you didn't have a proper theoretical reason for why it was important at the time.

On Multi-Sited Ethnography

Part of the reason your ethnography was taken up within anthropology was the perception within the discipline that we hadn't looked at class. This links to the question of doing what has come to be talked about as "multi-sited ethnography," of how you do ethnographic work of larger systems, of capitalism or globalisation, which seems to be even more pressing now than it was then.

I worry a little bit about multi-sited ethnography, and some American forms of anthropology. Through the new journal, *Ethnography*, I am learning about contemporary trends in the discipline. Many anthropologists are responding to the post–modern turn by adopting a version of contemporary history. You get a bit of political economy as an overall view of the country, you get a bit of institutional history, and then you get a snap of someone sitting on a verandah with somebody from a development agency. This is a kind of super-sophisticated journalism. The specific anthropological eye becomes the over-viewing eye of contemporary history. I see why this happens and it has a role. But I just don't want to lose the focus on situated human creativity, on "chunky" ethnography. With a lot of modern anthropology you don't quite know why you've been told stuff. It's interesting, it's a good story, but so what? What's the question or puzzle that the writer is wrestling with, and *from what vantage point?* What's specific about the mode of enquiry? The worry about the local-ness and the worry about narration, how the data is communicated, should not lead us to desert chunky, close, fine-grained, finely detailed, sensuous ethnography and head off towards an attempt to contain all levels of determination within a single descriptive frame.

There are other routes to understanding how the locality relates to the global, other routes of narration. There may be short circuits between global capitalist domination and some of the internal intricacies of experience. It is very important to record concentrated detail about subjectivity, about experiential intimacies, whatever the difficulties of representation and naturalness. Amongst other things this is in order to have a chance to be able to link them in theoretically reflexive ways, in compelling and nuanced ways, in ways that produce an "Ah-ha" effect, to a dimensionality and depth in how structural determination, change and continuity are understood and presented. The ways we live now are formed *both* through structuring forces and the increasing power and apparent viability of internal experiences and very local practices. There seems to me to be a danger in multi-sited ethnography and overview ethnography where external determination, influence and life-force, that which drives the whole thing forwards, is presumed as some kind of reservoir of global water. Waterfalls cascade down through a number of levels, starting off as global history, and you give that as a section, and then it flows into a national arena, then it dribbles down into politics and institutions. A bit more water dribbles down onto the town and the local economy, and a bit more dribbles down onto trade unions and a bit more water dribbles down onto specific sites and *finally* you get to creative groups and individuals and you've got no water. Certainly no counter-flows. One way of dealing with the problems is to try and understand the short circuits, to try and understand, for instance, commodity fetishism in the commoditised materials and communications which surround us and what it means for subjectivity. That stretches both to the global and to the highly particular. This would be, for me, a structural "force" that can be named at the subjective level, and analysed interactively there, rather than traced through millions of mediations. It is very odd that whilst everything is provided, nothing made locally, we've never held intimacy as more important. Yet you won't get to that intimacy by starting with global capitalism and then to national capitalism then Blairite politics etc.

Just as there is a kind of reductive and flattening "do-it-all" political economy, there is also a flattening "discursive-ism" still prevalent. If you focus just on narratives and discourses, then you understand consciousness and subjectivity on a very artificial and self-justifying rationalising level, insulating yourself from the possibility of recording and understanding sensuous activities and processes as containing depth and dynamism as well as subtlety and ambiguity. People are moved by passions that they can't explain. They are involved with musics, technologies, situations, things, that help them to hold and develop an expressive sense of themselves, sensuously, which might often be in tension with their discursive "positions."

Rather than a flow of structural determinations, economic and symbolic, trickling down, there is something around culture and consciousness and subjectivity at a particular stage of history struggling in its own creative ways to make sense of the mediations around intensely private and intimate experience. Even in the Third World which is going through a rapidly concertina-ing period of not only industrialisation but also the industrialisation of consciousness, the mediating levels may be as much determined by subjective changes as by larger structural changes. Of course I believe in and support "global ethnography." How else did it start? We can't now leave "globalisation" to capitalists and abstract theorists. But we need to try to define what *we* mean.

If the result of the critique of empiricism is to lessen the focus on concrete local experience and its own ways of dealing with world changes, then we've lost. We must really maintain a dialectical open-ness to the mid-range institutions being as influenced by culture and subjective change as by macro-change. Not least they have to adapt to try to control and contain pressures, restraints and resistances "from below." The journalists and historians and economists can do an equally good job of painting the overall picture, but the particular anthropological or ethnographic contribution should be to continue to focus on experience. Of course multi-sited studies and methodologies are important to a larger understanding, but they shouldn't be of multiple depth-less differences abstractly draped on a second-hand political economy clotheshorse. They should show how the same or similar tendencies are played out dialectically *in experience* and *local practices* in different ways according to power, location and interest.

Theory, Ethnography, and Ethics

Who would you say has most influenced your theoretical position?

So far as I've got a coherent theoretical position it has developed from my own interests, empirical interests, political interests and from protecting my humanism from, or justifying it with respect to, other theoretical positions. My recent book, *The Ethnographic Imagination* (2000), is in some ways my *first* attempt to systematise and theorise a position. *Profane Culture* grew out of the struggles to understand the biker culture within a humanist early cultural studies paradigm. The *Ethnographic Imagination* grows out of struggles to try to understand ethnographic specificity in relation to the the take-over of cultural studies and much of social science by linguistic paradigms and post–structuralism (which is a simplification but there's truth in it), re-thinking my naive practices in *Profane Culture*, for instance, in the light of subsequent debates. Staking out the possibility of fieldwork on sensuousness from my point of view.

For graduate students and people at the beginning of their career, "Theory" constitutes a major dilemma, you know: "Am I a Marxist?" "Am I a Bourdieuan now or a symbolic interactionist?" "An ethnomethodologist?" "A semiologist?" I have difficulties with all those categories. My own view is that ethnographers should have a healthy independence. I'm not against any of the theories actually. I've learned a great deal from all of the theoretical revolutions of the Centre, and I learn a great deal from the incredible range of Bourdieu's work now. But if I *hadn't* got my own groundings in a humanistic creativity and some, however limited, examples of my own field experiences to draw upon to, it would be very difficult not to get sucked into theory. Funnily enough I think Bourdieu would say something rather similar about his early Algerian fieldwork. The problem is if you're, for example, just a Bourdieu disciple before the fact of fieldwork, it's even *harder* to do creative fieldwork; you would be using a Bourdieuan system and looking for exemplifications and illustrations. Back to the importance of Hoggart's "immersion in the destructive element" again.

So, I am against joining a school. Grad students tend to feel that they need to belong to a school, it's very difficult not to get sucked in, to find a patron, theoretically and sometimes concretely. It's slightly dangerous in my view. The commitment of the ethnographer should in some way be to his/her topic and set of small "p" politics and priorities. Being principledly eclectic, rather than putting all their eggs into one basket. Theorists cluster, they are often saying rather similar things. Bewitched by their own importance, perfecting their own "unique selling propositions" they are just very, very clever at generating further relevant categories, salami slicing against the opposition. This can get in the way of sensuousness. You end up more bothered about figuring out what a theorist means rather than figuring out what culture means. You should only use theory if it creates illumination, casts light on things, help you to present a phenomenon more fully *in itself*. Too many ethnographies are shackled rather than liberated by theoretical obeisance. If there aren't illuminating categories around, don't shy away from developing or adapting your own categories in relationship to the world, which is *undoubtedly* developing ahead of us and developing forms, binaries, sensuousness, emergences, cultural forms which *aren't* going to fit easily into prior categories. The over-reification of theories and theorists is a big problem.

How do you get your own Ph.D. students to engage with theory without being overwhelmed by it?

By asking why they are interested in the topic and then reminding them of Hoggart's advice to me. By saying that I want, for all of the naturalistic dangers, to have some account of the topic that interests them. By encouraging wide readings and trying outs. This is where the intellectual vandal comes in. Try on lots of different theorists in however a primitive form and don't genuflect to Bourdieu or Marx or Althusser or Bhabha or Spivak, you know. Don't be a pedant! To try to get the essence of what they're saying in practical and useable form and throw the concept at what interests *you*, and see if sticks. If it is illuminating and interesting, fine, then remodel the concept, be a bit less of a vandal. If it doesn't fit, try throwing something else.

Has it been lonely doing the sort of intellectual work you've done? Has it been hard for you to stick to your guns, stick to your eclecticism?

Good question. If you asked me if I was an intellectual, I'd say no. I'd say I'm a person who lives in Wolverhampton and who does intellectual *work* some of the time. The work is not at the centre. I earn some of my money in the academy. I have some sense of a centre of existence or identity—not that I know what it is, I certainly wouldn't want to glorify it—that's *not* defined by the academy. If I were a person more defined by the academy it might be not just lonely but impossible to plough my furrow. But it's another kind of loneliness, oddly bringing its own kinds of solidarity, which insulates me from academic paranoi, from taking its endless debates too seriously. I don't know, aren't all ethnographers to an extent facing a problem? Being worldly and not worldly. Convinced of the necessity of fieldwork; inescapably doubting the human integrity of the human contracts it entails. Whether or not they join a theoretical school, they know this *dreadful* contradiction of the exploitative relations within the ethnographic encounter. You're a voyeur, you're trying to look around corners. You're also to an extent ventriloquizing the people you're talking with to make your account. You're undertaking an unequal exchange which is capitalistic in its own way, because it *appears* to be an equal exchange, but in fact it's *very* unequal. You take from trust-like and reciprocal relations something which is then one sidedly and academically "marketised" as public, exchangeable: ripped out of local use value for a particular kind of exchange value. You take it off and cash it in in the academy, such as *Learning of Labour* becoming a book that sells 100,000 after twenty years. I have all of these guilts. I'm driven still, though more in theory than practice at this point, to concrete interactions because that is the only way of trying to understand creativity, sensuousness, specificity, even though the very action undermines that with its second order motives.

These multiples of the normal social atmospheric pressure, uniquely felt by the fieldworker, sometimes make me think of our method as a kind of symbolic tank or submarine. Field roles are a bit like tanks or submarines, splendidly useful vehicles for getting to strange or dangerous places. You'll never know, till you try, how quickly a vehicle can become a death trap. You *are* the research instrument. That's the point. But also, by that, you are making of yourself an enclosure that can be crushed.

You don't often don't mention this other side, the ethical impossibility of ethnography. Isn't that the other angle of the ethnographic imagination, its impossibility ... ?

Maybe that's the debt that the imagination tries to pay off. What I'm saying specifically here, though, is that I've felt solidarity with ethnographers no matter what their leanings because I think we *are* in some kind of secret club, whose rites of passage and membership fees consist of handling unexpressed guilt. Perhaps it's mephisophelean. The higher the fees, the higher the achievement. I can feel the electricity, the tension when it's present, but invisible in a text; part of a fatefulness in how experience is described; experience *really* registering as *implicated* witness; part of the undischargeable debt which turns into a kind of politics agonisingly without closure.

I don't care whether they're called anthropologists, Marxists, ethnomethodologists or linguists. I do feel an *immediate* sympathy and solidarity with anybody who has attempted to the very odd thing of joining in a social situation for reasons which are entirely unique to our little club, and which may well be suspicious to social agents: our peripheral membership of a social group as the *centre* of something else. Though it never ceases to amaze me how open and honest people are when *you* know that *you* are trying to peer round corners. You are not trying to do dirty deals in a conscious capitalistic way as in exploiting surplus-value, but you've got these driven feelings, as I said before, not least, to "get some data." If I've got an academic home, it is with people who know that moral dilemma. You could almost say that theoretical schools are very unimportant compared with that. Also, yeah, I resent some of the pure theorists. I want to *force* them to go out and face those moral dilemmas. Get them by the scruff of the neck, "this is what you're talking about." Not that academic thing of, you know: "Show me some empirical data." Rather: "Have you *really* been in a situation where you're trying to generate data, relevant to the theory you're talking about, from the people you're talking about?" Especially doing that with people who aren't like you, safely encamped in seminar groupings, or about whom you want to say something critical or difficult for them to hear. On the one hand, can we possibly do social science *without* talking to and granting equal *interactive* humanity to the people we're talking about? On the other hand, *how* can we do that without, at some level, exploiting them? You know, under existing social relations, honesty forces us to be dishonest. That leads to a discussion of the commitments and pay-offs and politics of why we put ourselves in moral jeopardy to start with. There is a compromised but unmistakeably unique energy behind this framing and justifying that which seperates us from "the suits" of the social sciences. And it is this shared knowledge of the energies of moral jeopardy which is my solidarity within this strange group.

Acknowledgments

We would both like to thank Paul Willis for his support of this project. David Mills would also like to acknowledge the financial support of the Leverhulme Trust and the British Academy.

References

Hoggart, R. (1957). *The uses of literacy.* London: Chatto and Windus.

Willis, P. (1977). *Learning to labour: Why working class kids get working class jobs.* Farnborough: Saxon House.

Willis, P. (1978). *Profane culture.* London: Routledge and Kegan Paul.

Willis, P. (1986). *Youth and community education. The future role and organisation of local government*; Education Working Paper 2.4. Institute of Local Government Studies, Univeristy of Birmingham, Birmingham, UK.

Willis, P. (with S. Jones, J. Canaan, & G. Hurd). (1990a). *Common culture.* Buckingham: Oxford University Press.

Willis, P. (1990b). *Moving culture: An enquiry into the cultural activities of young people.* London: Calouste Gulbenkian Foundation.

Willis, P. (2000). *The ethnographic imagination.* Oxford: Polity Press

Willis, P., Bekenn, A., Ellis, T., & Whitt, D. (1988). *The youth review: Social conditions of young people in Wolverhampton.* Aldershot: Avebury.

Willis, P. (2001). Tekin' the piss. In D. Holland & J. Lave (Eds.), *History in person.* Santa Fe, NM: SAR.

Notes on Contributors

Jean Anyon teaches social and educational policy in the Doctoral Program in Urban Education at the Graduate Center of the City University of New York. Her last book, *Ghetto Schooling: A Political Economy of Urban Educational Reform*, was positively reviewed in the *New York Times* and in over 20 other publications, and is widely used and cited. She has written many scholarly pieces on the confluence of social class, race, and education. Several of her articles are classics, and have been reprinted in over 40 edited collections. Her forthcoming book is entitled *And We Are Not Yet Saved: Social Policy, Urban Education, and a New Civil Rights Movement*.

Michael W. Apple is John Bascom Professor of Curriculum and Instruction and Educational Policy Studies at the University of Wisconsin–Madison. Among his recent books are *Educating the "Right" Way: Markets, Standards, God, and Inequality* and *The State and the Politics of Knowledge*.

Madeleine Arnot is Reader in Sociology of Education and Fellow of Jesus College at the University of Cambridge. She has published extensively on the gender, race and class relations in education and has been actively involved in promoting equality policies and citizenship education. Her recent books include *Closing the Gender Gap* (with G. Weiner and M. David, Polity Press, 1999); *Challenging Democracy: International Perspectives on Gender, Education and Citizenship* (edited with J. Dillabough, Falmer, 2000), and *Reproducing Gender? Essays on Educational Theory and Feminist Politics* (RoutledgeFalmer, 2002).

Stanley Aronowitz is Distinguished Professor of Sociology and Urban Education at the Graduate Center, City University of New York. His latest books are *How Class Works* (Yale, 2003) and, with Heather Gautney, *Implicating Empire* (Basic, 2002).

Greg Dimitriadis is Assistant Professor in the Department of Educational Leadership and Policy at the University at Buffalo, SUNY. Dimitriadis is the author of *Performing Identity/Performing Culture: Hip Hop as Text, Pedagogy, and Lived Practice* (Peter Lang) and *Friendship, Cliques, and Gangs: Young Black Men Coming of Age in Urban America* (Teachers College Press). He is first coauthor, with Cameron McCarthy, of *Reading and Teaching the Postcolonial: From Baldwin to Basquiat and Beyond* (Teachers College Press). He is first coeditor, with Dennis Carlson, of *Promises to Keep: Cultural Studies, Democratic Education, and Public Life* (RoutledgeFalmer).

Nadine Dolby is Assistant Professor of Comparative/International Education and Foundations of Education at Northern Illinois University. She is author of *Constructing Race: Youth, Identity and Popular Culture in South Africa* (State University of New York Press), and has published in numerous educational journals, including *Harvard Educational Review, Teachers College Record, Educational Researcher*, and the *British Journal of Sociology of Education*. She is the recipient of a "Rising Scholar" award from the Kellogg Forum on Higher Education for the Public Good.

Robert Gibb received his PhD from the University of Edinburgh in 2001. He has carried out research on antiracist associations in France, with a focus on the relationship between antiracism, republicanism, and party politics. He was the Leach/Royal Anthropological Fellow at the University of Edinburgh in 2001–2002 and is currently working on a research project funded by the British Academy entitled *"Spontaneity" and "Organisation": Anti-Racist Mobilisation in France During and After the 2002 Presidential Elections*. He has published in the *Journal des anthropologues*, the *International Journal of Francophone Studies*, and *Migrations-Société*, and has a book *The Politics of Anti-Racism in Contemporary France* forthcoming with the publisher Berg.

Jane Kenway is Professor of Education at Monash University in Melbourne, Australia. Her most recent book is: Kenway, J. & Bullen, E. (2001). *Consuming Children: Entertainment, Advertising and Education* (Open

University Press). Her forthcoming books with Peter Lang include *Globalizing Public Education: Policies, Pedagogies and Politics* (with Michael Apple and Michael Singh, editors) and *New Generations: Arts, Humanities and the Knowledge Economy* (with Elizabeth Bullen and Simon Robb). She is currently completing *Masculinity beyond the Metropolis* with Anna Kraack.

Anna Kraack is currently studying law at the University of Otago in New Zealand. Prior to this she studied rural sociology and worked for 3 years at the University of South Australia as Research Fellow on the Australian Research Council project *Country Boys in Uncertain Times and Places.*

Peter McLaren is a Professor in the Division of Urban Schooling, Graduate School of Education and Information Studies, University of California, Los Angeles. His most recent books include *Che Guevara, Paulo Freire, and the Pedagogy of Revolution* and (with Dave Hill, Mike Cole, and Glenn Rikowksi), *Marxism Against Postmodernism in Educational Theory.* His forthcoming book, *Red Seminars: Pedagogies for Unlearning Capitalist Culture,* will be published in 2004.

Cameron McCarthy teaches mass communications theory and cultural studies at the Institute of Communications Research at the University of Illinois at Urbana.

David Mills is Anthropology Coordinator at the Centre for Learning and Teaching Sociology, Anthropology and Politics at the University of Birmingham. He no longer works in the Department of Cultural Studies and Sociology after the university pressured all of its existing staff into taking compulsory redundancy in June 2002. As well as completing a political history of social anthropology, he is currently carrying out research into disciplinary knowledge practices in contemporary UK higher education.

Kathleen Nolan is a Student in the PhD Program in Urban Education at the City University of New York Graduate Center. She is a recipient of the Spencer Social Justice and Social Development Fellowship. Her research interests include the political economy of incarceration and the relationship between urban public school policy and the criminal justice system. Kathleen taught ESL (English as a Second Language) and English at South Bronx High School for 4 years. Currently, she teaches at the City College of New York in the Bilingual Education program and mentors teachers in the area of reading and writing in a second language. Her chapter "The Power of Language: A Critique of the Assumptions and Pedagogical Implications of

Howard Gardner's Concept of Linguistic Intelligence" will be published in *Multiple Intelligences Reconsidered* (editor Joe L. Kincheloe, forthcoming).

Fazal Rizvi is Professor of Educational Policy Studies at the University of Illinois at Urbana-Champaign. Before coming to America he held a number of academic and administrative positions in Australia. He has written on issues of globalization and educational policy, democratic reforms in education, and the politics of race and multiculturalism. He is currently researching student mobility across national boundaries and the internationalization of higher education.

Valerie Scatamburlo-D'Annibale, an award-winning author and educator, is an Assistant Professor and Chair of the Graduate Program in Communication and Social Justice at the University of Windsor. Her first book, *Soldiers of Misfortune: The New Right's Culture War and the Politics of Political Correctness*, received the American Educational Studies Association's 2000 Critics Choice Award. She has also published in a wide variety of journals and edited collections in the areas of social theory and critical pedagogy.

Lois Weis is the Author or Coauthor of numerous books and articles pertaining to social class, race, gender, and schooling in the United States. Her most recent books include *Silenced Voices and Extraordinary Conversations: Re-Imagining Schools* (Teachers College Press, 2003, with Michelle Fine); *The Unknown City: The Lives of Poor and Working Class Young Adults* (Beacon Press, 1998, with Michelle Fine); *Speed Bumps: A Student Friendly Guide to Qualitative Research* (Teachers College Press, 2000, with Michelle Fine); and *Beyond Black and White: New Faces and Voices in U.S. Schools* (State University of New York Press, 1997, with Maxine Seller). She sits on numerous editorial boards and is the editor of the Power, Social Identity and Education book series with SUNY Press.

Trained in literary criticism at Cambridge, **Paul Willis** received his PhD in 1972 from the Centre for Contemporary Cultural Studies at Birmingham University, where he remained as Senior Research Fellow until 1980. During the 1980s he served as youth policy adviser to Wolverhampton Borough Council in the English Midlands. There he produced *The Youth Review* (published by the Council and Ashgate [1988]), which formed the basis for youth policy in that city and for the formation of the democratically elected Youth Council, both still functioning. During the 1990s Paul served first as Head of the Division of Media, Communications and Cultural Studies and then as a member of the Professoriate at the University of Wolverhampton.

Currently he is Professor of Social and Cultural Ethnography at Keele University. He has held a variety of consulting posts, including membership in the Youth Policy Working Group of the Labour Party (1989–1990); at the English Arts Council (1992–1993); and at the Tate Gallery of the North (1995–1996). In 2000, he cofounded the Sage journal, *Ethnography*. Paul Willis's work has focused on the mainly but not exclusively ethnographic study of lived cultural forms in a wide variety of contexts, from highly structured to weakly structured ones, examining how practices of "informal cultural production" help to produce and construct cultural worlds "from below." Currently he is working on conceptual and methodological ways of connecting or reconnecting a concern with identity/culture to economic structure, with particular reference to "shop floor culture." Books: *Profane Culture, Learning to Labour, The Youth Review, Common Culture, The Ethnographic Imagination.*

Index

A

Abnormal mental abilities, preoccupation with, 103
Aboriginal peoples, 13
Academic authority, 151
Academics, attention accorded in, 125
Academic success, 133
Achieve, 138
Achievement test scores, money and, 137
Adult
    identities, 115
    power, 7
African existence, time of, 45
Age of Reason, 85
American hospitals, distinction between animate and inanimate in, 52
American minds, testing of, 99
American time, 44
Angela Davis, 151
Animism, examples of, 35
Anthropology, 49
Anticolonialism, 18
Antifeminism, 74
Arab women, use of veil by, 70
Archaeology of silence, 66
Archeological retrieval, 19
Aristotle, 86
Aryan women, 55
Authority, inscribing of over others, 59
Autonomy, concept of, 94
Aztec Empire, 15

B

Baby in a box, Skinner's, 97
Bacon, 86, 89
Bias(es)
    awareness of, 3
    Enlightenment/modernist, 85
    reexamination of, 6
    Western, 95
Big business, American schooling and, 140
Bioethics, description of, 51
Black children, verbal exploration by, 106
Black civil rights workers, 20
Borderlands, definition of, 27
Border messages, 28
Boys
    nomination of for science enrichment children, 125
    toys marketed to, 126
Breastfeeding, 5
Britain, India's independence from, 13
British Gibralter, 13
British imperialism, 15
British Raj, classification practices of, 103
British settlements, 14
Business Coalition for Education Reform, 140
Business Roundtable, 140

C

Campaign of power, 65
Capitalism, 22, 85
    advanced, 46

Capitalism *(continued)*
  corporate, testing as avenue for, 144
  domination, 61
  industrial, 45
  market expansion, 26
  power, 7
  representation, hypercapitalism as form of,
    117
Cartesian dualism, 35, 86
Cartesian thought, separation of child from
  adult, 88
Categorization, representation through, 111
Chewong people, 35
Child(ren)
  beliefs as violence against, 2
  -centeredness, critique of, 95
  consideration of as colonizing construct, 84
  Freud's scientific notation of, 97
  incomplete, 8
  labels imposed on, 83
  sexuality, 116
  stereotypical theories labeling, 154
Childcare, out-of-home, 125
Childhood, *see also* Corporate structures of
  control, childhood as
  author-authorities of theories of, 125
  idealized version of, 107
  innocence, 88
  labeling of, 103
  normality, predetermined, 105
  Western scientific study of, 7
Childhood, colonization and, 83–97
  child as scientific object of empire, 95–97
  exploring childhood as colonizing construct,
    83–85
  reinscribing Western colonialist ideology on
    those who are younger, 85–95
    dualism, 88–89
    progress, 89–92
    reason, 92–95
Children of the National Longitudinal Study of
  Youth, 136–137
Christendom, 34
Christian church, interpretation of childhood
  as evil constructed by, 95
Christian doctrine, child-rearing and, 115
Christian theology, 86
Christian values, Eurowestern male, 34
Civil rights
  impact of testing on, 143
  movements, academics influenced by, 71
  workers, 20
Civil society, 17
Classroom
  teachers, impositions on, 154
  volunteers, female, 129
Colonial agents, sexual sanctions of, 42
Colonialism

Enlightenment version of, 32
  intellectual forms of, 47
  language used to describe, 118
  physical, 11
  unchallenged legacies of, 6
Colonialism/postcolonialism, historical and
  contemporary conditions, 11–29
  creating possibilities for decolonializing,
    28–29
  extent and impact of physical colonization,
    12–13
  illusion of understanding, 13–18
    colonialism and imperialism, 14–16
    neocolonialism, 16–18
  postcolonialism and postcolonial critique,
    18–28
    border knowledges and hybridity, 27–28
    related constructions, 20–27
Colonialist power, 7
Colonies, settler, 14
Colonization, undoing forms of, 29
Committee for Education Reform, 140
Commodity chain, 24
Concerned Women for America, 75
Concubinage, 42
Conquered lands, extraction of resources from,
  24
Consciousness, absence of, 35
Contemporary literacy, 40
Control, women as object of, 96
Co-optation, technologies of, 69
Corporate capitalism, testing as avenue for, 144
Corporate colonization, of public schools, 132
Corporate hypercapitalism, testing as product
  of, 138
Corporate structures of control, childhood as,
  99–119
  cautions and possibilities, 118–119
  colonialist power and representation of
    future citizens, 109–118
    children as instruments of hypercapi-
     talism, 117–118
    children as objects of moral
     theorizing/salvation, 114–115
    children as overt political tools, 112–114
    children as universalized global identity,
     115–117
  constructing and privileging expert discipli-
    nary knowledge, 100–102
  legitimizing surveillance and intervention,
    108–109
  predetermined normality, 103–108
Corrupt governments, 88
Country development, notions of, 16
Cree life, 37
Criminality, avoiding, 108
CTB McGraw-Hill, 139
Culture(s)

collision of, 27
dualist, 51
Hawaiian, 150
nondualist, 51
nonliterate, 52
regulation, act of, 48
wars, United States, 72
Curriculum requirements, 138

D
Dangerous social elements, control of, 63
Declaration of Independence, 20
Decolonialist practice, *see* Education, recon-
ceptualizing of as decolonialist practice
Defamiliarization, 151
Dependence, pattern of, 102
Descartes, 86
Developmentally appropriate practice, 2
Developmental theory, 4, 17
Disciplinary knowledge, expert, 100
Disciplinary power, 62
Disciplinary thinking, development of, 47
Discourses, demonizing, 74
Disney World, 107
Disqualified voices, 123
Domestic servants, dangers represented by, 116
Dominant values, Western, 65
Dualist culture, 51
Dutch Antilles, 13

E
Eagle Forum, 75
Earth, fragility of, 26
Economic expansion, U.S., 16
Economic theories, succession of, 17
Ecuador, Jivaroan tribes of eastern, 36
Education
expenditures, 136
girls and women in, 127
as ideological state apparatus, 114
learning theories, 4
Education, reconceptualizing of as decolonialist practice, 123–144
feminist perspectives in construction of
decolonialist education, 124–132
challenging gender and sex role stereotyping, 125–127
feminist challenges to teacher education,
130–132
focusing on girls and women in education, 127–128
recognizing how teacher work has been
gendered, 128–130
imposition of testing, 132–144
marshaling resistance, 141–144
testing and education practice, 136–138
testing as product of corporate hypercapitalism, 138–141

what standardized tests do not do,
133–136
Elián Gonzalez, 113
Emancipation, transformational liberatory
research and, 149
Emotions, play and, 105
Empire
basic tension of, 119
children as perfect objects of, 97
technologies for continuation of, 67
Energy reciprocity, 36
Enlightened adulthood, 46
Enlightenment
belief in progress, 89
logic, 18
philosophy, 49
spirit, imperialism located within, 16
theorizing, children as objects of, 95
Enlightenment/modernist
bias, 85
dualism, 13
logic of, 21
Equal Rights Amendment, 76
Ethics
power and, 7
research, 151
Ethnography, 145, 146
Euclidean geometry, 53
Eurocentric assumptions, 16
Europe
false fact of, 34
nationalism in, 32
European imperialism, orientalist ideology of,
84
European intellect, 12
European toy, origination of, 105
Expert(s)
hierarchy of, 102
notion of, 102
psychology, 101
understandings acknowledged regarding,
101

F
Family values, 74
Fascism, 12
Federal deficits, 76
Feminism, 18
challenge of, 57
disciplines, 54
goals and assumptions, 20
major contribution of, 56
science, themes of, 56
thought, 124
Feudalism, 31
First world, 25, 88
Flip the Stick, 106
Foundationalism, 40

Fourth world, 25
Freedom
  children's need for, 95
  enlightenment, 15
  resistance and, 64
  sexual, 76
French Guiana, 13
French imperialism, 15
French Revolution, 49
Freud, scientific notation of child, 97

G
Galileo, 86
Galton, nature/nurture binary, 100
Gay rights, 76
Gender
  natural division of, 46
  social structure and, 41
  stereotypes, 125
  toys color-coded according to, 126
Genocide, 33, 37
Girl(s)
  education of, 125
  epitome of hard-working, 125
  sexual harassment of at playgrounds, 127
  toys marketed to, 126
Good behavior, gendered notions of, 130
Good girl(s)
  sexual images conjured up by, 126
  women choosing not to be, 74
Goodness, questioning, 127
Government(s)
  classifying possessions by, 50
  corrupt, 88
Governmentality, 63
Graduate Record Exam (GRE), 134
Grand Valley Dani, game introduced to children of, 106
GRE, see Graduate Record Exam
Great anxiety, teacher education as, 130
Great dichotomy, 40
Greek philosophy, Christian interpretation of, 86

H
Harcourt Educational Measurement, 138
Harmonious pluralism, illusion of, 147
Hawaiian culture, 150
Houseless savages, world created by, 90
Human development, belief in progress through, 91
Humanity, fact/fiction of, 34
Human realities, 4
Human rights, 36, 37
Human truths, discovery of predetermined, 87
Hybridity, most positive feature of, 28
Hypercapitalism, 112
  characteristics of, 117

children as instruments of, 117
network of power, 124
public schools and, 132
testing as product of corporate, 138

I
Ideological state apparatus, education as, 114
Imperialism
  British, 15
  as economic endeavor, 16
  enterprises, magnitude of, 5
  first world, 88
  French, 15
  intellectual, 92
  last hideous gasp of, 17
  market forms of, 154
  notions, perpetuation of, 34
  outpost for, 16
  powers, 7, 12
  practice, impact of, 11
  result of, 16
  Spanish, 15
  undoing forms of, 29
  Western, influence of, 19
Imperial Russia, 15
India, independence of from Britain, 13
Indigenous people, 11
Indigenous research agendas, 150
Indigenous Tribal Peoples of the Tropical Forests, 152
Individualism, 53
Individualization, emergence of, 106
Industrial capitalism, 45
Industrialization, 87
Infant Health Development Project, 137
Influence, colonialist, 31–57
  construction of academic disciplines, 46–54
    anthropology and colonialism, 49–51
    bioethics, 51–52
    mathematics, 52–54
    scientific oversimplifications, 47–49
  feminist disciplines, 54–57
  postcolonial critique and challenges to accepted knowledge discourses, 33–46
    gender, 41–44
    humanity, 34–38
    language and literacy, 38–41
    time, 44–46
Inner war, 28
Inside voices, 1
Intellectual advancement, 115
Intellectual colonization, 119
Intellectual domination, 7
Intellectual imperialism, 92
Intellectual property, 152
Interpretive power, struggle for, 151
Investigations, types of, 150
Invisibility/silence, technology of, 67

Iowa Test of Basic Skills (ITBS), 139
IQ test scores, 136
Isolated phenomenon, childhood as, 3
Israel, conflict between Palestine and, 13
ITBS, *see* Iowa Test of Basic Skills

J
Jesuit priests, Native American cultures and, 43
Joint Standards report, caution of, 144
Judeo-Christian traditions, hegemonic
        masculinity of, 43
Junk-bond king, 141
Juridico-discursive model, power following, 60

K
Kant, 44
Kindergarten teachers, 133
Knowledge(s)
    categorizations of, 33
    disciplinary, 100
    discourses, challenges to accepted, 33
    expert, 101
    nonacademic, 128
    non-Western, 124
    psychological, 100
Knowledge Learning Group, 141

L
Labor
    international divisions of, 22–23
    protection of children from, 104
Language, 38
    male-defined models of, 129
    Western ways of using, 39
Latin America, Spanish imperialism in, 15
Legal sanctions, 62
Legitimate Mayan voices, 73
Literacy, 38
    complexity of, 40
    contemporary, 40
    will to, 39
Logic, independent expression of, 94
Logical-mathematical thought, Piagetian theo-
        ries of, 93

M
Male-haters, 76
Marriage
    control of women's bodies through, 21
    pushing poor women toward, 96
    requirement for, 77
Marxist economic dependency, 18
Masculine systems, 20
Mass dissettlement, 14
Maternal deprivation, 96
Mathematics, definition of, 52
McDonald's, gendered discourses and
        universal identity of, 126

Menchú, Rigoberta, 71
Mental testing, 103, 133
Mestiza, 28
Methodologies of contemporary colonization,
        59–79
    constructing and maintaining colonialist
            power, 60–67
        postcolonialism and campaign of power,
                65–67
        power as produced and producing, 60–64
        resistance and freedom, 64–65
    countering of reinscriptions of power,
            78–79
    domination and attempts to be heard, 71–78
        Rigoberta Menchú, 71–73
        U.S. Women and power, 73–78
    maintaining colonialist power, 67–71
        technologies of co-operation through
                representation, 69
        technology of invisibility/silence, 67–69
        technology of simplification, 70–71
Metric revolution, 48
Middle Ages, 35, 89
Middle-class mothers, 125
Middle-class values, 74
Mind versus matter/body, 86
Minority children, attendance of at school,
        133
Miracle child, 113
Misogyny, 42, 73
Model, juridico-discursive, 60
Modernism, 85
Modernization, importance of, 17
Monochronic times, 44
Monopoly, socialist, 139
Moral consciousness, 35
Moral decay, 74
Moral Majority, 75
Moral theorizing/salvation, children as objects
        of, 114
Motherhood, 54, 55
Mulattos, 28
Multitasking, women, 46

N
National Alliance of Business, 140
National Council on Measurement in Educa-
        tion, 143
Nationalism, European, 32
Native American cultures, Jesuit priests and,
        43
Native populations, dying out of, 33
Natives, view of in colonial situations, 68
Natural law, acceptance of, 86
Natural play, 108
Nature/nurture binary, invention of, 100
Nazi Germany, 55
NCS Pearson, 139

Need
    discourse of, 104
    institutionalized condition of, 110
Neocolonialism, 14, 16
New lands, discovery of, 32
New Right
    politics of resentment, 74
    scholars, 72
Nietzsche, 123
No Child Left Behind Act of 2002, 132
Nonacademic knowledge, school, 128
Nondualist culture, 51
Nonliterate cultures, 52
Non-Western knowledges, 124
Normality, predetermined, 103
Northern eyes, 68
Northern Ireland, Catholic minority in, 13

O
Objectivity versus subjectivity, 86
Observation
    child study through, 108
    necessity of, 109
    surveillance labeled as, 149
Occidentalism, 21
Opacity, 38
Orient, European invention of, 110
Orientalism, 42, 99
Orientals, 79
Out-of-home childcare, 125

P
Panopticism, prison, 63
Patriarchy, colonialism and, 20
Permanent provocation, freedom as, 64
Personal authority, erosion of, 102
Personhood, Euro-Western ideas of, 51
Physical colonialism, 11
Piaget
    notion of child-centeredness, 95
    stages of cognitive development, 91
    theory, 4
Play
    activity(ies)
        diverse cultural, 106
        scientific truths regarding, 106
    Disney, 107
    healing of emotions and, 105
    natural, 108
    power of, 105
    sensori-motor, 106
    visual illusion of as universal, 107
Playgrounds, sexual harassment of girls at, 127
Political agenda, Western thought, 22
Political economy, 23
Political power, children's lack of, 113
Political society, 17
Political theory, construction of, 110

Political tools, children as, 112
Population policy, 55
Postcolonial critique
    complicatedness of, 154
    purpose of, 148
    viewing childhood and education through,
        1–8
        explanation of book, 5–8
        who we are and what our perspectives
        are, 2–5
Postmodernism, 54
Poststructuralism, 54
Poverty, avoiding, 108
Power
    adult, 7
    campaign of, 65
    capitalist, 7
    colonialist, 7
    disciplinary, 23, 62
    discourse as mechanism of, 61
    ethics and, 7
    extreme impositions of, 3
    group-imposed forms of, 66
    hypercapitalist network of, 124
    imperialist, 7, 12
    interpretive, 151
    of oppression, 154
    political, 113
    psychological, 7
    regulatory, 63
    relations, 17
    resistance and, 64
    rules/technologies of, 62
    shift of by military force, 17
    U.S. women and, 73
    will to, 19
Predetermined normality, 103, 105
Predetermined reality, 148
Preemployment tests, worldwide market
        for, 140
Prelogical people, 53
Prison panopticism, 63
Privileged women, 77
Problem students, how teachers view, 130
Progress
    cultural ideology of, 49
    Enlightenment belief in, 89
Psychological Corporation, 141
Psychological knowledge, 100
Psychological power, 7
Psychology, practice of, 100
Public discourse, creation of, 78
Public schools
    corporate colonization of, 132
    hypercapitalism and, 132
Puerto Rice, United States as contemporary
        colonizing power over, 13
Purposeful underdevelopment, 25

Q
Queer theory, 54

R
Racial difference, discourses of, 42
Racism, 42
Ralph Nader's Commercial Alert, 143
Rare treasures, collection of, 33
Rational self-interest, pursuit of, 34
Reading instruction, two-stage model of, 41
Reason, privileging of, 101
Regulatory power, 63
Representation through categorization, 111
Reproductive regulation, 21
Republican Party, 78
Research agendas/methodologies, constructing
    decolonial, 145–152
    construction of postcolonial research ethics,
        151–152
    existence of decolonial research, 147–151
        epistemological goals of research,
            148–149
        questions and purposes that drive
            research, 149–150
        recognizing and countering attempts that
            would discredit, 151
        reconceptualizing research models,
            150–151
Resistance, freedom and, 64
Rhodesia, process of settlement in, 14
Riverside Publishing, 139
Roman Empire, 15
Roman philosophy, Christian interpretation of,
    86
Rousseau, 95, 115
Russia, Imperial, 15

S
SAT exams, 134
School(s)
    curricula, centers of care included in,
        127
    minority children attending, 133
    nonacademic knowledges in, 128
    number of children expelled from, 133
Schooling, as political act, 142
Scientific forestry, 47–48
Scientific heritage, colonialist, 13
Scientific intellectual advancement, 115
Scientific method, 92, 146
Scientific truth, 103
Second world, 25
Self-actualization, 115
Self-interest, 31, 34
Sensori-motor play, 106
September 11, 2001, attacks, 114
Serial killers, future, 74

Sets of preference, difference converted into,
    23
Settlement, colonies established for purpose
    of, 14
Settler colonies, 14
Sexism, 42
Sex role stereotypes, 125
Sexual freedom, 76
Sexual images, good little girl conjuring up,
    126
Sexuality, children's, 116
Sexual orientation, 64
Simplification, technology of, 70
Sisterhood, 54, 55
Skinner, baby in a box, 97
Slavery, 12
Social class histories, 128
Socialism, 86
Socialist monopoly, 139
Social justice, 123
Social sciences, uncovering of truths assumed
    by, 104
Social structure, gender and, 41
Social struggles, postdevelopment theory and,
    26
Society, threat to change, 69
South Africa, process of settlement in, 14
Space, definition of, 45
Standardized tests, 133
Stanford Achievement Test, 141
Stanford-Binet Intelligence test, 136
Subaltern
    discrediting of individual, 71
    voices of, 67
Subject people, 84
Subordinate status, 13
Superiority, imperialist assumption of, 20
Superstitious values, 31
Surveillance, 60
    legitimizing of, 108
    manifested, 64
    objective, 90
    society, 109

T
TAAS standardized test, *see* Texas Assessment
    of Academic Skills standardized test
Teacher
    education
        basics of in U.S., 131
        feminist challenges to, 130
        reconceptualization of, 8
    quality, problem of, 131
Teaching, effects of standardized tests on, 135
Test(s)
    lawsuits challenging legality of, 143
    preparation, 141
    resisting of, 142

Testing
  common assumption behind, 135
  education practice and, 136
  impact of on civil rights, 143
Testing (continued)
  public awareness about, 142
  resistance to, 142
Texas Assessment of Academic Skills (TAAS)
      standardized test, 136, 139
Theory of equilibration, 93
Think tanks, 78
Third world
  countries, power relations between, 17
  representation of, 25
Thought(s)
  Cartesian, separation of child from adult,
      88
  feminist, 124
  logical-mathematical, 93
  revolutionary, 154
  ways of organizing, 13
  Western
    influence of colonialism on, 47
    political agenda of, 22
Time
  of African existence, 45
  linear conceptions of, 44
  social construction of, 44
  universal, 46
Toy(s)
  color-coded according to gender, 126
  origination of European, 105
Toys R Us, gendered discourses and universal
      identity of, 126
Truth-oriented disciplines, 12
Truth versus nontruth, 86
Tunnel vision, 47
Tutoring, 142

U
Un-American voices, 78
United States culture wars, 72
Universalist child development, challenges to,
      153
Universalized global identity, children as, 115
Universal time, notion of, 46
Unmarried women, labeling of, 96
Unthought-of-possibilities, 3
UN "Universal" Declaration of Human Rights,
      36
U.S. Virgin Islands, 13
Utopian beliefs, modernist, 145

V
Vast right-wing conspiracy, 75
Verbal exploration, 106
Victims revolution, 77

W
War, functioning without, 37
Warped tongue, 147
Welfare Queens, 76
Welfare reform, 76
Weschler Intelligence Tests, 141
Weschler Preschool and Primary Scale of
      Intelligence—Revised (WIPPSIE-R),
      136
Western culture, aura of universality, 50
Western disciplinary thought, influence of
      colonialism on, 47
Western discourse, creating citizens within,
      118
Western expansion, Enlightenment/modernist
      projects that legitimated, 29
Western feminist discourse, first wave of, 43
Western imperialism
  influence of, 19
  project, 18
Western languages, characterization of, 38
Western notion of theory, 8
Western perspectives, limitations of, 79
Western society(ies)
  dominant values of, 65
  play and biases of, 107–108
Western thought, political agenda of, 22
Wet nurses, dangers represented by, 116
White colonizer, 21
Wifehood, 54, 55
Wife-mother role, feminism's devaluation of,
      70
Will to literacy, 39
WIPPSIE-R, see Weschler Preschool and
      Primary Scale of Intelligence—
      Revised
Women
  histories, 126
  labeling of unmarried, 96
  as object of control, 96
  privileged, 77
  status held by in indigenous societies, 43
  teachers, vulnerability of, 129
  technology view of, 52
Work discipline, 46
Working mother damage to children, 96
World
  division of into hierarchical categories, 25
  Enlightenment view of, 32
  Greek understanding of, 86
  language and ways of viewing, 38
  mercantile view of, 50
  ways of classifying, 50
World Bank, 24
World Trade Center attacks, 114
World War, I, 12
World War II, 12, 16, 96